Educational Technology in
Curriculum Development

Educational Technology in Curriculum Development
Second edition

Derek Rowntree
Professor of Educational Development
The Open University

Harper & Row, Publishers
London

Cambridge
Hagerstown
Philadelphia
New York

San Francisco
Mexico City
Sao Paulo
Sydney

First published 1982
Reprinted 1983

British Library Cataloguing in Publication Data

Rowntree, Derek
    Educational technology in curriculum
    development.—2nd ed.
    1. Curriculum planning—Great Britain
    2. Educational technology—Great Britain
    I. Title
    375'.001   LB1564.G7

    ISBN 0-06-318169-X
    ISBN 0-06-318170-3   Pbk

Printed and bound in Great Britain
by Butler & Tanner Ltd
Frome and London

Derek Rowntree's other books include:

Assessing Students: How Shall We Know Them? (Harper & Row)
A Dictionary of Education (Harper & Row)
Statistics Without Tears (Penguin)
Developing Courses for Students (McGraw-Hill)
Learn How to Study (Macdonalds)

ACKNOWLEDGEMENTS

This book is dedicated to the many Open University colleagues, especially in the Institute of Educational Technology, the Arts Faculty, and the Centre for Continuing Education, with whom discussions and collaboration over the last dozen years have provided so stimulating a climate in which to practise and think about educational technology. My special thanks are due to Nick Farnes and Dave Harris whose comments on early drafts of the first edition were invaluable and, subsequently, to Jack Field, Janet Gale, Mary Geffen, Graham Gibbs, Roger Harrison, David Hawkridge, Gill Kirkup, Clive Lawless, Tim O'Shea and Rob Waller, all of whom took the trouble to consider and comment on the first edition and so helped give me the impetus I needed to achieve this second edition. I must also express my thanks for the patience and continuing encouragement of my publishers. As always, however, despite the thought-provoking comments I so gladly acknowledge, both from colleagues and from reviewers of the first edition, the responsibility for content and treatment remains entirely my own.

Contents

PROLOGUE TO THE SECOND EDITION

> The end of all our exploring
> Will be to arrive where we started
> And know the place for the first time.
>
> T.S. Eliot, *Four Quartets*

The first edition of this book was published in 1974. In re-reading the book, with a view to preparing this new edition, I have become aware of how much my own beliefs and strategies as an educational technologist have changed since then. These changes are reflected in this new edition and give it a somewhat different flavour from the original. All the same, I have resisted the temptation to start over again, as if I had never previously written a book about educational technology, and so offer a radically new and idiosyncratic view of the subject. To have abandoned entirely the basic version of educational technology embodied in the earlier text might have been fun for me but would have been unfair to the many readers who might still benefit from it.

What if I personally no longer apply educational technology in quite the pristine form in which I first presented it? I may believe that my practices have become more subtle and sophisticated. I may feel some temptation to demonstrate that my own ideas have moved on in the last few years, that I am not being left behind by the flow of new thinking. However, I am not writing with a view to impressing my peers. Rather, my purpose is to introduce *newcomers* to the field. This purpose, I believe, is best served by presenting them with a coherent, if basic, model of educational technology which, once come to terms with, they can adapt and develop (as I have done) to suit their own pedagogic style and intentions. (Those who have already reached that stage may be interested in the personal model I put forward in Rowntree 1981.)

Too often in education, pioneers tire eventually of their innovation and look around for a new bandwagon to start or join. This is reasonable enough, so long as they do not then publicly deride or disown their earlier concerns simply because they no longer identify with them personally. My own educational thinking would not have reached the

stage it has today without having been metabolized through the educational technology I present in this book. Far be it from me to pull the
ladder up behind me, preventing others from following a similar route.

But please be assured that the educational technology presented here is
no historical curiosity. It is firmly embedded in the curriculum planning
of institutions like the Business Education Council and the Technician
Education Council, not to mention the Open University and countless
curriculum development groups in schools and colleges around the
world. It is also recognizably present in most courses on educational
technology and in the practices of the majority of educational technologists. And many teachers are only now beginning to realize the extent to
which their students can benefit from its application.

In fact, educational technology has become more varied over the years
since I first wrote about it. We may even find it practised under different
banners: educational development (which is my own preference), staff
development, applied educational science, instructional design and so on.
Different practitioners have evolved their own variations on the basic
themes. These reflect their various beliefs and values and theories about
knowledge and learning. Some educational technologists, what we might
call the 'existentialists' among us, resist discussion of their philosophical
stance. Their beliefs, values and theories are defined by their actions.
They are the sum of their deeds. But most of us have become convinced
that we need to be able not only to act appropriately but also to explain
and justify our actions or the advice we might give to others on how to
act.

Many concerns in educational technology have emerged more strongly
in the last few years. Educational technologists are showing more interest
than once they did in the nature and structure of the knowledge that is to
be taught. They are expressing views about the 'what' as well as the
'how' of learning. Their views of the student are also diversifying. At one
time, the behaviourist model, derived from experimental psychology,
dominated the field; the student was seen as a relatively passive
responder to stimuli. More recently, an 'information-processing' model,
derived from cognitive psychology, has become more popular. This
model sees the student as an active problem-solver who has his own
individual purposes and develops his own ways of connecting new
knowledge with what he has already learned. To this has been added a
view derived from humanistic psychology (see Maslow 1954 and Rogers
1969) that sees the student as capable of 'realizing' himself through

significant learning. It stresses the need for personal relevance in learning and a non-threatening milieu in which the student can take a good deal of the responsibility for his own studies and learn as far as possible through experience that involves the feelings as well as the intellect.

In parallel with these changes, educational technologists are now less prone to think of the teacher as a passive recipient and implementer of curricula and 'packages' developed by specialists elsewhere. The teacher's role as a curriculum developer in his own right is increasingly being encouraged. Broadly speaking, where once educational technologists leaned most heavily on individualist psychology for technical inspiration, they are now drawing more and more on philosophy to clarify their purposes and on *social* psychology to understand the social context in which people work together in developing and pursuing curriculum purposes.

I believe these developments were all discernible in the first edition of this book. Indeed, having been used so widely, it may have done something to foster them. Nevertheless, when I compare what I said about such developments in the 1974 edition with the understanding I now have of them and the extent to which they have since permeated and humanized educational technology, I seem now to see that field as if for the first time. Hence, while the basic model presented in this book is the same as that in the earlier edition, it is presented more knowingly.

When I first wrote the book I believed myself to be talking directly to *teachers* – hoping they would see the sense of considering an educational technology approach to their own work. To a large extent this has happened, of course. But, in addition, the last few years have seen the establishment of specialist educational technologists/developers. Their prime role is not to teach but to advise teachers on aspects of teaching. That is, the educational technology message does not always go direct to the user but is often mediated through advisers. I am somewhat wary about such division of labour. I would prefer to see every teacher as at least a 'general practitioner' of educational technology, even though he might well call on a specialist for a second opinion in particularly tricky situations, or for initial guidance when embarking on any new kind of teaching.

As such a specialist adviser myself, I aim always to be working towards my own superfluity. The old proverb has it that if you give a man fish, you feed him for a day; whereas, if you teach him how to fish, you feed him for a lifetime. Accordingly, I would hope that educational technologists working with teachers will act so as to enable each client to develop his own educational technology and so become less dependent on advice from outside experts. I am happy to note that such de-mystification and appropriation of the message has been widespread among my academic colleagues in the Open University, however much many of them might resist being labelled as educational technologists, preferring simply to think of themselves as having become better teachers.

So, once again, this book aims to appeal to the classroom teacher as well as to those who plan to specialize as educational technologists. However, it does not offer a set of 'handy hints' on how to educationally technologize their teaching. This is not a 'how-to-do-it' book. It is not a manual providing step-by-step guidance on developing learning materials and systems. (If this is what you need, see Rowntree and Connors 1979.) What I hope to do here is to provoke thought rather than to prescribe actions. Different teachers might well use educational technology in different ways to produce different, but equally pleasing solutions in a particular situation. This book is about the issues that need to be considered, the factors involved, and the kinds of procedure that teachers may be able to draw on in their curriculum discussions and decision-making.

And what of the connection with curriculum development? One of the reviewers of the first edition suggested that its title should be not *Educational Technology IN Curriculum Development* but *Educational Technology IS Curriculum Development*. I would not wish to go this far. Curriculum studies is another new field with a huge literature of its own, and it supports many different approaches to the work of curriculum development (see Stenhouse 1975). Educational technology is one of these and, in my personal experience, the most generally applicable. Indeed, being a somewhat pragmatic and eclectic approach, it has been influenced by other approaches that exist separately in their own right. This book is about educational technology as one form of curriculum development rather than about curriculum development in general. So I limit myself to the one approach, albeit with occasional digressions. However, as Robert Louis Stevenson once said: 'To state one argument is not necessarily to be deaf to all others; and that a man has written a book of travels in Montenegro is no reason why he should never have been to Richmond.' Nor, I might add, is it reason to suppose that he might wish to deter other travellers from exploring different routes towards different destinations.

A Note on Terminology

This book is intended for teachers at all levels of education. Thus, when the word 'teacher' appears in the text, it can also usually be taken to imply 'tutor' or 'lecturer'. Similarly, when I refer to what may happen in 'school', this can usually be read as shorthand for 'school, college, polytechnic, university or other educational institution'. To refer to the person who, we hope, is doing the learning, I sometimes use the word 'learner'; sometimes, where I am speaking specifically of young schoolchildren, I use 'pupil'; but the word I use most frequently – to represent people of all ages from kindergarten to post-secondary and continuing education for whom teachers are to any degree responsible – is 'students'. (To my mind, the term 'student' seems to beg fewer questions about effectiveness than the term 'learner' and also to allow of more autonomy for the person than does 'pupil'.) Finally, like all professions, educational technology has no shortage of technical terms (jargon); these I have tried to define and explain wherever I have needed to use them.

End-of-chapter Questions

In response to requests from teachers who have been using the earlier edition of this book in education courses, I am including some discussion questions in this edition. At the end of each chapter, and at the end of the book, is a set of questions relating to the ideas put forward in the preceding pages. These can serve as discussion questions for a class session or, if you are reading the book on your own, should be useful in helping you evaluate the book's ideas, chapter by chapter, and relate them to your own experience of teaching and learning.

Many of the questions ask you to relate a chapter's ideas about teaching and learning to a course with which you are familiar. This could usefully be a course you are teaching, or planning to teach, yourself. Alternatively, or additionally, it could be a course you have taken, or are taking, as a student. Indeed, if this book is 'required' or 'recommended reading' for a course you are taking now, you might find it illuminating to relate the book's ideas to that course.

My questions, however, are just a few of the many that could be raised in relation to each chapter. I doubt if any of them will be as pertinent and probing as those you will be able to generate yourself. If you are working with a class, you may find it useful to think up further questions that interest you and which you believe would be worthy of group discussion.

References

At the back of the book, you will find an extensive list of the articles and books referred to in the text. In compiling the list (as one of my final tasks in putting this edition together), I was amazed to find that I needed to add about 140 items since the time of the first edition (1974) – a revealing indicator of the voluminous output of 'literature' relevant to educational technology in curriculum development.

Where items in the list of references are particularly useful as background reading to one of the seven chapters, I have indicated the chapter number in the margin alongside it. Where an item is of relevance to educational technology as a whole, I have put an asterisk (*) in the margin.

I have also added a list of some of the many journals and periodicals that regularly contain articles of interest to educational technologists.

CHAPTER 1

WHAT IS EDUCATIONAL TECHNOLOGY?

We start, I say, with a problem, a difficulty. . . . At best we have only a vague idea what our problem really consists of. How, then, can we produce an adequate solution? Obviously, we cannot. We must first get better acquainted with the problem. But how? My answer is very simple: by producing an inadequate solution, and by criticizing it.

Karl Popper

This book is *not* about audio-visual aids. My aim is not to promote television, teaching machines, computers and other instructional devices, ancient or modern. Educational technology is not to be confused with electronic gadgetry. A cynic has remarked that many things have happened in this century and most of them plug into walls. But even if the sockets were to be filled in and the secret of electricity lost for ever, we should still need educational technology. For educational technology is as wide as education itself: it is concerned with the design and evaluation of curricula and learning experiences and with the problems of implementing and renovating them. Essentially, it is a rational, problem-solving approach to education, a way of *thinking* sceptically and systematically about learning and teaching.

From Tools to Systems

Why is it so necessary to begin by putting the 'media' in their place? Because the label 'educational technology' once looked like being attached exclusively to a tools technology whose emphasis was on audio-visual aids to the teacher – film, television, tape-recorders and so on. Usually, the 'hardware' (like film projectors and tape-recorders) was developed outside education, but teachers were promised 'software' (films and tapes and so on) designed specifically to meet their needs. It was a technology devoted to supporting and enhancing the status quo providing teachers with the tools that would enable them to teach the same things more effectively or to larger numbers of students. It was a failure. High cost and unreliability of equipment; over-selling; shortage of suitable software; fear, scorn or indifference among teachers and, above all, the lack of a sufficient incentive and rationale for audio-visual innovation have prevented widespread acceptance.

Of course, there are some schools making good use of their newer media. But most have machines lying gathering dust in cupboards – except on open days when they still provide something 'modern' for the visitors to exclaim over – while teacher soldiers on with chalk and talk. Not surprisingly, educational technologists are less than gratified when people in education expect them to be propagandists for the latest electric nostrum.

Nevertheless, we have all had to recognize that the sheer variety and enormous bulk of new materials and media raise vexed questions of evaluation and choice for the teacher. This pressure from media, especially those mass media esteemed in the student's private life, has allied itself with others – spending cuts, youth unemployment, student cynicism, parental concern, employer anxiety, government pronouncements on education and the economy, and the uncertainty of the future ahead of our pupils. Together, they encourage us in renewed thinking about what education is and might become, and what we should be doing about it. Hence the need for a technology in the Greek sense of a *systematic treatment of an art* – in this case, the art of education. The purpose of such a technology would be (to use another Greek term) *telesis:* 'progress intelligently planned and directed; the attainment of desired ends by the application of intelligent human effort to the means' (Hawkridge 1981).

For generations, children, parents, employers, teachers, headteachers and inspectors of schools have, in decreasing order of confidence, assumed that, in general, education knows what it is doing, and that, despite occasional lapses and misadventures, it has all been thought out, rigorously evolved, and perfected in the light of experience. The assumption of *telesis* is delusory, and people are beginning, vociferously, to notice.

During the last twenty years, more and more sophisticated tools (like programmed learning and microcomputers) and teaching materials (like new 'curriculum packages') have entered the classroom. They have not always added much to the amount of learning taking place and have sometimes antagonized teacher and student alike. Hence, many educationalists have begun to look beyond the individual components and strategies of the teaching/learning system. They have become concerned with understanding the *system as a whole*. Identifying aims and objectives, planning the learning environment, exploring and structuring the subject matter, selecting appropriate teaching strategies, helping students develop new ways of learning, evaluating the effects and effectiveness of the teaching/learning system, and using the insights gained from evaluation to understand that system and, where possible, improve it – this is now the province of the educational technologist. While the earlier 'tools technology' continues to live on independently in many educational or training establishments, it has been largely superseded by a new and more powerful '*systems* technology'.

In fact, the 'tools technology' was always a good deal less unified than the name might suggest. The various media grew up separately and so did their followers. The programmed learning people had little to say to the film people and the language laboratory people spoke to neither. Not surprisingly, this fostered a bits-and-pieces approach in which curricula and courses might be tinkered with and marginally improved but would never be scrapped or replaced. By contrast, the systems technology, in its sceptical analysis of the whys and wherefores of the whole operation, and its willingness to entertain radical alternatives, is almost subversive. With their zeal to promote the total educational environment (not to be identified with 'educational institution') and the harmonious and successful interactions of all the people and things within it, educational technologists might almost be thought of as pioneers of educational *ecology*. Without such a global and committed approach to education, we certainly cannot hope to solve the central problems of curriculum planning outlined by Philip Taylor (1970):

Planning a course of study for pupils, and constructing the curriculum they will follow is central to the whole educational process. Upon this planning hinges a very great deal. It defines, directs and co-ordinates what the pupil is intended to learn, gives direction and purpose to teaching, provides it with justification and gives it order and coherence. About how this planning is done, what criteria may best be used to decide between alternative possibilities, and how to judge the effectiveness of the planning, we know next to nothing. In periods of educational continuity such knowledge may be unimportant but in times of educational change when teachers are being called on to develop new approaches to teaching and new courses of study it is likely to be of crucial value. . . . There is a need to make explicit the principles by which effective planning is achieved, and to communicate these principles so that they may become, in time, part of the professional expertise of all teachers.

I write this book in the belief that the principles of educational technology should be part of the 'professional expertise' of teachers. I would hope to see them capable of using educational technology in the curriculum development which is likely to become an increasingly important part of their work. Educational technology can help the teacher whether he is planning individual 'lessons' or a complete course, or even a programme of connected courses.

The principles of educational technology are not new. They were vigorously heralded by curriculum reformers like Ralph Tyler as early as the 1930s and since (Tyler 1971), and the moving spirit of 'scientific method' goes back through John Dewey's 'stages of problem-solving' to Roger Bacon and Aristotle. Many diverse streams of influence have helped shape educational technology – e.g., media research, systems analysis, educational psychology, 'progressive' (child-centred) educational theory, communications theory, management by objectives, educational measurement, skills analysis, curriculum development and programmed learning. It also has much common ground with the literature of what might be called 'educational pathology', which seeks to lay bare all the diseased tissues of education (see Blishen 1969, Goodman 1971, Hansen and Jensen 1971, Henry 1971, Holt 1969 and 1970, Illich 1971, Reimer 1971, Rubinstein and Stoneman 1972, Postman and Weingartner 1971, Pateman 1972, Smith 1977, etc.). Tracing the intellectual ancestry of educational technology is a popular pastime in the journals; rather than devoting time to genealogy here, let me simply refer you to a few examples: Hawkridge 1981, Morgan 1978, and Saettler 1978.

Programmed Learning's Contribution

Of all the contributory influences, programmed learning has probably given most of the impetus if not of the original thinking. But, paradoxically, the nature of its contribution was not apparent until most of its initial features had been stripped away. Only then did educational technology emerge from the chrysalis.

It was once easy to recognize a programme. Students worked through sequences of highly verbal material, each at his own pace, using a teaching machine or programmed textbook, without help from a live teacher, writing down an answer at each small step (which was either 'linear' or 'branching') and, like as not, being taught a narrow range of subject matter by rather didactic teaching strategies.

By the mid-1960s all this had changed (Leith 1968). Most of the early identifying features were either being discarded or else absorbed into other media – television, textbooks, lectures – and so on. Many programmes then being written involved visual, tactile and auditory stimuli; practical work; group pacing; multi-media learning – from pictures, recorded sound, and real objects to be handled; interaction with a live teacher and with other students; steps as large as possible; answers not necessarily written; mixing of linear, branching and newer frame-writing techniques; new areas of subject matter; and more emphasis on learning by discovery (Rowntree 1968). With this crossing of the boundaries between media, it became necessary to look beyond the teaching programme and think instead of programmed teaching.

The mythology and folklore of programming began to float away, along with the narrow-minded behaviourist psychology that had both sustained and inhibited the movement in its infancy. Many programmers realized that they had been programming things that should never have been taught at all, or that should have been taught by some other method or combination of methods. More and more they saw the folly of setting out with a medium in search of a message. They began to concentrate on deciding first what might be learned (the message) before deciding how it should be taught (the medium). This is where systems technology took over from the tools, and the change of emphasis may prove to have been programmed learning's greatest gift to education. In planning their courses, teachers have customarily begun by thinking up ways of motivating their students and providing acceptable classroom activities. Only later, *if at all*, would they go on to spell out the purposes or objectives of this teaching and consider means of evaluating whether those purposes or other outcomes had materialized (Taylor 1970). Programmed learning reversed these priorities, and educational technology now revolves around the idea of *evaluation*, and usually, but not exclusively, evaluation in terms of objectives.

Changing People

The purpose of education is to help people *change*. The bluntness of this statement may alarm some teachers. Yet it is surely apparent that, when we are acting as teachers (rather than as friends, acquaintances, colleagues, entertainers), our purpose is not (or not only) to help people pass the time, or to feel good, or to be amused or stimulated. We intend our interventions to have more than a passing effect. Indeed, we wish people (especially young people) to develop differently from how they might if they were left to themselves. For their own good – and for ours, if we are honest, and conceivably for society's – we want to help them develop the way they think, act and feel – in short, to change their capabilities and dispositions. We want them to become more knowledgeable, more skilful, more confident, more independent, more empathetic, more rational and so on. We therefore develop curricula that, we hope, will encourage personal growth in our students and bring about the desired changes.

You may well ask 'Who says what changes are to be desired?' Teachers, pupils, parents, examining bodies, the government, potential employers? Different educational technologists will give different emphases to the various possible influences, according to their own educational and social beliefs and the pressures to which they feel subjected.

Let us be clear, however, that saying the central purpose of education is to enable people to change is not to say that one would necessarily desire every person to change along the same lines, let alone that they must be lines we would desire for ourselves. As St. Thomas à Kempis pointed out some five hundred years ago: 'If you cannot mould yourself as you wish, how can you expect other people to be entirely to your liking?' In some cases, we will wish to influence the direction of the change; but in others we might see our role as that of the professional who can best help the student towards goals of *his own* choosing. At the very least, we can scarcely avoid taking into account his wishes, beliefs and understandings as we pursue whatever changes we do wish to bring about.

Certainly it would be unethical, no matter how often it is done, to expose people to a changing influence (i.e., to education) without our being able (in principle) to discuss with them (or with their parents in the case of very young children), and agree with them, the kinds of change we would propose. For one thing, they may prefer not to change in the kind of way proposed. For another, they may rightly claim to have already attained some of the skills and qualities we propose to help them towards. And clearly we cannot discuss with a student the kind of changes we might aim for in his knowledge, skills and attitudes unless we can first spell out our purposes. This we might well do in the form of a set of *learning objectives*, describing as precisely as necessary what capabilities and dispositions the student might acquire, in what ways he might 'grow'.

The Importance of Objectives

It was the writers of programme learning materials who first brought home to us the possible benefits of outlining at least some of the objectives of the learning before we embark upon the teaching (Mager 1962). By objectives we mean not the broad purposes or aims of the teaching, or what form it will take, or even what subject matter it will cover, but simply: 'What should the student be able to do (or do *better*), as a result of the teaching, that he was unable to do (or do so well) before?'

Here, for example, is a broad *aim* that might be expressed by a teacher:

'I will teach the student to think critically'.

Contrast that with the kind of objectives that he might draw out from such an aim:
'In his area of interest, the student should be able to:

- actively seek out problems
- define his problem
- search for more than one possible approach to solving a problem
- identify sources of relevant data
- reject irrelevant data
- distinguish between facts and opinions
- point out further problems arising from his investigations
- withold or temper judgements where data is insufficient . . . and so on'.

Whether or not these coincide with what *we* think of as 'critical thinking', they would leave us considerably less room for doubt about what the teacher means by it. They are reasonably precise objectives whose attainment and exercise we should be able to observe in the activities of the 'educated' student.

The value of objectives, urged upon us long before the programmed learning boom (Tyler 1934), is that they can provide both a goal for the teaching and a measure of its effectiveness. Once we know what we are trying to accomplish, by way of enhancing the student's knowledge, skills and attitudes, we can be more confident about what to say to him.

Only when we know what we are trying to bring about can we tell the extent to which we have been successful in achieving our purposes.

Ten years ago, many might have argued further that all our objectives should therefore be fully defined before starting to teach. Nowadays, most educational technologists have softened their attitude: while they would expect to see some consideration of possible objectives beforehand, they would recognize the need to be responsive to possible objectives that suggest themselves only once the teaching is well under way.

The existence of objectives means that, as with programmed learning, any attempt at teaching can be empirically evaluated and revised until it achieves satisfactory results. If students do not reach the objectives, we do not blame the students. If we remain convinced that the objectives are both worthwhile and attainable, then we assume that the teaching is faulty and must be re-thought and modified until it is successful. By 'teaching', here, I mean to include any intervention the teacher makes that is calculated to aid the student's learning. Thus, giving the student direct instruction or sending him off to find out on his own would equally count as 'teaching', if consciously chosen as being the optimum way of enabling the student to reach the objectives in different circumstances. For many practitioners, this focus on objectives has come like a Copernican revolution in educational thinking (a 'paradigm shift' in the language of Thomas Kuhn, 1970) – in which the educational process is now seen to revolve not around the teacher teaching but around the learner learning.

Problem-solving

In effect, programmed learning's emphasis on objectives has fostered in education the 'hypothesis-testing' approach of 'scientific method'. Using this approach, we tackle curriculum development as a *problem-solving* exercise. We follow steps not unlike those of the scientist who begins by identifying a problem, then comes up with a hypothesis to solve it or explain it, and who finally performs some test or experiment that allows him either to accept that hypothesis or else reject it in favour of an alternative which he then puts to the test in the same way. Like the scientist, we hope eventually to reach a satisfactory (if never perfect) solution to our problem.

Our 'problem', of course, is how to achieve the educational purpose that we have identified – or, more specifically, how to get our students to their objectives. Our 'hypothesis' will be that certain learning experiences will bring this about. And we 'experiment' by actually exposing the students to these learning experiences and then checking to see whether they do in fact reach the objectives as a result. If the objectives are reached, then the 'hypothesis' (the learning experiences) can be considered valid and effective; we can accept it as a solution to the problem whenever we have similar students facing similar objectives. If the objectives prove not to have been reached satisfactorily we must reject or modify our original hypothesis and start thinking up an alternative: that is, we must re-think our teaching.

It is this scientific *method* (and *not* scientific knowledge, because a prescriptive science of learning is still nowhere within sight) that has enabled us to lift off from the old tools technology, and its preoccupation with individual bits of hardware, into the new systems technology in which both old and new media can be selected and combined to form learning experiences that fit together as a self-checking, self-improving system. We may not know as much as we would like about how individuals learn; but we do know enough to find out *whether or not* they have learned – and to try again differently if they have not. Nevertheless, the dream of an applied science of teaching is still pursued by some (see Reif 1978).

So the educational technology approach has these four basic strands or phases:

1 Identify purposes, especially in terms of objectives.
2 Develop the necessary learning experiences.
3 Evaluate the effectiveness of those learning experiences in achieving the purposes.
4 Improve the learning experiences, in the light of evaluation, so as to better achieve the purposes.

In each of these four phases, the teacher forms hypotheses and makes decisions. His hypotheses will be based on his own insight and experience, together with the illumination afforded by literature and anecdote (e.g., Kaufman 1966, Kohl 1972, Holt 1970) and by the findings of researchers into learning (e.g., Gage 1963, Travers 1973). For guidance on how to use the research findings as a teacher, within just such an hypothesis-testing, experimental approach to teaching, see Stones (1979) which, despite its intimidating title (*Psychopedagogy*), is highly readable and replete with down-to-earth examples from the classroom. See also Stenhouse (1975) for his discussion of the teacher as a researcher in his own classroom.

Although the four-phase educational technology approach is systematic, it is not magical. It is a vehicle, not a substitute, for imagination and hard thinking. It is a recipe not for instant success but for cumulative self-improvement. As Coladarci (1956) explains:

> Intelligent hypotheses are not chosen randomly nor are they found full blown. An intelligent hypothesizer thinks along the lines of the following model: *On the basis of what I know now* about individual differences and the reading process, I hypothesize that this kind of grouping-for-reading will lead to the kind of pupil-progress in reading that I would like to bring about.

The 'what I know now' may never be perfect but it should always be developing, through evaluation of the quality of 'pupil-progress', leading the teacher to better and better hypotheses about how to help his students learn. These hypotheses will, nevertheless, continue to differ from teacher to teacher. Each will build them out of his own experience, imagination and values, using his own metaphors, analogies and imaginative leaps (see Cowan 1980). The test lies not in how they originate but in how they are justified, evaluated and improved upon.

So, to the extent that educational technology *is* what educational technologists *do*, educational technology is educational problem-solving. Among the diversity of aims and methods espoused by particular educational technologists, this is a commitment they do tend to have in common. You may feel that this problem-solving, educational technology approach is not very revolutionary. Nor is it, unless applied by someone brave enough to face up to all the disturbing hypotheses that can arise in the course of it. (More of this later.) In fact, the approach looks (and is) commonsensical. Obvious enough, some would say, without all the ballyhoo. Many's the time, having explained the approach to someone outside education, I have been asked: 'But isn't that what all teachers do?'

Well, no doubt the best teachers have always done something of the sort, though rarely have they had time and facilities to do so as rigorously as the modern pressures on education would seem increasingly to make necessary. Michael Eraut and Geoffrey Squires (1973) describe educational technology as a 'response to complexity different in degree rather than kind from the older "good" method'.

Meanwhile, the majority of teachers still ask: 'What shall I do?', rather than: 'What shall my pupils become?' (Popham and Baker 1970); still come to objectives and evaluation as an after-thought, if at all (Taylor 1970); and as Jules Henry (1971) has said in talking of the ill-effects school has on the mental health of children (in the USA):

> . . . educators have been unwilling to inspect the products of their work; and for this reason the everyday, average, run-of-the-mill transactions between teacher and pupil in the classroom have remained hidden from scientists, not to mention educators themselves, who are, of course, among the most unscientific professionals in the world.

In truth, education is a profession where self-evaluation tends to be minimal and benign. Given the apparent inflexibility of the systems most of us work in – e.g. syllabi to be covered, colleagues to be kept in with – it is scarcely surprising that we are rarely inclined to spend much time or energy in self-criticism. Our most common assumption is: 'I've taught them, so they should have learned.' Yet, if the teacher is essentially a generator of hypotheses, it may be only the failure to test these hypotheses that has kept teaching as a 'nebulous art' rather than permitting it to evolve into an activity at least as scientific as, say, medicine where, despite the unsolved problems, the unpredictabilities of the human psychosoma and the pressure of numbers, each new generation of practitioners becomes a little more proficient than the last. Admittedly, this analogy has its dangers, since many people would argue that medicine itself has become *too* scientific – treating diseases rather than people, preferring technological rather than psycho-social therapy. However, the commitment to systematic learning from experience does not necessarily prevent that learning from being applied in a humane and personal manner.

Educational technology does differ from most technologies, though, in that it gets focused on *specific* systems or situations. The educational technologist sets out to develop a particular system, not to generate and test general principles that can be applied in routine fashion in other situations. Of course we may well draw on and adapt experience gained elsewhere, perhaps by other educational technologists; and our own explorations are almost certain to have something to teach other educational technologists; but such exportable knowledge is a serendipitous by-product, not the object of the exercise.

Educational Technology and Systems Thinking

Because it is concerned with systems as a whole and because some workers have brought into it the techniques of systems analysis (Pfeiffer 1968) the educational technology approach is sometimes called the systems approach. ('Systematic approach' would generally be more apt, and certainly less pretentious.)

The systems metaphor is undoubtedly a fruitful one. Education clearly is enmeshed in a net of systems which form the context and constraints for our activities. Education itself can be viewed as a system – a self-adjusting combination of interacting people and things designed by human beings to accomplish some predetermined purpose. Yet, at the same time, education (like industry, the trade union movement, government, mass media, public health and so on) is but a subsystem when compared with the *supra*system – society as a whole – from which it receives its 'input' (students, teachers, material resources and ideologies) and which expects from it a certain kind of 'output' (people possessing certain skills, attitudes and understandings). Then again looking the other way, education itself is also a suprasystem: a system in which intermesh a number of subsystems – e.g., the administrative system, the catering system, the examination system, the in-service staff-training system, etc. – all of which must work together and facilitate the purposes of the most important subsystem of all, the learning system.

Systems analysis teaches us to look beyond what seems to be the horizon and to anticipate the future problems that will result from our present solutions. Consider the whole as well as the part; consider not only the system but also its subsystems, its companion systems, and the suprasystem which they comprise. Everything relates to everything else, 'inputting' and 'outputting', and if you alter one part of a system you may get unwanted repercussions elsewhere. Teach primary school children to think and question, and they may suffer rebuff in secondary school. Introduce a new curriculum, and teachers may need retraining. Enforce an extra year of schooling, and discipline problems may intensify. Make all secondary schools comprehensive, and parents may press all schools to ape the grammar school élitism. Abandon examinations, and prospective employers or further education institutes need new selection procedures. Buy tape-recorders, and you may run out of money for pencils and paper.

Sometimes, if anticipated, such new problems can be prevented, sometimes not. Little wonder that one of the jargon words much used in systems analysis is 'trade-off' – how much of one desirable thing you're prepared to give up in order to get more of some other desirable thing. Anthony Oettinger (1969), while recognizing that attempts to change systems can be met with prevarication and resistance, goes on to say:

> . . . whenever society has wished to change itself, the educational process has come to mind as an agent of social change. Systems analysis has helped us to realise that because the schools are now tethered by many strings, they find it hard to change themselves, hence still harder to induce changes in society. Although systems analysis offers no magic, it can further help to lead us from this realisation to the acquisition of sufficient knowledge about the strings – what they are made of, how they are inter-connected, who pulls them, how much they can stretch, and so on – to provide, first, understanding and, second, mechanisms for turning toward agreed-upon and explicitly defined goals.

The dominant 'liberal' tradition in educational theory takes little account of such systems thinking and tends to focus more narrowly. Many educational technologists have followed this tradition and, for various reasons, have been systematic without wholeheartedly embracing the systems approach. Clifton Chadwick (1979) suggests that this lack of wholehearted commitment to the systems approach has prevented educational technology from being as influential as it should have been. It might be fairer to say that it is their relative lack of influence that has prevented many educational technologists from pursuing their systems approach to bring about changes as radical as they would wish.

Interestingly, systems explanations seem to be sought both by the Marxists and by the libertarians whose critical views tend to dominate the 'alternative press' in education. As Mike Smith (1977) puts it:

> What is common to both positions is a willingness to move quickly from the particular to the general, from the individual instance to explanation in terms of system. If one is attempting to deal with a problem within the accepted frame of reference one tends to explain away difficulties as problems to do with individual performance; an inexperienced teacher, 'difficult' children, discipline, etc. Both libertarians and Marxists are likely to argue, on the other hand, that while you attempt to deal with the problems in terms of the existing frame of reference, the difficulties are likely to continue. They are problems to do with the system, not with particular people.

Marxists and libertarians differ, of course, in that the former are likely to suggest that the problems must be solved within society before they can be solved within the school; while the latter might feel that much can be done by exerting appropriate pressures within the existing suprasystem (e.g., by setting up a 'free school' or simply by individual teachers relating to their pupils in new ways).

Beware the Rhetoric

Bela Banathy (1968) describes the systems approach as 'commonsense by design' and his book makes both a commonsensical and a very lucid introduction to the systems view. The fields of education and communication perhaps attract more than their fair share of unreadable writing, and educational technology is far from immune. Sometimes this may be due to the author's anxiety to win respect for what, if they were comprehensible, might be thought rather mundane observations; sometimes, as George Bernard Shaw noted, we are assaulted by:

> . . . the jargon of those writers who, because they never really understand what they are trying to say, cannot find familiar words for it, and are therefore compelled to invent a new language of nonsense for every book they write.

Sometimes, however, I suspect that the opacity of the prose and the elaborate jargon is used not as a window-dressing, nor as a result of the author's shaky grasp of his ideas, but in order to anaesthetize the reader against the full impact of what is being said. This is especially noticeable in the works of some American writers whose experience of systems analysis has been in industrial, business and military contexts and who are convinced that education can be 'engineered' in the same kind of way. The 'engineering' approach to education can offer useful insights that would otherwise be unattainable, but its dehumanized rhetoric is often too evocative of the assembly line, and of factory ethics and commodity economics, to win much of a hearing from teachers. Without wishing to sound 'more humanistic than them' it must be emphasized that this undue stretching of the systems metaphor occurs far less in Britain than it does in America. Raymond Callahan (1962) in *Education and the Cult of Efficiency* analysed how the inept application of business mores had resulted in what he called the American tragedy in education:

> . . . that educational questions were subordinated to business considerations; that administrators were produced who were not, in any true sense, educators; that a scientific label was put on some very unscientific and dubious methods and practices; and that an anti-intellectual climate, already prevalent, was strengthened.

He might have noted also the conformity and suppression of individuality induced by scorning emotional and aesthetic education and by treating students as raw material to be processed.

All that of course was done without benefit of educational technology. The constant danger, however, is that educational technology – especially some of the tools like television and computers, and some of the systems concepts like 'trade-off', and 'cost-benefit analysis' – will light a spark in the eyes of those who are keener to minimize costs than to maximize effectiveness. We must always be vigilant. Like most technologies, ours is ethically neutral. Thus, educational technology can be liberal, libertarian, Marxist or whatever, according to the beliefs of its different exponents. From my humanistic and 'woolly libertarian' perspective, I have often enough been disturbed by what I would regard as 'misapplications' of the technology, e.g., powerful teaching techniques being developed to bring about learning of dubious legitimacy. Faced with such cases, my remedy is not to abandon educational technology but to show how it can be used to attain other ends or utilize other means. I must know the technology at least as well as those who might misapply it; and thus make sure that both the purposes and the processes of our educational systems are as humanistic as society can be persuaded to allow. As William Blake expressed it: 'I must create a system, or be enslaved by another man's.'

Yet, whatever its ideologies, education has always played its cards 'close to the chest'. It abounds with vague or unstated goals, implicit acceptance of constraints, hidden assumptions about students and society, private teacher/student transactions in closed classrooms, secret modes and unexplained rationales of selection and assessment of students, and an equivocal attitude to institutional self-improvement. Much of the thinking and feeling that goes into education may be good and honourable, much may not; but the vast majority of it rarely gets debated, even among teachers, except at the most superficial level. And it is difficult to be vigilant about what is hidden from view.

Behavioural Not Behaviouristic

Having already, I hope, disposed of the popular misconceptions that educational technology is either (merely) audio-visual aids or (worse still) a form of 'human engineering', this may be an opportune moment to dismiss another false connection that is all too easily made. It is a fact that educational technologists make much use of the word 'behaviour' and its derivatives. We may talk, for example, of learning being 'a long-lasting change in a person's *behaviour*'; or we may urge the value of *behavioural* objectives. It is also a fact that *early* educational technology, largely because of its programmed learning ancestry, was rather *behaviouristic* in its approach to teaching and learning. That is to say, it leaned heavily upon the kind of psychology popularized by B.F. Skinner (1968), whose practitioners, arguing by analogy from the training of rats and pigeons, often seemed to view the human learner also as if he were a thing to be worked upon, with a view to changing (shaping) his behaviour, a process that could be accomplished without any need to speculate about or take into account his intentions, desires or other aspects of his 'mental state'. This provocative but simplistic conception soon crumbled in the face of classroom realities and was replaced by conceptions of the learner as a purposeful participant in the making of knowledge and as a social being whose purposes and strategies are influenced by what he perceives about the people around him and the demands of the institutional setting in which he is operating.

Nevertheless, we may still talk of changes in students' behaviour and of behavioural objectives. To talk thus is not to imply that we are interested only in what students do, ignoring what is going on in their minds. We can use the term 'behaviour' to include not only students' physical actions but also what they *say* (their vocal behaviour) and what they seem to *mean* by it. As McIntyre (1980) points out in discussing research into classroom interactions:

> Researchers commonly describe themselves as observing classroom 'behaviour' but it is in practice very rare for observation systems to be limited in their concern to the physical movements or sounds made by the participants: almost without exception, meaning and purpose [i.e., from the participant's point of view] are attributed to what is observed.

The fact is, people's behaviour – what they say and do – is our only way of getting to know their beliefs and capabilities and understandings. We have no direct access to anyone's state of mind, except our own – and even there one may sometimes be deceiving oneself. Hence the power of educational technology's suggestion that learning objectives be expressed in behavioural terms. If we can say what we expect the learner to be able to do, we shall be in a position to observe whether or not he has learned. Of course, we must not be naïve about this. We must always ask what lies behind the behaviour. A student is quite capable of producing the expected behaviour (e.g., giving a 'right' answer) but for any of several possible 'wrong' reasons. For instance:

- he may be recalling the answer from having seen the problem tackled before
- he may be copying the answer from a book or a colleague without understanding it
- he may be guessing, wildly or intelligently
- he may mean something different from what his answer appears to suggest
- he may believe something different from what he has chosen to convey
- he may despise the answer he chooses to give.

John Wilson (1972) gives a particularly elegant example of how behaviour may belie understanding:

> The child that puts down *animale* as the ablative singular of *animal*, on the grounds that ablative singulars of most third declension Latin nouns end in -*e*, knows more Latin than the child who thinks they all end in -*i* and therefore puts down *animali*: even though *animali* is right and *animale* is wrong (the word is an exception to the general rule).

There must also be some capabilities that we cannot observe in behaviour. For example, one objective in geography might be that the learner should be able to 'visualize the terrain represented by a topographical map'. Now if we observe that the student can *describe* the terrain verbally, or *draw a sketch* of what it must look like, we shall certainly know that he can visualize it. Unfortunately, he may not be adept either at verbal description or at sketching, yet *nevertheless* be able to visualize the terrain. In such a case, only the student will know whether the behaviour (mental behaviour only here) has been attained.

So, and this is the point of the digression, we can seek behavioural changes in our students, we can help them towards behavioural objectives, *without using any teaching strategies derived from or reminiscent of behaviourist psychology*. Our use of behavioural terminology does not require that we ignore our learners' intentions or treat them as things. In the language of continental philosophy (frequently echoed in the 'alternative press' on education), we are ultimately concerned not with the *process* of behaviour (the physical events) but with its *praxis* – what it means to the learner. Please do not assume, however, that behaviourism has been entirely banished from educational technology; some practitioners still seem to find it an adequate model of human learning.

Educational Technology in Curriculum Development

As I have already suggested, educational technology can serve any of a variety of values. But it does embody one crucial value of its own – that it is a good thing to say as clearly as possible what it is you are trying to do, how and why you propose to do it, and in what manner you will judge the effectiveness of the subsystem you thereby create. Thus, the four-phase problem-solving approach asks that the design and implementation of learning be shown to relate to explicit purposes and that the process be treated as one of systematic trial-and-error with clear evaluation criteria leading to honest, non-dogmatic attempts to improve the hypotheses on which the learning system is based. The approach can be used to detect the nonsense in other people's teaching as well as to minimize it in our own.

Before going on in the following chapters to explore each of the four phases of our model, it can be usefully displayed in a form much loved by the systems analyst, a flow chart (Figure 1.1). More succinctly than prose, this flow-chart reveals the cyclical nature of the model and the 'feedback loops' through which 'improvements' are made to the learning design and also perhaps to the objectives and even to the evaluation process itself.

I have acknowledged the systems view by showing the model ringed about with the constraints imposed by the suprasystem within which we are working. These constraints include the structure of schooling, the expectations of students, parents, employers and other educators; the knowledge, skills and attitudes with which students reach a given point in education; the space, time and money available; the learning media available; the power and influence of mass media; our knowledge of how to facilitate learning; government decisions on educational priorities; and so on. Different teachers may well be conscious of different constraints. Whatever the constraints, they influence and limit our decisions in every phase. The ring is broken to show that the constraints are not immutable.

Even in the short term we can often remove a constraint by exerting special pressure; for example, by proving that a certain set of valued objectives can only be attained by the usually prohibited means of taking a class abroad for a time. In the long term, of course, the constraints are modified by flux in society which is itself partly due to education, e.g., education responds to the expectations of the present generation of parents and employers while at the same time helping to shape the expectations of what will be the next generation. At any one moment of decision, however, we act in accordance with what we perceive to be the existing constraints.

At the time of writing (1982), expenditure cuts imposed by government policy are the paramount educational constraint in the UK.

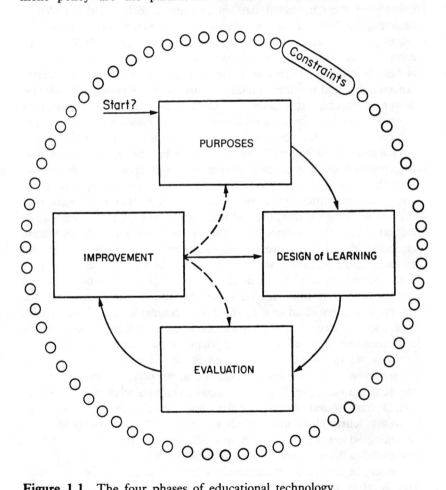

Figure 1.1   The four phases of educational technology

Another considerable constraint may be that the very curriculum planning process itself takes place 'against the clock', with school staff finding that inadequate time is available for debating what could be far-reaching curriculum decisions (see Weston 1980).

The basic approach shown in Figure 1.1 is capable of as much elaboration as the situation demands and as the prevailing constraints allow. It can help with all kinds of educational 'problems' ranging from teaching pre-reading concepts to deprived five-year-olds (Maguire 1971); to developing the 'integrated day' in primary schools (Clarke 1969); to designing a curriculum in environmental studies for ten-year-olds (Kefford 1970); to setting-up a new university (Neil 1970); to the complete overhaul of a country's educational system (Richmond 1969). It is flexible enough to allow both for long-term planning and for instantaneous decision-making. Thus, in curriculum development and the design of learning experiences, we may well launch the first phase of the approach days, weeks or months before the students are to be exposed in the resulting learning experiences. For example, we may design a new course during the summer vacation in time for the following term. But the approach can also be used extempore at high speed when *face-to-face* with the student, e.g., if a student's comment or question reveals, at one and the same time, ignorance of vital subject matter, inelegance of expression, illogical thinking and undesirable attitude to classmates, our response and how we evaluate its effects will depend on whether we can correctly identify the several possible learning objectives open at that moment and can choose which of them can be tackled there and then. This sort of application can occur dozens of times every day. While it may seem odd to link such an apparently simple interchange with the design of a curriculum or the reform of a country's educational system, each calls for decisions to be made about the priorities between diverse ends and the relations to them of whatever means are available.

What we do in each of the four phases of problem-solving – the evidence we look for and the questions we pose – varies from one application to another. Figure 1.2 shows an amplification of the approach that I have found useful in curriculum development. As we know, however, 'curriculum' may include anything from a five-year programme of studies down to a forty-minute lesson or an even briefer episode of planned teaching. Most of my remarks in this book will, for convenience, be related to an intermediate level – the development of *courses* (the level at which educational technologists are most often working).

But please note that the principles discussed will usually apply also, to some degree or other, to the design both of lengthier and of briefer learning experiences. Figure 1.2 shows the kinds of task that need to be performed within each phase of course development. Before we go on to examine these tasks one by one in the ensuing chapters, it will be helpful to run through the four phases and notice the kinds of question that can arise.

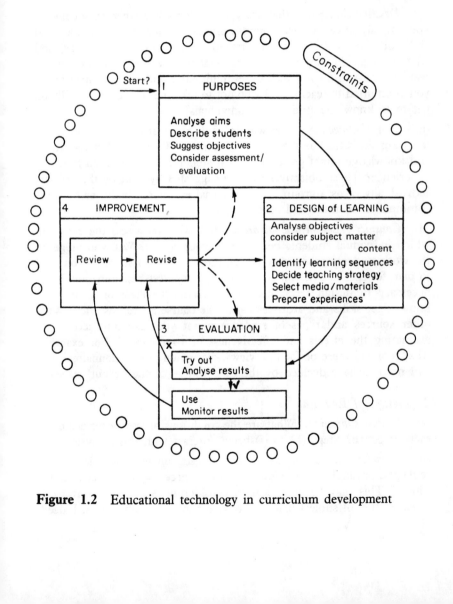

Figure 1.2 Educational technology in curriculum development

1   Purposes

(a) *Analyse Aims.* What should be the broad aims of the course? What kinds of people are you helping your students to become? How may these educational aims be justified? You may also have other, non-educational aims, e.g., making a name for yourself or trying to attract additional students or funds to your institution. Such aims may well affect what follows.

(b) *Describe Students.* What are your students like when they come to you? What range of backgrounds, interests, knowledge, attitudes and skills do they have? What understandings (or misunderstandings) and what feelings do they already possess about the subject matter of the course? Can you/do you wish to set minimum standards for entry; or are you committed to teaching all who opt to take the course? How will you get to to know the students as individuals?

(c) *Suggest Objectives.* In view of (a) and (b), what might students learn to do (or do better) as a result of the course? What new skills, attitudes and knowledge might go to prove that students have benefited from the experience? These objectives may be suggested by you, by the learners individually or as a group, by an external examining body, or by some combination of these and other sources.

(d) *Consider Assessment/Evaluation.* How will you assess the extent to which individual students benefit from your course? Will you judge by the work students produce as they go through the course; or do you need to plan for special assessment events – quizzes, tests, examinations? Is it necessary to design tests that will ascertain the state of a student's knowledge, skills and attitudes *before* the course as well as after? What other sources and types of evidence might you take into account in evaluating the effects and effectiveness of your course? For example, what role will there be for interviews, discussion or questionnaires? You will need to have decided by the time you reach the 'tryout' stage.

2   Design of Learning

(a) *Analyse Objectives.* What are the conditions necessary for achieving each objective? Steps (b) to (f) below interact with this analysis.

(b) *Consider Subject Matter.* What subject matter coverage (topics, concepts, principles, examples, etc.) will be necessary or sufficient in the course? This may become clear in considering objectives. Conversely, consideration of subject matter may give rise to new objectives. Indeed, if your course is one geared to 'getting across' a body of knowledge, this step may need to precede (but not substitute for) the specification of objectives.

(c) *Identify Learning Sequences*. From your analysis of the objectives and any necessary subject matter coverage, can you identify the elements to be learned and find effective ways of sequencing them? Is there scope for individual students to sequence and structure their learning for themselves?

(d) *Decide Teaching Strategy*. What will you do to help the students learn? Is it preferable, for example, to tell or show the students how to reach the objectives or to give them resources that will enable them to find out for themselves? Teaching strategy should be determined by the nature of the knowledge, skills and attitudes you are aiming to develop and by the individual needs of students.

(e) *Select Media/Materials*. If you are going to prepare new learning experiences, what will be the most effective combination of teaching methods or media: lectures, discussion, field-trips, practical work, textbooks, audio-tape and so on? If you are going to use materials that exist already, e.g., a programmed text or a series of television tapes, how do you ascertain that they tie in with your students' objectives?

(f) *Prepare 'Experiences'*. Do you need a detailed script for each learning experience (e.g., in the case of a television programme or a self-instructional text), or do you merely need, say, a set of key questions and an adaptable contingency plan, e.g., for a discussion group or a field-trip?

3 Evaluation

(a) *Try Out*. Engage students in the learning experiences you have designed. Assess how individuals have developed as a result. Observe the effects and effectiveness of the course – what is it like to teach and learn within the subsystem you have created?

(b) *Analyse Results*. What has resulted from the learning experiences? How have they themselves changed? Which objectives have been most widely attained? Which objectives remain unattained by which students? Does this matter? Have any unplanned-for outcomes been observed?

– To the extent that you are satisfied with the results go, on to 3(c) below.

– To the extent that results are not as satisfactory as you would wish (x), go on to 4(a) below.

(c) Use. Carry on implementing the course, or component learning experience within it, on a regular basis (and encourage its use in suitable learning environments elsewhere); *but*

(d)   *Monitor Results.* Continuously evaluate to make sure that students continue to benefit; and go on to 4 if necessary.

4 Improvement

(a)   *Revise.* According to which objectives have been achieved and which not, and the difficulties and distastes experienced in teaching and learning within the course, where are its strengths and weaknesses? The objectives may be too optimistic. It may be overloaded with subject matter content. The learning design may be at fault. The evaluation may have been insufficiently sensitive. Check back over the earlier phases, identifying and remedying weaknesses. Then try out the revised learning experiences and evaluate anew.

(b)   *Review.* Some of the constraints you took account of in planning the course or component learning experiences may now have changed and the course may need updating. If so, start again at whichever phase might be affected.

Some Cautionary Remarks

Although they are useful in grasping the broad flow of events, such flow-charts as Figure 1.2 always oversimplify the processes. For example, I have ordered the steps above in what is usually the most productive sequence for the *initial* planning of a course. If, however, you are *re*-designing a course or trying to build on teaching that has already been done, you may enter the sequence in a different way – through 'evaluation' perhaps, or through an ad hoc or unavoidable alteration to the 'design of learning'.

Do not assume either that these steps are the only ones possible, or that, once taken, a step can never be retraced. The approach is dynamic and iterative, and always leaves room for second thoughts. For example, although one should certainly make a *first* attempt to define objectives very early in the planning, one inevitably needs to come back and re-define or add to them after having worked through some of the later steps. In practice, while the decisions taken at each step are affected by earlier decisions, they are themselves liable to cause some of those earlier decisions to be changed.

Again, the separateness of the boxes in the chart may imply that the phases and the steps within them are also clearly separable. There may also be an implication that they can be considered at leisure, away from the hurly-burly of the actual teaching/learning situation. Neither of these assumptions is necessarily true. While chiefly addressing any particular step, one almost inevitably has several of the others more or less in mind at the same time. Similarly, while one can sometimes enjoy the luxury of armchair curriculum planning, much of the decision-making must take place 'on the wing', with students, administrators and other teachers breathing down one's neck.

So, here we have an approach that can be used any time an episode of teaching is being planned. It can apply, in some form or other, to long-term planning for a whole course lasting weeks or months, to daily lesson planning, or even to on-the-spot planning for a learning experience of but a few seconds' duration. It can be applied by a *group* of teachers designing a one- or two-year course as well as by an *individual* preparing his or her lessons. The approach can also be applied *retrospectively*, by teachers (or students) who are analysing a previous teaching/learning encounter and trying to understand the intentions and assumptions of the participants: what must have been their objectives? how did they relate their learning activities to those objectives? how did they evaluate the outcomes? And so on.

Notice that the approach does not demand that the learning experience comes through programmed learning, mechanical aids or any specific medium, but merely that the teacher should think systematically, and in terms of purposes and objectives agreeable to his students, about the multitude of means and media available. On occasion, analysis will even suggest that the objectives are best attained through chalk-and-talk. But no one medium will be ideal for all objectives, or even for all students interested in any given objective. The task of selecting media and combining them – not just to liven up a dull lesson but to satisfy a defined need – will make the utmost demands on the insight and imagination of the teacher. He will need to regard his job not so much as 'teaching' but rather as 'arranging for learning to take place'. He will be a director of learning resources, one of which is himself. But, like the director of a film or play, he will not always give himself the starring role.

Notice also that there is nothing to prevent exchange of roles between student and teacher. Indeed, I would suggest that one of the teacher's prime aims should be gradually to reduce his students' dependence on teaching and help them take responsibility for organizing their own learning. Thus the student will often be teaching himself (and his colleagues) just as the 'teacher' will often find himself in a learning role – learning not only with his students but also from them. The systematic approach of educational technology is, after all, but a specific application of the five stages of problem-solving proposed as part of the curriculum by John Dewey in *How We Think* (1910). If we agree that students should be taught to think, and about education as well as more remote matters, perhaps they too need to become educational technologists?

Whose Educational Technology: Whose Objectives?

The suggestion that students might learn to teach themselves may alert us to an emerging watershed in the evolution of educational technology – one more fundamental perhaps than that which separated systems thinkers from the 'audio-visual-aiders'. Traditionally, the educational technologist's role has often been to help the 'subject matter expert' clarify his objectives and develop learning experiences through which they could be achieved by 'the average student'. But many educational technologists are now asking: 'Why *these* objectives and not others? How can we suit the ends as well as the means to the needs of individual students?' Having won some reputation as specialists in effective learning, they are anxious not to become the kind of specialist described by Marshall McLuhan as 'one who never makes small mistakes while moving towards the grand fallacy'. They are beginning to ask whether effectiveness is sometimes misdirected. Particularly, many are now uncomfortably aware that their systematic, problem-solving methodology can too easily be put to improving the effectiveness of teaching/learning systems that are basically authoritarian and manipulative, and which they would prefer to help replace with democratic and facilitative systems, devoted to helping the learner clarify his own purposes and develop his own best ways of attaining them.

Out-and-out manipulation is, of course, seen only at the indoctrination end of the teaching/learning spectrum. There the 'victim' is unwittingly learning to fulfil someone else's expectations of him. When the student knows he is preparing to meet others' expectations and broadly concurs with this, as typically happens in the training area of the spectrum, manipulation may still predominate but, to the extent that his individual purposes are respected, may be tempered with facilitation. It is only at the truly educational end of the spectrum, where the student is being helped to enhance and fulfil expectations of his own, that facilitation becomes paramount. Reginald Archambault (1967) reminds us that the manipulation/facilitation divide is by no means new, even among 'progressive' educators: '. . . for Rousseau, the process of educating was still a subtle one of moulding a child to a conception of what the tutor wanted him to become. Tolstoy saw education as striving to maintain and enrich the child's original spirit.'

Negotiating the Curriculum

In practice, teachers and students tend to move to and fro over some middle ground between the two extremes, with humanistic ideals pulling them one way and the pressures for standardized qualifications and certification pulling them the other. Certainly the objectives pursued by a given group of teachers and learners can rarely be identified as emanating solely from one extreme or the other. Choice of objectives is a complex 'transactional' process in which the participants reach some kind of 'agreement' as to what is to count as valid educational knowledge (see Young 1971 and Apple 1979). Through persuading and influencing one another, through bribery and coercion, through trust and compromise, teachers and students strike a balance between what 'the system' requires, what the student wants to learn about, and what the teacher feels capable of teaching.

The teacher's willingness to negotiate curriculum must be seen as part of his professional world-view, his *pedagogic paradigm*. According to their values and beliefs about education, knowledge, learning and the student, different teachers can be seen as taking up different positions along a continuum whose opposite extremes are hinted at in such dichotomous terms as: authoritarian *v.* libertarian; closed *v.* open (Bernstein 1971); teacher-centred *v.* student-centred; dominative *v.* integrative (Flanders 1970); realist *v.* idealist (VanderMeer 1969); objectivistic, psychometric *v.* subjectivistic, phenomenological (Esland 1972). Very crudely, one end of the continuum tends to attract the teacher whose first loyalty is to a public corpus of pre-existing knowledge (which he knows everyone ought to acquire) and the need to 'get it across' to a succession of students who learn, as far as their finite capacity and motivation will allow, by absorbing and reproducing the *products of other people's experience*. The other end of the continuum attracts the teacher who avoids generalizations about what everyone ought to know and who, believing people to have unlimited capacity for growth unless 'discouraged', gives his first loyalty to individual students and encourages them to exercise their own developing motivation and purposes in the *process* of thinking and feeling their way towards making sense of *their own* ideas and experience. Of the two paradigms (whose myriad beliefs are merely sampled above), I suspect the former is more typical of secondary schools, the latter of infant schools; perhaps, also, the latter paradigm is more typical of arts-based subjects than science-based subjects, and more typical of women than men.

Only those teachers sympathetic to the latter paradigm are likely to strive towards facilitation. To do so has a number of far-reaching implications, not least in the procedures for choosing objectives and strategies for learning, in using communication media, and in student assessment. To begin with, facilitation requires of the teacher some shift of attitudes from 'Here is what I'm going to teach you and it's your job to learn it' towards 'How can I use my personal interests and expertise to help you enrich your understanding of, and reach out from, whatever you are interested in?' In literary studies, for example, one manifestation of this latter emphasis would be to say to students not 'Read *this* book by *this* author (and we'll discuss it)', nor even 'Read *any* book by *this* author', but 'Read *any* book by *any* author (or write your own), and we'll discuss it'.

We certainly cannot facilitate the student's attainment of his own purposes without opening ourselves to *his* perceptions, *his* experience, *his* point of view. In doing so, we risk being changed ourselves. A colleague, Nick Furbank (1973), expects his literature students to be able to 'say something which makes the tutor radically rethink his own conception of an author or literary work'. Graham Holderness (1973), rebuking those teachers who regard students' personal viewpoints and anecdotes as an 'irrelevant' interruption to their teaching, illuminates the process:

> Discussing *The Rainbow* with a group of [Open University] students and hearing the personal responses, the individual contributions of a wide variety of ages and occupations – the 'irrelevant anecdotes' of a farmer, an ex-miner, an engineer, a schoolteacher, a single woman, a married woman, a woman with children – to my mind enriched the reading of that book infinitely. It came to life as I had never seen it before – and I had taught it many times.

Wherever one sits on the spectrum between manipulation and facilitation, one thing seems certain: the kinds of purposes to which both teacher and students will fully devote their mental energies (rather than simply going through the motions) can emerge only out of a responsive human relationship – what Paulo Freire calls 'the convivial dialogue' – in which, even when the teacher takes the initiative, his concern is for the student's developing autonomy. Where this dialogue is absent from a teaching/learning system, the unresolved, and often unacknowledged, tension between manipulation and facilitation will produce conflict and inconsistency.

Educational technologists are no more unanimous than other educators as to how far (and when, for whom, in what circumstances, etc.,) they should be helping the student reach the system's objectives and how far (etc.,) they should help the system meet those of the student. Both tendencies co-exist and often intermingle. Although I leave no doubt as to which one I incline to, you will find reflections of both, and of the tension between them, in the ensuing chapters.

Questions on Chapter 1

1 How do you feel about the proposition that the central purpose of education is to change people? If it is not that, what would you say is the central purpose (if you believe it can be said to have one)?

2 To what extent would the author's idea of a hypothesis-testing, problem-solving approach fit in with your own ideas and experience of what it means to be a teacher? Give some instances from your own experience that could be explained in these terms or, alternatively, that could not.

3 Considering a course with which you are or have been concerned (either as teacher or student), what might it mean to take a systems view? How would you do so? Can you see any advantages in doing so?

4 How convinced are you by the author's distinction between behavioural and behaviouristic? Do you feel uncomfortable about talking in terms of the learner's 'behaviour'? If so, why is this? On the other hand, perhaps you feel the author is being unfairly dismissive of behaviourism?

5 With regard to the course you have in mind (from question 3), list six different constraints that would influence the objectives, the teaching methods, or the ways used to assess students. Can you think of an apparent constraint that might yield fairly readily if pressure were applied in the right place?

6 What are your initial reactions to the four-phase educational technology approach as outlined by this chapter? What would you see as the possible benefits and difficulties in attempting to apply such an approach in *your* situation?

7 Have you observed or experienced any teaching that the author would classify as manipulative or as facilitative? Think of some teachers you know (of yourself too, if you are one). Towards which end of the alleged continuum would you say each one normally operates? Why would you say this is?

8 Given that this first chapter is a 'trailer' for the rest of the book, does it contain any ideas that you would not have expected to see discussed in a book on 'educational technology'? Conversely, does it seem to propose excluding any issues that you would have thought essential? Make a list of words and phrases indicating surprise inclusions and omissions. Does this suggest that your present conception of educational technology is much different from that of the author?

CHAPTER 2

A CLOSER LOOK AT OBJECTIVES

Education does not mean teaching people to know what they do not know.
It means teaching them to behave as they do not behave.

John Ruskin

Objectives generate both the light and the heat in educational technology. Their light is that in which we design, evaluate and improve our learning experiences and curriculum plans. Their heat is less productive, arising as it does out of confrontations with those educators who deem it somewhat improper to speak plainly about the changes in thinking, feeling or ability that they hope to encourage in students. In this chapter we shall discuss the benefits to be had from a clear specification of objectives, and examine some of the oft-spoken objections to objectives. But first let us sharpen our focus on just what objectives are.

Aims *v.* Objectives

The literature of educational intention is a minefield of terminological confusion. Statements of purpose operate at several different levels and there are many different words used to denote the levels, e.g., aim, goal, objective, standard, learning outcome, criterion, etc. Unfortunately, some writers are liable to bundle all the levels together under one label while some, although giving the levels separate labels, happen to label them differently from other writers. Thus, what one calls an 'aim' is for another an 'objective', for a third a 'criterion' and so on. Especially when actual examples are thin on the ground, a pseudo-controversy can easily arise between two educators who cannot see that their only real disagreement is over choice of labels. I think we can save a lot of trouble if we restrict ourselves to two labels ('aim' and 'objective'), making distinctions within these categories and supporting them by specific examples.

Aims and objectives can best be thought of as being at opposite ends of a ladder of abstraction. For example, one of the curriculum aims of a school might be 'to open out the child's imagination and sympathies'. A teacher of English might translate this into a course aim (still very broad) 'to foster an appreciation of some novels of D.H. Lawrence'. He might then decide that appreciation would be demonstrated by attainment of such objectives as the following.

The student should be able to:

- Identify with Lawrence's characters.
- Relate Lawrence's viewpoint to his own experience.
- Analyse the story elements that have provoked his involvement.
- Describe an incident from his own experience as if seen by Lawrence.
- Assume the persona of Lawrence in responding to hostile contemporary criticism.
- Make and justify a personal statement as to Lawrence's 'meanings'.
- Seek out and read more of Lawrence's novels than are set for assignments, and so on.

He could make these objectives even more concrete by thinking up possible test questions, e.g., 'What would you have done if you had been Mrs. X in such-and-such a situation?', or 'Reply as Lawrence to this review in *The Times*', or 'Why does Lawrence end the novel with that particular paragraph?', etc. Perhaps he might also consider *situations* in which he might observe pupils' individual or group responses to Lawrence, e.g., a role-playing exercise or dramatic enactment of a scene, or records of pupils' book-borrowing.

Notice that objectives are not only more precise (and more numerous) than either curriculum or course aims, they also switch the emphasis from the teacher's teaching to the learner's learning. They tell us what to look for in the student, whereas the aims do not.

In fact, aims represent the most abstract level among statements of educational purpose. They are to be found in school and college prospectuses, speech-day orations, the works of the great educators, and are particularly clearly exemplified in the reports of government committees. For instance:

- Skills, qualities of character, knowledge, physical well-being, are all to be desired . . . certain skills of communication in speech and in writing, in reading with understanding, and in calculations involving numbers and measurement. . . . All boys and girls need to develop, as well as skills, capacities for thought, judgement, enjoyment, curiosity. They need to develop a sense of responsibility for their work and towards other people, and to begin to arrive at some code of moral and social behaviour which is self-imposed. It is important that they should have some understanding of the physical world and of the human society in which they are growing up. . . .

Newsom Report (1963) *Half our Future*, HMSO

– One obvious purpose is to fit children for the society into which they will grow up . . . for such a society, children, and the adults they will become, will need above all to be adaptable and capable of adjusting to their changing environment. They will need as always to be able to live with their fellows, appreciating and respecting their differences, understanding and sympathising with their feelings. They will need the power of discrimination and, when necessary, to be able to withstand mass pressures. They will need to be well-balanced, with neither emotions nor intellect giving ground to each other. . . .

Plowden Report (1967), *Children and their Primary Schools*, HMSO.

And here, as part of the UK government's consultative document towards a 'core curriculum', are six aims suggested for schools (DES 1980):

– to help pupils develop lively, enquiring minds, the ability to question and argue rationally and to apply themselves to tasks, and physical skills;
– to help pupils acquire knowledge and skills relevant to adult life and employment in a fast-changing world;
– to help pupils to use language and number effectively;
– to instil repsect for religious and moral values, and tolerance of other races, religions and ways of life;
– to help pupils understand the world in which they live, and the inter-dependence of individuals, groups and nations;
– to help pupils appreciate human achievements and aspirations.

Similar statements of aim, often no less embracing, can be found in the syllabuses teachers have written for individual subject courses. For example, you are likely to be told that a particular history course will not only develop the student's historical sense and enable him to practice the skills of the professional historian but will also encourage tolerance of others, racial sympathy and international togetherness. But wherever we find a statement of aims, common themes recur: the intellectual and emotional development of the individual, preparation for adult life in society, acquisition of a common culture and so on. The statements quoted above hint at a conflict which is rife at this level of abstraction: we apparently want children to develop their individuality and yet to fit into their place in society; to become original, critical thinkers and to subscribe to conventional mores; to prize their gift of rational thinking and to treasure their emotions and imagination; to learn how to enjoy leisure and to believe in the dignity of work; to be responsive to innovation and to hold dear the eternal verities in a changing world; and so on.

The Limitations of Aims

The government's consultative document mentioned above (DES 1980) offers the opinion that: 'Schools are likely to be more effective in achieving their curricular aims if these aims are clearly set out in writing, are generally known and accepted by staff and pupils, and are systematically pursued through curriculum organisation and day-to-day teaching.' True as this may be, something more is needed.

Abstract statements of purpose – aims I have called them though you may find other writers calling them goals, objectives, curriculum purposes or simply pious hopes – are too vague and ambiguous to be of much help in planning actual learning experiences. Two teachers can be agreed that helping the child 'to appreciate human achievements and aspirations' or 'to develop capacities for thought, judgement, enjoyment and curiosity' are important educational aims – and yet they may hold quite different views as to what would constitute such appreciation and development. Thus, each may set about his teaching in ways that the other would totally deplore.

Vague and abstract aims, especially if they sound obviously worthy, can give the kiss of death to a curriculum. Because we can never be certain as to whether or not the long-term purposes have been achieved, just about any set of teaching activities and any set of short-term learning outcomes can be justified as appropriate. We can thus settle down into a change-resistant status quo. The educator who operates exclusively with such aims allows himself all the fine ideals and noble goals of a minority political party that knows it will never get into office and be put to the test. Vagueness and multiple ambiguity is his best protection against charges of incompetence. He will be able to get away with the tactics of a swimming instructor who pushes all his novices in at the deep end – for those who survive he takes the credit, while those who sink from sight have no one to blame but themselves.

According to Albert Bandura (1970), vagueness of aim is equally prevalent in psychotherapy:

> One of the major obstacles to the development of effective change programs arises from the failure to specify precisely what is to be accomplished, or the more common practice of defining the intended goals in terms of hypothetical internal states. When the aims remain ambiguous, learning experiences are haphazard, and whatever procedures are consistently applied tend to be determined more by personal preferences of change agents [*psychotherapists or teachers*] than by clients' [*patients' or pupils'*] needs.

And he is sceptical about the extent to which the ambiguous aims are achieved:

> The criteria upon which judgments of therapeutic efficacy are based leave much to be desired. In many instances psychotherapists' global impressions of their results serve as the major indicants of outcome. Considering that such ratings reflect upon therapists' professional competence, it is reasonable to assume that therapists do not underrate the therapeutic value of their methods.

There is similar scepticism about the achievement of general aims in education (see Musgrove 1971, De Cecco 1972, Hajnal 1972). Whatever is learned in school, it does *not*, for most people, seem to lead to the lifetime of creative and critical thinking, devotion to inquiry and the pursuit of learning, moral autonomy, personal expression, aesthetic discrimination, tolerance, flexibility, developing awareness of self and others, etc., etc., envisaged by the great educators. Clearly, much of this shortfall of educational intent is due to the fact that the social system is a more powerful 'change agent' than is the educational system. But a large part of it is, I fancy, due to our unwillingness to spell out, examine, and make public the *objectives* we would take as necessary or sufficient for the achievement of our general aims. As a result, where behavioural changes are brought about, they are not always those we'd have wished for. Benson Snyder (1971) describes how students adapt their behaviour to what the system actually *requires of them* (not necessarily what its participants profess), acknowledging the reality of a 'hidden curriculum' unconsciously transmitted by the total social context.

The Value of Aims

For open curriculum planning, and some opportunity to attain our general aims where they are attainable and abandon them where not, we need to push for more precision, saying: 'Your aims sound fine but what would the student have to *do* to convince you they are being attained? What do you look for in students who have benefited from your curriculum? What are the objectives?

On the other hand, you may feel inclined to ask: 'Why bother with aims at all? Why not go straight into the objectives?' Unfortunately, this would be to ignore a fact of life. People characteristically do conceive of broad aims before they analyse them into a precise specification, though they may modify their aims once they've produced some objectives. There is nothing to be gained, either when thinking out one's own educational intentions or when helping someone else think out his, to pretend that the thinking is 'aimless'. Better to start from where people are than to pretend they are somewhere more convenient.

Besides, aims do help establish the *ethos* of a curriculum. Although for different teachers (or students) a given set of aims may imply different sets of objectives, for any one teacher (or student) his aims are likely to help him in judging the worthwhileness of the objectives. Aims provide the ethical standard against which objectives are justified. Thus, if a student or teacher questions the value of one of your objectives you can only discuss the matter in terms of your overall aims. Without such a standard, as the Newsom Report says:

> Discussions of the educational objectives too easily lose themselves in the weighing of rival claims between this subject and that, or in emphasis on the practice of basic skills at the cost of excluding all variety or relevance of interest.

Even where a set of aims does not infallibly pin down a set of appropriate objectives, they may still help us assess the appropriateness of the means through which we teach. As James Hoetker (1970) eloquently puts it:

> We cannot teach critical independence by insisting on the mechanical application of memorised critical formulas. We cannot teach respect for thought by attending only to mechanics and forms of expression. We cannot teach honest self-expression by punishing disagreements with established opinions. We cannot teach students to be free citizens by teaching them as witless ninnies. And, above all, we cannot teach students to honour the common humanity of all men by expressing contempt for the student's own humanity in our every word and gesture.

Headmasters who prohibit girls from wearing jewellery on the grounds that 'they've got such terrible taste' or who insist on boys' hair and girls' skirts being of a length abnormal in the students' peer group, please note: aims like 'cultivation of the aesthetic sense' and 'development of personal judgement and self-respect' are best not mentioned in your speech-day orations.

From Aims to Objectives

But if we are to know what to strive for in the behaviour or observable activity of students, aims must be translated into objectives. For example, John Wilson (1969) considers the aim of *helping the pupil to think and act morally*. This, he says, implies that the pupil should:

- Demonstrate to an adequate degree the belief that the feelings, needs and interests of all other people are equally important to his own.
- Be able adequately to discern what other people's feelings, needs and interests are, and also what his own feelings, etc., are.
- Possess sufficient knowledge (e.g., of social norms and of things dangerous to humans) to be able to predict the outcomes of his possible choices of action.
- Possess adequate social skills with which to communicate, cooperate and interact with other people.
- Be able to decide course of action based on his own moral principles (and not on expediency, rules, impulse, guilt-feelings, etc.).
- Possess sufficient alertness, courage and motivation to consistently carry out the moral actions he has decided on.

John Wilson goes to great lengths in 'operationalizing' these objectives, specifying them in futher detail and suggesting relevant 'criterion tests' and learning experiences. Despite the further explication, it remains clear that the teacher will need sensitive assessment skills to check that such objectives are being attained. He may also need to recognize that he is capable of growth in this area himself. So too with the 'self-actualization' objectives suggested by Carl Rogers (1961):

- The person comes to see himself differently.
- He accepts himself and his feelings more fully.
- He becomes more self-confident and self-directing.
- He becomes more the person he would like to be.
- He becomes more flexible, less rigid in his perceptions.
- He adopts more realistic goals for himself.

- He becomes more acceptant of others.
- He becomes more open to the evidence, both of what is going on outside of himself and what is going on inside of himself.

Notice also, both in Wilson's set of objectives and in Rogers', the frequent use of words like 'sufficient', 'adequate', and 'more', indicating that each objective must be specified with yet further precision to relate it to the present and possible future states of particular *individual* students. But, and this is the point, despite the relativistic nature of these objectives and the problems they will pose for assessment, they are already far more suggestive of appropriate teaching strategies and learning experiences than are the high-minded platitudes and woolly generalizations that usually preside over curriculum planning.

General curriculum objectives like those of Wilson and Rogers are not tied to any specific subject content. Indeed, they could be pursued without studying any of the traditional subject disciplines in the school curriculum. If, however, we ask a subject teacher about his purposes, we are again likely to be presented with vague, ambiguous statements largely in terms of what the teacher intends to do to his students and often incorporating the subject matter which is to be 'covered'. This is just as likely in science-based subjects as it is in arts-based subjects. For example, here is a set of 'aims' compiled from the science syllabuses of a number of secondary schools by Philip Taylor (1970).

- Knowledge of scientific principles and their application to everyday life, for example electrical principles useful in household electricity, heat conductors, air pressure.
- To give a training in scientific method, progressing from known information through observation to a conclusion. To emphasize the need for accurate observation, recording and interpretation of data.
- To encourage a sense of responsibility in the individual, e.g., looking after animals.
- Providing an understanding of nature and man's use of it, e.g., lightning.
- To link science with other subjects, e.g., biology with gardening (plant life).
- Fostering interests in, and an awareness of plant and animal life around the pupil.
- The basic science course acts as a basis on which a more detailed approach to individual subjects can be built.
- A general science course should give a grounding in scientific principles necessary for a pupil's future work, e.g., apprenticeship electrical engineering.

From this we get a general indication of the criteria by which the course content will be selected and of the pedagogic tone. But we can form no clear picture, or rather (and worse) we may all form *different* clear pictures of what the 'graduate' of such a course should be able to do as a result. Take the first item of Taylor's list for instance. How should the student *demonstrate* his knowledge of the scientific principles and their application to household electricity, heat conductors, air pressures, etc.? What might be some possible objectives? Taking just the example of heat conductors, the author of the course aims might spell out precise objectives as follows.

By the end of the course the student should be able to:

- State which of ten given examples of heat transfer are due to conduction, which to convection and which to radiation.
- Provide one example of his own for each.
- Given ten substances, indicate which are good conductors and which are good insulators.
- Describe or design simple experiments to show that:
  (a) Water is a poor conductor of heat.
  (b) Dark surfaces absorb radiant heat more easily than light ones.
  (c) Radiators heat rooms by convection as well as radiation.
- Etc.

Of course there are many alternative objectives he could spell out and still be consistent with so broad a description of the course aims. But without some such objectives for each area of the course neither teacher nor students will know where they are going, let alone how to get there.

To be operationally useful, then, general curriculum aims and course aims must be translated into objectives. Some objectives will need to be attained by every student in a group, others will be of relevance to only some of the group. Take for example the curriculum aims published by the National Art Education Association in the USA in 1968:

Each student should demonstrate, to the extent that he can, his capacity to:

(1) have intense involvement in and response to personal visual experiences; (2) perceive and understand visual relationships in the environment; (3) think, feel and act creatively with visual materials; (4) increase manipulative and organizational skills in art performance appropriate to his abilities; (5) acquire a knowledge of man's visual heritage; (6) use art knowledge and skills in his personal and community life; (7) make intelligent visual judgments suited to his experience and maturity; and (8) understand the nature of art and the creative process.

Lloyd Bishop (1971) 'operationalizes' these aims by turning them into course objectives for his teaching in ceramics:

As a result of the art program, each pupil should demonstrate to the extent that he can, his capacity to:

1. Have intense involvement in and response to personal visual experiences:
   a. by voluntarily attending ceramics classes and labs an average of three hours a week for at least one semester;
   b. by voluntarily attending an exhibit, display, or studio of ceramic work and discussing it with others.

2. Perceive and understand visual relationships in the environment:
   a. by being able to describe the relationship between foot, belly, neck, and rim in any given ceramic pot;
   b. by being able to identify and discuss examples of good form/function relationships in objects of everyday use.

3. Think, feel and act creatively with visual art materials; by voluntarily making ceramic objects of his own design.

4. Increase manipulative and organizational skills in art performance appropriate to his abilities:
   a. by being able to prepare and care for clay and objects of clay from construction through the final firing;
   b. by being able to properly construct unique objects of clay.

5. Acquire a knowledge of man's visual art heritage:
   a. by being able to describe generally the differences in the construction of pottery from basket-maker to the wheel, and the general relationship of these methods to the culture of the times;
   b. by being able to distinguish and discuss the differences between the pottery of the American Indian, the Hellenic Greek, the medieval Japanese, and the contemporary American.

6. Use art knowledge and skills in his personal and community life:
   a. by voluntarily purchasing or trading his own work for a piece of pottery for himself or for someone else;
   b. by voluntarily sharing his points of view about the existing examples of ceramics in his community with others.

7. Make intelligent visual judgments suited to his experience and maturity:
   a. by being able to discuss, on the basis of judgments formed while taking this class, what are examples of good pottery from a group of given examples;
   b. by making objective critiques of the relationship between form and material in his own and the pottery of others;
   c. by keeping that work of his own which is good and by voluntarily destroying that which fails to meet the criteria which he has set for good pottery.

8. Understand the nature of art and the creative process:
    a. by voluntarily attempting projects that are unique to him;
    b. by voluntarily discussing with others events or objects which seem both unique and important to him.

(NAEA 1968)

He goes on to further analysis of these course objectives and shows how to derive from them even more specific (lesson) objectives related to the needs and interests of an individual student. Here are the objectives he works out with one particular student relating to the 'prepare and care for clay' objective in 4a above:

– Given the proper formula, the student will be able to mix ten pounds of clay from dry materials and slurry in fifteen minutes, observing all the restrictions and safety precautions regarding the equipment use.
– The student will be able to describe how to store clay properly so that it loses none of its working qualities over a period of several days.
– The student will be able to wedge five pounds of freshly mixed clay into an homogeneous mass in ten minutes.
– The student will be able to identify plastic clay, leatherhard clay, and bone-dry clay from a group of twenty samples in a period of ten minutes.

There is no profit to be had from trying to stipulate at what point of precision a statement becomes an objective rather than an aim. (When does fog become mist become clear visibility?) The essential thing to recognize is that the nearer we get to an objective, the more likely it is that 'interested parties' or 'experts' will be able to agree as to whether or not a given student's behaviour indicates attainment, or at least improvement. And it is at this end of the ladder of abstraction we need to be in order to design appropriate learning experiences for individuals and groups.

The Variety of Objectives

So far I have spoken of objectives as if they were all comparable descriptions of student activity, differing only in the precision with which they are stated. Perhaps it is time we noted other differences.

Types of Activity

One rough distinction between objectives is based on the kind of activity or behaviour involved: *thinking, feeling* and *doing* behaviours give rise, respectively, to what are known as cognitive, affective, and psychomotor objectives. Cognitive objectives involve the learner in thinking processes like remembering, evaluating, and problem-solving. All the 'heat transfer' objectives (page 39) are cognitive objectives. Affective objectives, on the other hand, involve the learner's feelings and attitudes. Carl Rogers' 'self-actualization' objectives are clearly affective, as are those objectives in the ceramics course that refer to what the student *will* 'voluntarily' choose to do, as opposed to what he will merely be *able* to do. Affective objectives often relate to the learner's dispositions rather than to his capabilities. Finally, psychomotor objectives are those involving the learner in some kind of muscular activity – like the above-mentioned objectives of mixing and wedging clay.

Many objectives, of course, are an amalgam of cognitive, affective and psychomotor. For instance, we might ideally expect the student who is competently mixing clay to be, at the same time, remembering the principles involved, entertaining some kind of attitude or feelings about the safety requirements, and enjoying the tactile satisfaction he gets out of handling the material. But it often makes sense to recognize a given objective as falling *primarily* into one category or another. Our decision about where the emphasis lies may help us decide on appropriate means of teaching and learning.

Schooling in our northwestern corner of the world has for centuries concentrated on the cognitive. The intellectual nature of the enterprise is well described by Sterling McMurrin (1970):

> The cognitive task is not only the achievement and communication of knowledge. It is discipline in the habits of reason, in the ways of knowing; a discipline in perception, in the inductive, deductive, and intuitive processes and in the techniques of analysis and generalization. It involves both sensory knowledge and abstract thought. And for the lower schools, it entails especially the cultivation of the skills of literacy – the capacity for reading, writing, oral expression and computation – which make the acquisition of knowledge possible.

With all this to accomplish, little wonder that affective objectives have been neglected – on the assumption either that they were no business of the teacher or that they would somehow take care of themselves. Rational thought and detached verbal understanding have traditionally been prized above feeling, action and involvement. This imbalance has long concerned many educators, therapists, and imaginative writers (see Jones 1972). Roger Harrison and Richard Hopkins (1967) have blamed it for the culture shock, and the initial inability to cope with ambiguous situations or to take action under stress, experienced by Peace Corps volunteers. They argue that people who are to work with people from other cultures – teachers obviously, but, to an even larger extent, all of us – need educational experiences that 'have a more direct connection with life as it is lived in our relativist, kinetic, peripatetic, crisis-ridden society'. They describe an experience-based training for 'connecting head and guts' which has very wide applications.

The determination among some US educators to get thinking and feeling objectives flowing together again gave birth to the concept of 'confluent education' (see Brown 1971). As for psychomotor objectives, with the exception of those involved in such prestige occupations as surgery and in certain sports, they too have generally been held in low esteem. Certainly, the psychomotor and, to a large extent, the affective (where they have been given any emphasis at all) have been objectives for the working classes – wood-hewing and water-drawing and related arts – together with the gentling, affective influence of scripture and compulsory acts of worship. Educational and class status, meanwhile, has been offered and pursued only through escalating cognitive accomplishment and certification (Dore 1976).

Levels of Complexity

Another way we can distinguish between objectives is in terms of their level of complexity. Are they high-level or low-level objectives? Within each of the three main categories of objectives we can see that some skills or abilities are more difficult to attain than others. This may be because the 'more difficult' abilities need more preliminary practice. Usually it is because the student must first have acquired a number of lower-level abilities, or 'enabling objectives' as they are sometimes called. This is very obvious in the psychomotor area. For example, jumping to catch a ball is likely to be more difficult to learn than standing still and catching a ball, because the former objective can be attained only by someone who can *already* both catch and jump.

But the same holds for the other categories too. Cognitive objectives range from simply remembering factual information, up through skills like analysis and evaluation (using earlier knowledge), towards the creative recognition and solution of problems, perhaps generating new knowledge in the process. In the affective category the humblest objective may be to get the student to pay attention or 'reach out' towards a new experience; at a higher level his experience may persuade him to attach value to what he is learning; at the highest level it may even bring about a change in the student's aspirations and life-style. At each level of the hierarchy we meet objectives that can be attained only by students who have already attained certain objectives at lower levels. This has clear implications for the structuring of learning experiences which we'll explore in Chapter 4.

The most-quoted classifier of objectives is undoubtedly Benjamin Bloom who, with his co-workers, has produced two handbooks (Bloom 1956, Krathwohl, Bloom and Masia 1964) offering taxonomies of educational goals in the cognitive and affective categories or domains. A taxonomy for the psychomotor domain has since been provided by Harrow (1972). In the cognitive domain, Bloom identified six levels of objective, with 'knowledge' as the lowest level and 'evaluation' as the highest:

1.0 KNOWLEDGE
    1.1 Knowledge of specifics
    1.2 Knowledge of ways and means of dealing with specifics
    1.3 Knowledge of universals and abstractions in a field
2.0 COMPREHENSION
    2.1 Translation
    2.2 Interpretation
    2.3 Extrapolation
3.0 APPLICATION
4.0 ANALYSIS
    4.1 Analysis of elements
    4.2 Analysis of relationships
    4.3 Analysis of organizational principles
5.0 SYNTHESIS
    5.1 Production of a unique communication
    5.2 Production of a plan or a proposed set of operations
    5.3 Derivation of a set of abstract relations
6.0 EVALUATION
    6.1 Judgment in terms of internal evidence
    6.2 Judgment in terms of external criteria

In the affective domain, Bloom identifies the following five levels:

1.0 RECEIVING (attending)
    1.1 Awareness
    1.2 Willingness to receive
    1.3 Controlled or selected attention
2.0 RESPONDING
    2.1 Acquiescence in responding
    2.2 Willingness to respond
    2.3 Satisfaction in response

3.0 VALUING
    3.1 Acceptance of a value
    3.2 Preference for a value
    3.3 Commitment
4.0 ORGANIZATION
    4.1 Conceptualization of a value
    4.2 Organization of a value system
5.0 CHARACTERIZATION BY A VALUE OR VALUE COMPLEX
    5.1 Generalized set
    5.2 Characterization

Without wishing to be as rude as R.S. Peters (1969) about Bloom's efforts ('a dog's dinner . . . full of muddled conceptualization'), one must admit that they do not give the kind of help we might hope for in formulating our own objectives. There is an overlap between the levels and even between the domains; there are gaps; the examples quoted are too few, are usually too vague to be useful, and redolent of the multiple-choice style of questioning on which the taxonomies were based. Also, the very format perpetuates the fallacy that cognitive and affective objectives can be attained independently of one another. Nevertheless, as the first attempt to identify some kind of structure and cohesion in a highly flabby area, Bloom's taxonomies can still help illuminate curriculum discussions, and the elaborated attention given to levels above or other than 'knowledge' is still, in itself, a new message for many teachers. (For further criticism, see Ormell 1974, Pring 1971, and Rowntree 1977, pp. 103–106; and for a review of other workers' taxonomies, see Glenn 1977.)

Dealing with Variety

But might we really need to specify objectives at as many as six different levels; or eight levels if we follow Robert Gagné (1965) whose scheme we'll be looking at later? Edgar Stones (1972), in his thorough and systematic analysis of teaching objectives in educational pscyhology, uses three levels. He expects students to recall principles of educational psychology, then to identify applications of the principles, and finally to apply the principles themselves in solving classroom problems. In Stones (1979, pp. 160–162) he shows how this three-fold classification can be widely useful in school learning.

Certainly (following Scriven 1967) teachers must recognize and distinguish between at least two levels of cognitive objective – recall of information and the higher-level intellectual behaviours. Too many teachers talk vaguely of purposes that could be spelled out as high-level objectives – e.g., 'I teach my students to think mathematically' – and then test their students on low-level objectives only – e.g., requiring them to memorize formulae or perform mechanical computations. As we all know, most students learn only what they think they are going to be tested on. As Neil Postman (1970) puts it:

> At present, the only intellectual skill the schools genuinely value is memorizing and the student behaviour most demanded is *answer-giving* – giving someone else's answers to someone else's questions.

In his review of research on teacher questions in the classroom, Hargie (1978) confirms that teachers usually ask questions to which they already know the answers. Most researchers report that teachers ask mainly low-level questions, stressing factual recall rather than thinking and evaluation. Educationally this is sad, but it is quite understandable where the teacher sees himself as responsible for training students to tackle public examinations that are themselves based almost totally on factual recall.

The discontinuity between remembering and thinking behaviours was well illustrated by Margaret Abercrombie (1969):

> It was found that students who . . . were well-grounded in the facts of biology, physics and chemistry, did not necessarily use scientific ways of thinking to solve problems presented in a slightly new way. They might be able, for instance, to recite all the lines of evidence for the theory of evolution but yet be unable to use this material to defend the theory in argument with an anti-evolutionist. They might know what the function of a certain organ is believed to be but did not always know why, nor did they clearly understand on what kind of evidence a belief of that sort was based. When asked to describe what they saw in dissecting an animal or in looking through a microscope, they often did not distinguish sufficiently sharply between what was there and what they had been taught 'ought' to be there. It seemed that scientific ways of thinking did not automatically result from learning the facts of science.

Also, even if teachers deny responsibility for the more 'therapeutic' of affective objectives, they must recognize that their cognitive objectives have an affective aspect which should influence their teaching style. That is, every teacher would hope that the student finishes a course with at least as much (and preferably more) *interest* in the subject as he had at the beginning. In the useful terminology of Robert Mager (1968) the teacher should be aiming to encourage 'approach' rather than 'avoidance' tendencies. We are not interested merely in what the learner can do (immediately the course is over) but, more importantly, with what he *will* do (when the course is long past and he is free from the threat of assessment). It is the affective element that turns 'can do' *capabilities* into 'will do' *dispositions*. That this does not happen often enough is lamented by Everett Reimer (1971) as follows:

> Schools are obviously as much designed to keep children from learning what really intrigues them as to teach them what they ought to know. As a result, children learn to read and do not read, learn their numbers and hate mathematics, shut themselves off in classrooms and do their learning in cloakrooms, hangouts, and on the road.

One distinction between objectives that I often find useful in course planning (especially when considering assessment) is to ask whether they concern primarily *knowledge, attitudes* or *skills*. (Again, mixtures are possible within a single objective.) Thus, in a course on drug therapy for trainee doctors, three of the objectives might be that the doctor should:

– be concerned to respond to the patient's ideas and feelings about his symptoms and possible treatments *(attitude)*
– be able to review a range of possible treatments *(knowledge)*
– be able to elicit the patient's expectations and judge his likely compliance with possible treatments *(skill)*.

It is important to point out, however, that this is *not* the same distinction as that made by Bloom between cognitive, affective and psychomotor objectives. Knowledge can be knowledge of one's own or another person's feelings or of how to perform a physical task (whether or not one can actually perform that task competently). Attitudes refer to people's values, preferences and dispositions as suggested by their actual behaviour – as opposed to what they might profess in a questionnaire or interview. Skills can be cognitive or affective as well as psychomotor; including, for instance, the skills of literary criticism or scientific problem-solving, of violin-playing or cutting a dove-tail joint, of chairing a meeting or counselling a patient. By skills I am referring to demonstrable ability in a pursuit, as opposed to knowledge about the principles involved or about the practice of other people.

I am not suggesting here that skills necessarily represent a higher level of objectives than knowledge about a skill. They are certainly separable in that one may possess the knowledge but be inept in applying it. Similarly, one may have an intuitive competence (e.g., in certain social skills) without being able to elucidate the principles one is following or place them in any kind of theoretical context. As White and Mayer (1980) argue, certain types of knowledge (what they call 'productive knowledge') enable one to *understand* the skill in such a way that one can extend one's competence, e.g., by applying the skill in novel or more demanding situations.

As we have seen already, there are many ways of classifying objectives and I shall be discussing yet another classification in the next chapter. The various classifications cut across one another, and none is superior to others for all circumstances. Sometimes one seems most helpful in generating objectives or analysing what has been attained, sometimes another. As in so many areas of teaching, having a variety of models on which to draw can help us with the creative task of imagining how things might be different from the way we first see them.

The Benefits of Objectives

What is to be gained from spelling-out one's educational purposes in the form of explicit objectives? There are four main areas of benefit: communication, content and structure, teaching and learning methods, evaluation and assessment.

Communication

First of all, objectives may enable you to *communicate* about the intentions of the teaching and learning. To begin with, one can communicate with the student. Research by Mager and Clark (1963) has shown that students who know the objectives of a course, and who are given appropriate references and resources, may be able to *teach themselves* in half the time taken by normal classroom methods. (This much-quoted finding does need to be interpreted with care, however. It could amount to no more than students saying: 'Tell me what test questions you are going to ask, and I'll go and look up the answers.') But whoever does the teaching, students will still learn faster and contribute more if they knew where they are supposed to be heading. Ideally, of course, the students should be encouraged to formulate their own objectives as well as accepting the teacher's. In this case, objectives will help them to communicate their needs to the teacher and he will see more clearly what he can do to assist. But, whatever the source of the objectives, they will be more likely to be achieved if they are known to the students as well as the teacher.

Teachers sometimes point out that, especially in a highly technical subject, it is difficult for a student to grasp the implication of certain objectives until he has actually achieved them. There is often much truth in this; but it is usually possible, and well worth the imaginative effort, to give the student some kind of gloss on such objectives. Perhaps one can describe typical examples of the capabilities required, the context in which they are relevant and possible results. This may be sufficient to convince the student of their appropriateness and value. If students are merely left guessing, they are likely to play safe and act as though the objectives were to memorize the teacher's words of wisdom or to score a pass mark on an examination.

Objectives also enable you to discuss educational purposes with your colleagues. This opens up all kinds of opportunity for dispute, argument and cooperative thinking. Broadly phrased curriculum and course aims usually sound far too worthy to quarrel with. Yet when they are translated into objectives the illusion of consensus is often shattered. Only then may teachers enter into a productive debate about what exactly is to be taught and what are the implications for the system *as a whole* of the objectives that different teachers want achieved. Such communication is clearly essential in any team-teaching situation. It is essential also where students pass from one teacher to another as they progress from phase to phase within a course. Otherwise, some objectives may be needlessly tackled by more than one teacher and, worse still, other important objectives may be skipped by every teacher on the mistaken assumption that someone else is tackling them. The confusion about who is responsible for achieving which precise capabilities probably accounts for the frustration behind the rueful epigram:

> Juniors schools say they get sent children who can't read.
> Secondary schools say they get sent children who can't write.
> Colleges of education say they get sent students who can't think.
> All schools say they get sent student teachers who can't teach.

It is particularly vital for those objectives that cut across different subject matters – e.g., critical thinking skills, cooperative learning skills, etc. – to be agreed by all teachers who work with any given group of students.

Not least, objectives also enable you to communicate your teaching purposes to yourself. As Robert Mager (1962) puts it: 'If you don't know where you're going, you're liable to land up some place else!' Or, of course, no place at all. But even if the some place else were useful and interesting (and often it is not) you would probably find yourself with no time or resources left to get to the place you later wish you really had tried to reach. This is not to deny that an eventful voyage may be more educational than the actual landfall; but one must then ask what are the capabilities and dispositions that the voyagers must draw upon and promote in order for the 'events' to have significance. Self-awareness about objectives often leads to more purposeful and sensitive teaching; and, in so far as the student is teaching himself, to more purposeful and sensitive learning.

Content and Structure

A second benefit of objectives is that they may help you to select and structure the content of your teaching. As you probe into possible objectives you will find they delineate the important topic areas of your course and even suggest possible paths through it. Very often you will find that you can rearrange the list of objectives in such a way that they suggest a sequence of attainment – with the later objectives building on and developing out of the earlier ones. (More of this in Chapter 4.)

Teaching and Learning Methods

Thirdly, objectives may help you decide on appropriate learning activities and teaching media. In teaching ceramics, for example, how do you decide on the best combination and permutation of group and individual work; explanation, demonstration and practice; lecture, discussion and use of packaged learning materials (books, films, etc.)? It is difficult to do this rationally without reference to specific objectives (as will be discussed further in Chapter 4). Take one specific example from ceramics. If students are to be able to 'distinguish between the pottery of the American Indian, the Hellenic Greek, the medieval Japanese and the contemporary American', should they learn by comparing verbal descriptions, photographs, cine-films or real pots? This depends on whether you want the student to be able to distinguish verbally, pictorially or 'in the flesh'. Perhaps you want all of these. The point is that the student who can make verbal distinctions between the types of pot may not be able to distinguish between actual specimens, and vice versa. These are different objectives and will be achieved through different learning activities and media. Knowing just what the students should be able to do as a result of the course helps you decide what experiences they should have during it. The constraints come in here, of course, affecting both objectives and methods, e.g., can you actually get access to real Japanese pots?

Evaluation and Assessment

The fourth and final value of objectives is that they help you decide on appropriate means of evaluation and assessment: on ways of monitoring the effects and effectiveness of your course and of finding out what and how well your students are learning. (The distinction between evaluation and assessment is discussed more fully in Chapter 6.) While identifying objectives you'll probably have tentative assessment schemes coming into mind all the time. And the specificity of the objectives will help to ensure that your method of assessment is appropriate to the skills being tested. You won't, for example, make the obvious but frequent mistake of assessing whether a student can carry out some practical task – like being able to distinguish between specimens of Indian, Greek, Japanese and American pottery – by asking him to write a short essay describing how he would do it! A classic example of this is encountered in driving tests where, in effect, the examiner sets out to test the candidate's ability to *recognize and name* different road signs seen while driving a car by asking him to *describe from memory* the features of the road signs named by the examiner (while not driving a car)! Unless you have some means of realistically testing the strengths and weaknesses of your course, and what students do and do not get out of it, you will be in no position to make rational improvements to it.

Some Objections to Objectives

Despite the apparent benefits of explicit objectives, they have not been clasped to the bosom by all educators. Objections are raised by some. I believe that these objections usually reflect ignorance (of what form objectives can take), or fear (of what objectives may disclose), or impatience (with pundits who claim too much for them). There is frequently some substance in the objections, but it usually reflects not on objectives as such but on the way some people have used them or over-promoted them. One of the most articulate commentators in recent years has been a colleague of mine whose critical review (MacDonald-Ross 1973) is guaranteed to stimulate; though it is best read with a suitable antidote, like Calder (1980) or even the following paragraphs, kept close at hand. See also the criticisms of objectives offered by Stenhouse (1975).

The lines of attack on objectives are various: They are too difficult to formulate, especially in arts-based subjects. They put too much stress on trivial and easily measured behaviours. It is dangerous to focus on behaviour anyway. Not all desirable results can be specified in advance. It is undemocratic to pre-specify. Objectives are too difficult for the teacher to work with. And so on. Let us look at some of these objections.

Recognizing Worthwhile Objectives

Some critics take umbrage because there are no clear rules for generating objectives. I am not sure why this lack should be found surprising, let alone daunting. There are no clear rules for doing many of the things we feel are worth doing in education. As I make clear in the next chapter, nobody pretends that objectives are easy to come by. The pinning down of clear and worthwhile objectives demands even more mental effort and research from teachers than they demand from their students. But, unless he so exerts himself, the teacher may find he is in the unfortunate professional plight of being unable to prove that his 'teaching' has any results. And it is a myth, dispelled by the experience of science-based curriculum development teams, to suggest that science yields up non-trivial objectives more readily than the arts. In all subjects and at all levels, the task is difficult. This is a reason not to abandon it but to seek ways of cooperating over it, improving our efforts and making them more productive.

A linked, but more serious, objection is to suggest that objectives over-emphasize trivial and easily measured behaviours. Trivial objectives are certainly the easiest to identify. This is partly because they are the kind that, without having been explicitly specified, are those most widely attained in education already. Fortunately, the educational technology approach can help focus attention on the low level and shallowness of such objectives, and should thus enable us to eliminate them. So what do we aim for instead? Are we really so incapable of saying how we would recognize higher-level capabilities in students?

Quite honestly, I believe that much of the criticism in this particular area arises because the critics are looking only at what I would call 'masterable objectives'. Such objectives (like those relating to heat transfer on page 39) one has either attained or not attained. It is not possible to 'improve' at such an objective as, for example, being able to name the author of *Wuthering Heights*. But to concentrate on such objectives is to ignore those that I talk of as '*infinitely improvable*'. Look at John Wilson's or Carl Rogers' objectives, for instance (pages 33 and 37). Could one ever expect to attain 100 percent mastery of such an objective as being able 'to discern what other people's feelings, needs and interests are' or 'to become more the person one would like to be'? Such objectives can scarcely be dismissed as trivial. If we wish to plan for a learner's 'growth' and 'development' in terms of objectives, then those objectives must surely be chiefly of the infinitely improvable variety.

The teacher who attempts to clarify his objectives is probably less likely thereafter to teach and test the trivial and easily measured than he was before. He is likely to have a better vision of what might be achieved. Robert Mackenzie (1970) describes how and why he resisted pressure to introduce into his school a classroom course on sea-navigation – 'much value to be got out of a navigation course, even if you never get a boat', he was told – because he clearly saw the objectives as relating rather to real-life problem-solving – 'what to do if things went wrong in the Firth estuary; if, for example, a fog came down and they lost their way':

> The great advantage of chartwork and astronavigation and these things, from the Education Department's point of view, is that it is so easily examinable. John Smith gets 68 per cent and James Thomson gets 75 per cent and down go these accurate-seeming figures in the report that will be sent to the prospective employer. But the value to these boys of going out in a boat and gradually gaining confidence in their ability to meet with emergencies and to pull out everything they've got in the fight with nature – that value is not so accurately measurable.

A teacher with lesser awareness of his true (and 'infinitely improvable') objectives might well have capitulated. To do so would have been to commit McNamara's Fallacy (named after the one-time US Secretary of Defence) – making the measurable important rather than the important measurable (or at least observable).

Behavioural v. Behaviourist Again

A special blast of wrath is directed at those objectives calling themselves 'behavioural'. I have already dealt in Chapter 1 with the assumptions that often lie behind this attack – especially the suspicion that the term implies behaviour*ist* conceptions of the learner and a predilection for teaching him to *do* things without a care for whether he is able to explain or justify, or acquire any 'productive knowledge' about, his actions. In real life (as distinct from the journals of academic debate), most proponents of behavioural objectives, on hearing of such suspicions, would look, if they truly had not done so already, for means whereby the 'missing' explanations, justifications and productive knowledge might *also* be expressed in observable behaviour.

If we actually examine the kind of objectives that are presented as behavioural, we find that they rarely do specify behaviour in ways that would allow action to be considered separately from intention. Never, for example, do they take the form: 'The student will move his pen across the paper, beginning by forming the letter "B", then . . . etc.' Rarely even do they imply that every student must necessarily demonstrate his attainment of the objective in exactly the same way as every other student. Very often, they will be no more specific than this: 'The student will learn to solve quadratic equations.' This latter objective, while appearing to allude to a behaviour (solving), actually indicates only the intended result of behaviour – that a solution should have been reached. The student behaviour involved may have taken the form of factorizing, of completing the square, or of using the general quadratic formula. Even if the behaviour had been specified more explicitly – 'The student should be able to solve quadratic equations by factorizing' – we should lose no sleep over the fact that different students might well 'behave' differently, but to equal effect, while doing so.

So, for many objectives, 'behavioural' is something of a courtesy epithet – but they are none the less useful for that. Especially with higher-level and affective objectives, the 'behaviour' is often indicated fairly broadly, leaving the teacher or assessor room to use his professional experience in deciding, with each individual student, how amply or in what manner that behaviour is demonstrated. This is particularly necessary with what I have called 'infinitely improvable' objectives – those which one never fully attains but goes on improving at for as long as one practises in the relevant field.

Some writers have tried to avoid the connotations of 'behavioural' by talking instead of 'performance' objectives. Unfortunately, this is open to almost the same kind of assault: 'So you're treating your students like performing animals, are you?' Despite the infelicities of language, the aspiration behind such objectives is clearly not to assert a particular view of the learner or approach to teaching. Rather, it is meant to concentrate attention on how learning is to be recognized in the student rather than be merely assumed as an inevitable, but regrettably invisible, concomitant of the teacher's teaching. If only we could have it fully understood that 'assessment' need not involve measurement, marking or competitive comparisons between one person and another (see page 84), we might do better to talk of *assessable* objectives instead.

Appraising Creativity

Undoubtedly, most of the agonizing is over affective objectives and the higher-level cognitive objectives, especially where they involve originality and creativity. This is one of the key problems raised by Elliot Eisner (1967) and Lawrence Stenhouse (1971), both of whom seem to prefer structuring courses around the dictates and traditions of the subject discipline rather than by outlining how the students might develop as a result. Certainly we have a lot to learn about describing and exemplifying high-level and creative abilities. Yet it would surely be nonsense, and flying in the face of a discipline's critical standards, to assert that there are no ways of stating in advance the kinds of quality one would look for, and the errors one would expect to see avoided, in a student's painting, essay, short story, musical score, research report or whatever. Professionals constantly make such appraisals and judgements about their colleague's work, and examiners likewise, with even greater show of accuracy, for candidates in the arts. So what capabilities and dispositions are they looking for? If and when they are willing to externalize their criteria for judgement, we shall have our objectives. Eisner admits that such judgements take place: 'One must judge after the fact whether the product produced or the behaviour displayed belongs in the novel class'; and Stenhouse even seems to relent and admit under another name what we are calling 'objectives': 'One could also sharpen and define the *criteria* [my italics] by which students' work might be judged.'

   To set the student off in pursuit of an unnamed quarry may be merely wasteful, but to punish him for failing to catch it is positively mischievous. Do we sometimes appear to say to the student: 'I can't say precisely what skills or knowledge I want you to acquire from this course. Just do your own thing (guessing what might come into my mind) and I'll give you a grade according to how I feel about it'? If there really are abilities that cannot be spelled out reasonably clearly in advance, even after we've observed similar abilities in previous students, let's not belabour the student with them afterwards.

Democracy and Enjoyment

Is it undemocratic to specify learning objectives in advance? One answer to this is to point out that all education is undemocratic in that the student is either literally forced or, at higher levels, economically persuaded to partake and be 'groomed for society'. Explicit objectives at least let the student see what is expected of him and he can, or should be able to, propose supplementary or alternative learning objectives of his own. And nor need the joy go out of learning – not that the majority of students notice much joy in it at present. I take it for granted that we should help students enjoy what they are doing; otherwise, they are unlikely to go on doing anything like it when they leave us. The chances are that they will enjoy it more if the objectives are clear – especially if the objectives are clearly their own. But beware of the teacher who says that interest, enjoyment and pleasurable activity are his only objectives. How does he convince himself and his students that school is the best place, and 'learning' the best means, to achieve them?

Managing Objectives

Do objectives really make the teacher's job more difficult? Certainly it is less easy to 'muddle through' if you are aware that you are not achieving what you set out to achieve. But some critics suggest that even the dedicated teacher cannot be expected to keep aware of the progress of a number of different students towards a number of different objectives. This to me would indicate that the teacher should modify the system rather than abandon his statement of purpose. He should perhaps go for fewer objectives, keep fuller records on each student and perhaps delegate some of the task of monitoring progress to a 'helper' or to the students themselves. If important objectives get skipped because it is difficult for one person to keep track of them all, this would suggest that more people should be aware of them rather than fewer. Writers like Joan Dean (1972) describe how systematic recordkeeping can be organized even in primary school, with children contributing through regular self-assessment.

There is, of course, an associated fear expressed by some teachers: that explicit objectives may lay them open to being judged by results. Personally, I would prefer to be judged by how effectively I help change the capabilities and dispositions of my students rather than by my 'qualifications', appearance, beliefs or even my methods. Many student and probationary teachers are judged unfairly because their teaching style is at variance with the prejudices and favourite practices of the person judging them. Conversely, many relatively ineffective teachers are rewarded for their orthodox behaviour in the classroom. What we should be judging the teacher by is the growth and development among his students.

Some critics fear that objectives may blinker the teacher, rendering him incapable of taking advantage of educational opportunities that occur without warning in his classroom. Again, education is too full of this already for objectives to worsen the situation. As I have said before, one's initial statement of objectives is not final and immutable: indeed it should make one more rather than less aware of the claims of the *new* objectives that arise urgently out of encounters with students in a learning situation. Awareness of all the important objectives that he has identified already may well make a weaker teacher think twice (and rightly) before swimming after red herrings. But it should not deter any teacher from recognizing an unexpected educational opportunity and a new and valuable objective to which it relates. Ralph Tyler (1964) clearly sees objectives as part of a dynamic, responsive style of teaching:

> . . . as you work with objectives and your efforts to reach them you frequently have a basis for re-definition of your objectives. As you see what is really possible, you may see more clearly the kinds of things the pupils need in addition to those you thought of in your original planning. The process of clarifying goals, then working towards them, then appraising progress, then re-examining the goals, modifying and clarifying them in the light of experience and the data, is a never-ending procedure.

Another related but equally conquerable fear is that having objectives to evaluate a course by will make the teacher blind to other, unplanned-for results. In fact, such results are no more likely to be overlooked than are side-effects in drug trials, provided a conscious effort is made to seek them out. If beneficial, the side-effects can be recognized as objectives and, in future, be built into the system. If harmful, then the learning system will be revised with a view to prevent their occurring again.

Beware of Implicit Objectives

Whatever you feel about the strength of objections to objectives, let's be quite clear about one thing. The denial of behavioural outcomes does *not* mean that none are being achieved. The teacher who refuses to identify his objectives, or to admit that he has any, is nevertheless acting as an 'agent of change' on the capabilities and dispositions of his students. His every communication with students contributes to the achievement of some implicit objective. It is unlikely, for instance, that teachers spelled out the objectives that constitute the learning described by writers like Everett Reimer (1971):

They learn that what is worthwhile is what is taught and, conversely, that if something is important someone much teach it to them.

and Philip Jackson (1968):

. . . our student learns to subjugate his own desires to the will of the teacher and to subdue his own actions in the interest of the common good. He learns to be passive and to acquiesce to the network of rules, regulations, and routines in which he is embedded. He learns to tolerate petty frustrations and accept the plans and policies of higher authorities even when their rationale is unexplained and their meaning unclear. . . . From kindergarten on, the student begins to learn what life is really like in The Company.

and Harold Taylor (1960):

The usual kind of education . . . is designed to give answers to questions which nobody asked and to inhibit the student in discovering his own truth and insight. The lectures and the texts do all that sort of thing for you. They provide a way in which the student can cover up his true self by finding a vocabulary acceptable to most people and a set of facts which are generally known among people generally considered to be generally educated.

Once this skill of covering up has been acquired, the student may never be called upon to say what he really thinks or feels at any point in his education or later life. This is what makes bores, and produces college graduates who are ignorant and dull, but successful and plausible.

The hidden curriculum marches on. If we don't specify the objectives we want, we'll have to put up with those we get.

In general, then, it seems to me that 'objectors' do not identify fundamental weaknesses of objectives but merely warn us of possible pitfalls in their formulation and use. Certainly, we cannot afford to ignore the warnings – they indicate the need for vigilance. But the dangers are minimal compared with those already rampant in content-based curricula presented to students in the hope that 'something useful's bound to rub off on them'. At any rate, the concept of behavioural (assessable?) objectives has surely generated the most powerful approach to curriculum development that has yet become available to us.

Alternative Ways of Curriculum Planning

Although in this book I am presenting an approach to curriculum development that is heavily dependent on an early formulation of objectives, we know there are other approaches. So, let me finish this chapter by simply reminding you of a dozen alternative ways of beginning to develop a course:

- Sitting and reviewing one's own knowledge of the proposed subject.
- Asking other teachers and subject matter experts.
- Analysing similar courses elsewhere.
- Reading textbooks aimed at students working at about the same level as ours will be.
- Reading more advanced books and scholarly articles on the subject.
- Reviewing films, radio and television tapes, newspaper and popular journal articles, etc., relating to the proposed subject.
- Asking prospective students what topics they would like to see the course include.
- Discussing with students their existing conceptions of, and attitudes to, the key concepts of the subject matter.
- Choosing books (or other source materials) around which the course will be organized.
- Thinking of essential activities that students need to engage in as part of the course.
- Considering how student attainment on the course might most sensibly be assessed.
- Studying an examination syllabus, the question papers, and examiners' reports from previous years, and so on.

These alternative approaches, and others, are discussed at length in Rowntree (1981) and to do so here would not be appropriate. However, one or two of them are touched upon later in this book; and it is worth noting, in the context of our present discussion, that many of them are attractive to people who would spurn objectives – and yet they can rapidly lead into discussions about how students might be expected to demonstrate the knowledge, skills and attitudes that are likely to be enhanced by their experience of the course.

Questions on Chapter 2

1   Consider the aims (if any have been expressed) for a course that you know about. How far do they illustrate the limitations and benefits

described in the first few pages of this chapter? Do you think different teachers convert them into similar learning objectives?

2 Again thinking of a course you are familiar with, what are its objectives? If no objectives have been made explicit, ask yourself what student capabilities are tested in its assessment procedures. How would you classify those objectives – e.g., in terms of cognitive/affective/psychomotor or levels of complexity or knowledge/attitudes/skills, etc?

3 In what respects do you agree with the benefits claimed by the author as likely to arise from a clear specification of objectives? Can you give examples of such benefits from your own experience? Have you experienced any benefits that the author has not mentioned?

4 Which of the objections to objectives mentioned by the author do you feel he deals with *least* convincingly? Why? How would you argue the case against him or, alternatively, strengthen his argument against the objection?

5 Are there any important objections to, or anxieties about, objectives that you feel the author has neglected to mention? If so, what are they? And what do you think the author might want to say if he were asked about them?

6 Think of a course you have planned or are otherwise familiar with. Which of the 'alternative ways of curriculum planning' mentioned on page 59 might have been most useful in planning? Could they have usefully been associated with the use of objectives? How? Or why not?

CHAPTER 3

DEVELOPING OBJECTIVES

'Stephen major,' he once said to my brother [about his writing of Latin verse], 'if you do not take more pains, how can you ever expect to write good longs and shorts? If you do not write good longs and shorts, how can you ever be a man of taste? If you are not a man of taste, how can you ever hope to be of use in the world?'

Leslie Stephen

In this chapter we discuss the origins of objectives, and how they can be developed into criteria that will help in judging the effectiveness of the learning system.

Sources of Objectives

Where do objectives come from? How do they arise? They arise in the perceptions of teachers, students, parents, employers and all who have a stake in education. They come from the views we all hold about the future needs of people in society and about the skills and insights that have found expression in the various arts, crafts and sciences, and they relate such views to the here-and-now needs and interests of individual students. We can make a model (Figure 3.1) to help us explore these sources and the kinds of objectives that come from them.

Our views about what is worth learning are very largely determined by our beliefs or assumptions about the future roles of people in society. These beliefs and assumptions may be tacit or ill-formulated, and they may even amount to little more than a thoughtless extrapolation of the status quo. They may relate generally to society as a whole, or recognize the many different sub-societies to which an adult will have loyalties – ethnic, occupational, social class, sex, age, family, sporting loyalties and so on. They may concern themselves with society as it is, as it may become or as it 'ought' to become. Whatever their slant and emphasis, these beliefs and assumptions about the learner's needs in society may provide the ultimate justification for both the ends and the means of education. Needless to say, people's differing beliefs and assumptions lead them to differing views about what ends and means are desirable. No consensus can be expected except through negotiation, and even then it may be tenuous and brief.

I   Life-Skill Objectives

From such beliefs we can derive broad aims in the curriculum like those of Plowden or Newsom (see page 33). We can then exemplify these behaviourally and operationally in terms of curriculum objectives. I have labelled them 'life-skill' objectives in Figure 3.1. But what life-skills will our students need in the months and years ahead? What can they conceivably learn now that will be of survival-value next year, a decade hence, and in the twenty-first century – when children now beginning school should be in the prime of adult life? Futurology is a perilous business and the only safe prediction about the year 2000 is that the future then is likely to seem even more uncertain and full with possibilities than it does now.

Yet some factors keep recurring in all discussions of the life ahead: children maturing earlier, people living longer, less demand for unskilled labour, more leisure time, fewer role differences between the sexes, more multiracial and other cross-cultural encounters, lifelong education, more emphasis on integrated teamwork and the pooling of skills and resources in solving the many problems in social welfare, the environment, business and research, that prove resistant to specialist approaches. And all this contributes to and is influenced by the continuing explosion of knowledge – not the least influential of which being knowledge about other people and how they live – which will be constantly outdating people's earlier ideas and attitudes, skills and roles.

Despite the interest in 'alternative futures' (see Hack et al. 1971, Kogan 1976) and the pleas for relevance still being heard from students all around the world, I know of no radical attempt in recent years to systematically reconstruct the aims of the curriculum. Neither the UK government's consultative document (DES 1980) nor the Scottish Munn Report (1977), to mention two recent efforts, suggests any aims that might not easily have been lifted from a pre-war report. This is no doubt because both seem to confine themselves to asking only what can be achieved with the existing teacher provision and in a system predicated

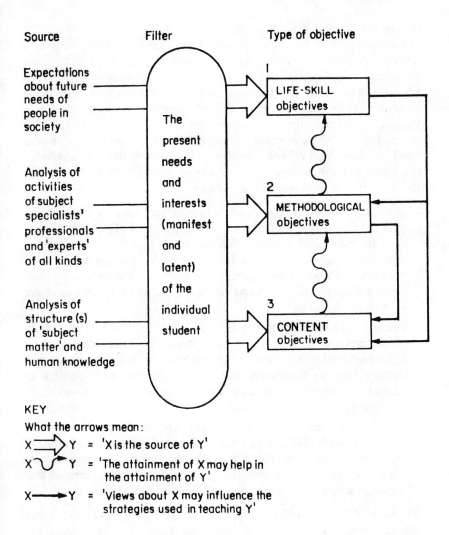

Figure 3.1   Source of Objectives

on the teaching of existing subjects.

Certainly, there has been no recent attempt to translate aims into worthwhile objectives. Something of the sort has been tried in the past, for example by Franklin Bobbit (1924) whose 'task analysis' of everyday life suggested 160 major objectives, and by the Russell Sage Foundation (Kearney 1953 and French et al. 1957) whose objectives filled two volumes. But those lists were never very useable and are anyway long outmoded. A future-oriented catalogue of worthwhile learning would need to offer well-defined objectives in response to such aim-laden questions as the following (which run from cognitive life-skills, through the affective, to psychomotor life-skills):

– How far can we increase a child's intelligence? Can we maintain the growth? Can we teach him how (not what) to think? Can we teach him how to learn, and relearn? Can we teach him all man's ways of 'knowing'? Can we teach him how to share his learning and to communicate with others non-verbally and verbally, in speech, in writing, graphically, symbolically, using all media, old and new, as a producer as well as consumer?

– Can we teach children how to live with uncertainty and stress, how to avoid emotional damage and stunted growth, how to channel fear and aggression, how to believe in themselves and others, how to give therapy both to themselves and others? Can we teach children to empathize with others, to enjoy the diversity of people's life-styles, to get involved, to commit themselves to cooperative courses of action?

– Can we teach physical skills that will continue to be useful to the student in adult life? Can he learn sufficient kinaesthetic confidence to go on enhancing these skills and to take the risk of trying to learn new ones? Can we introduce students to sports and physical exercises that they can safely and beneficially practise throughout their lives?

To some of these questions, especially in the middle paragraph, many teachers would answer 'No' or 'It's none of our business'. Certainly, educational technologists have been slow in bringing their approach to bear on such life-skill considerations. Fortunately, a few writers have already given us a start in digging out the underlying behavioural objectives. Carl Rogers' objectives (pages 37–38) are clearly affective life-skills. The 'critical thinking' objectives (page 7) may be recognized as cognitive life-skills. John Wilson's 'moral behaviour' objectives (page 37) combine affective and cognitive. Both cognitive and affective objectives are again obvious in the 'What's-Worth-Knowing Questions Curriculum' proposed by Neil Postman and Charles Weingartner (1971) where the teacher:

> . . . measures his success in terms of behavioural changes in students; the frequency with which they ask questions; the increase in the relevance and cogency of their questions; the frequency and conviction of their challenges to assertions made by other students or teachers or textbooks; the relevance and clarity of the standards on which they base their challenges; their willingness to suspend judgements when they have insufficient data; their willingness to modify or otherwise change their position when data warrant such change; the increase in their skill in observing, classifying, generalizing, etc.; the increase in their tolerance for diverse answers; their ability to apply generalizations, attitudes and information to novel situations.

Allied skills for exploring and mastering the student's environment are suggested by Alan Bishop (1971) who wants the student to be able to construct and apply mental models of the real world as follows:

A   Model construction and exploration:
- To search for, and find, similarities occurring in a variety of situations.
- To isolate and define the variables underlying these similarities.
- To determine and define the relationships that exist between the variables.
- To establish the necessary validity of statements of these relationships.
- To search for the axioms from which this model can be logically derived.
- To vary the axioms in order to produce other consistent models.

B   Model application:
- To recognize that a given situation is one in which a certain model is applicable.
- To make assumptions about the variables defined in the model.
- To manipulate the model in order to solve the problem.
- To verify that the chosen model is the best analogue of the given situation.
- To use the model for making new predictions.

Although these few examples give some taste of what is needed, the work of realistically deriving possible aims and then objectives from our expectations about the learner's life in society has yet to be done. As is implied in Figure 3.1, whatever the Group I aims and objectives we eventually come up with, or even if we stick to those implicit in current curricula, they will affect the way we set about achieving the Group II and Group III objectives. Don't assume, however, that all Group I objectives are somehow grander than those in II and III. Group I, like any other set of objectives, is hierarchical. The high-level life-skill objectives we have looked at above are underpinned by lower-level (but equally life-skill) objectives such as being able to read and write, tie one's shoelaces, and respond to the mention of one's name.

II Methodological Objectives

Until now, not a word about subject matter. In designing a curriculum we need not start by taking a 'subject' and asking: 'What are the relevant objectives?' We can just as well begin with the objectives and ask: "What, *if any*, are the relevant subjects?' So, we have already established that various life-skills (like the ability to classify, infer, suggest analogies, form testable hypotheses and so on) can be harnessed to the student's feelings and experience in his efforts to make meaning out of his environment. Having done so, we can go on to help the student identify any subject *areas* (not necessarily established subject disciplines) in which he can acquire and practise such life-skills. In this, we may draw upon an analysis of the activities of scholars, professionals and practitioners in all kinds of arts, crafts and sciences, seeking out correspondences with the emerging interests and enthusiasms of our student. Probing into his chosen subject matter – which may be *part* of an established discipline like geography, calculus and biochemistry, or which may be a subject area of the student's own devising like 'an analysis of television advertising', 'designing things to help our handicapped neighbours' and 'life in our town during the Second World War' – the student will be in a position to acquire a variety of *methodological* objectives.

By methodological objectives I mean the specialized 'modes of inquiry' and 'ways of knowing' which writers like Hirst and Peters (1970) and Philip Phenix (1964) see as being embodied in the various subject disciplines. They would argue that the different disciplines exemplify differing methods of investigation, differing forms of response to experience, differing criteria for proof and truth, differing modes of explanation and justification – all of which contribute to the growth of mind, but along different dimensions. Notice that I am talking here not of the concepts peculiar to the various disciplines but of any distinctive ways in which each discipline can be seen to generate and manipulate its concepts.

For example, Bell and Staines (1981) bemoan the fact that psychology students are often reduced to 'accumulating a large body of "facts", techniques and precisely stated generalizations which can be reproduced on demand (i.e., in essays and examinations)'. This refers to what I shall be going on to call 'content objectives'. As for the methodological aspects of the subject, say Bell and Staines:

> Students are merely *assumed* to know rather than explicitly taught, how to construct, analyse or evaluate the kind of argument which is characteristic of psychological discussion. We feel it is unrealistic to expect students merely to 'pick up' such an ability by some apparently magical process.

Unfortunately, we are rarely given enough examples from which to determine precisely how the methodology of, say, a chemist or a literary critic differs from that of an historian or a psychologist, except in using a different 'tool-kit' of concepts on different 'raw material'. We know especially little of how their supposedly different modes of perception affect their respective approaches to problems outside of their 'subject' – the kinds of problem that adults other than academics are facing most of the time – like: 'Am I doing right by my kids?', 'What can we do about the way things are around here?', 'How am I to cope with redundancy?', or simply 'Why won't the damn car start?'

If we ever do get down to compiling that 'catalogue of worthwhile learning' we may well find ourselves shifting many objectives out of the methodological group and into the life-skills group. For example, an historian might include, among his methodological objectives, that the student should learn to:

- Distinguish between examples of primary and secondary sources.
- Suggest possible primary sources for various kinds of required historical information.
- Arrange various types of primary source in the accepted order of credibility.
- Ask appropriate questions to determine the usefulness of any source.
- Distinguish between valid and invalid inferences that might be made from a source, etc.

Yet how far is he describing methodological skills peculiar to the historian and how far those life-skills used by the lawyer, the detective, the civil servant, and business executive and, indeed, anyone 'acting on information received'?

Paul Hirst (1968) rightly points out that one can't have, say, 'critical thinking' or 'problem-solving' without reference to some subject matter. However, this is not to say that the subject matter must be recognizable as belonging to some one *established* discipline. We should not be surprised if practitioners in the different disciplines have more in common than is sometimes supposed. For example, the 'manipulation of models' objectives (page 65) were conceived by Bishop as mathematics objectives. Yet in how many other subject disciplines might these also be regarded as essential methodological objectives? Are they not also appropriate even, say, to deciding why the car won't start? Was I so misguided in purloining them for the curriculum as a whole? Interestingly, many workers like Covington, Crutchfield and Davies (1966) and Edward de Bono (1973) have been producing materials and schemes for teaching 'thinking' as a 'subject' in its own right, based on the application of newly learned mental tools to everyday problems.

However, many teachers, especially above primary level, owe their allegiance to a single 'established' subject and (especially if working to a public examination syllabus) give their students only limited freedom to develop their own subject areas within it. Even as a group, teachers are restricted in the subjects they can sponsor. As Frank Musgrove (1971) points out, subject disciplines are not all equally prestigious. Subjects are social as well as intellectual systems:

> A subject is a social institution with its sense of identity and loyalty exacted from its members. In conflict with other subjects it defines its boundary and its sphere of interest. Subjects are highly organised, hierarchic, bureaucratic. They are busy discovering reasons for their existence and importance. They develop their own defensive systems against encroachment.

It has not escaped my notice that, since the first edition of this book, educational technology has itself grown into a 'subject'. It has its own courses and slots in college timetables, its own examinations, diplomas and professional associations, and even its own national bodies sponsored by government ('quangos' in the UK). Most of the features mentioned by Musgrove can now be discerned among the practitioners of educational technology.

Certain subjects are firmly entrenched in the curriculum, with an integrated examination/career-prospects system acting as a very institutionalized barrier to change. Yet we cannot all accept the rationalizing approach of those curriculum apologists who seem to suggest that the present mixture of subjects (essentially the English grammar school curriculum) must be the most worthwhile or it would not be taught. We want to ask: 'why history, algebra and chemistry? Why not ecology, astronomy and criminology? Or why not psychology, politics and anthropology?'. Of course the student should be encouraged to follow an interest in such well-defined disciplines where they impinge on his experience and so seem relevant to him. But equally relevant may be 'non-subjects' like pollution, sex, community development, television, science fiction, football and car mechanics, and the one subject of direct relevance that never gets discussed in school – education! In encouraging the student to define Group II objectives (Figure 3.1) of his own, we may be helping him construct *his own* subject.

Several decades of curriculum reformers have learned how difficult it is to squeeze 'new' subjects (like technology, sociology and economics) into the secondary school curriculum, let alone try to develop a Deweyan 'emergent curriculum' out of the experiences and interests of individual children. But the pressure has produced some results. Subjects as such now have little foothold left in the primary schools. At university and college levels too, the unexpected wealth of insight generated in such interdisciplinary or boundary areas as psycholinguistics, ecology, bionics and cybernetics, oceanography, industrial archaeology, period studies in the humanities and so on, are helping to soften the demarcation disputes between established subjects. Secondary schools are still mostly organized around the teaching of separate subjects; but cross-disciplinary curriculum projects do have their adherents, and the public examination system in England and Wales does provide assessment for teachers who want to develop with students their own 'integrated studies' curriculum (e.g., CSE mode 3).

If the student is working on a recognized subject, whether established or emerging, he should be developing the methodological skills peculiar to that subject or its parent disciplines. If, on the other hand, he is carving out a new subject area of his own, the methodological skills he needs may well be those typical of *several* disciplines, together with some that are freshly generated out of his own style of inquiry. Take, for example, a student who wants to investigate the effects of the Second World War on the local civilian population, perhaps because he is intrigued by the disparities between what appears in his school history books and what his family tell him. He could well find himself borrowing from whatever methodologies are used by the historian, statistician, sociologist, economist, social research interviewer, art historian, literary critic, political scientist and the philosopher, to name but a few. The conceptual richness of his study will greatly depend on the freedom and competence with which he can pull together a variety of approaches. The point is that he does not first need to learn each of the parent disciplines separately, in some sort of entirety, before he can draw upon their methodologies in formulating and answering questions of his own.

So, in so far as we can isolate distinctive modes of inquiry and ways of knowing in and around the disciplines, these are what we mean by methodological objectives (Group II) and on these the student will depend quite heavily for his future learning. Despite examination papers that continue to emphasize the recall of factual knowledge, educators are more and more committed to the belief that knowledge is becoming obsolete so fast that almost the only thing worth knowing is how to acquire new knowledge. As Jerome Bruner (1960) puts it: 'Methods of inquiry are more durable than facts and even generalizations.' Bruner (1964) goes on to explain it like this:

> To instruct someone in these disciplines is not a matter of getting him to commit results to mind. Rather, it is to teach him to participate in the process that makes possible the establishment of knowledge. We teach a subject not to produce little living libraries on the subject, rather, to get a student to think mathematically for himself, to consider matters as a historian does, to embody the process of knowledge-getting. Knowing is a process, not a product.

III Content Objectives

At the same time, students may well be held to need a grounding in basic concepts and principles (especially those that are unlikely to go out of date very fast) to help them make sense of new experiences and acquire new ideas reasonably efficiently. This brings us to the Group III objectives in Figure 3.1. Given that certain life-skills are to be aimed for, and that certain methodological objectives are important to the student's line of inquiry, what is the subject *content* of the student's learning, and what content objectives might he achieve as a result?

By content objectives I mean aspects of the student's ability to recognize and expound the concepts, generalizations and principles that make up the substance and structure of his subject area. The D.H. Lawrence and heat transfer objectives mentioned in Chapter 2 are of this type; so too are the objectives implied in the 'accumulations' criticized by Bell and Staines (page 66). Content objectives can be prescribed by a subject matter expert (e.g., a teacher) if the subject is an established one, or they may be allowed to emerge from the student's developing interests.

Jerome Bruner (1960 and 1966) is renowned for his assertion that children of almost any age and level of ability can develop a grasp of the nature of a discipline, provided the emphasis in teaching is not on isolated facts but on the fundamental concepts and unifying principles of the subject. These concepts and principles are the outcome of the discipline's modes of inquiry discussed above. Concepts like counter-vailing power in politics, food chains in ecology, conservation of energy in physics, salvation in religion, stimulus and response in psychology, form and function in art, behavioural objectives in education, together with an ability to apply the methodologies, enable the student to make sense of new experiences in the subjects. Each subject discipline can be regarded as a network of many such concepts and principles related together in some kind of systematic structure. Often, several alternative structures can be identified according to the viewpoints of different observers (including the students). With Group III objectives we are asking what the student has to do to demonstrate his grasp of these concepts or principles, and how he can explain and justify their relation-ships. Such behavioural objectives can be derived, as Bruner implies, from an examination of the structure (or structures) of the relevant discipline.

But Group III objectives can also be initiated by the student. To have him learn the teacher's structure would be little better than having him learn isolated facts. Instead, he can be encouraged to develop structures of his own, building analogies, examples and even new 'subject matters', out of his personal interests and experience. Without this he is unlikely to be developing the over-riding life-skills and methodological skills. Thus, the student investigating civilian life during the Second World War may find himself able to describe and suggest cause-and-effect relationships among such topics as social organization and adaptation; age-, sex- and class-variations; public disruption and personal loss, health, nutrition and living standards; employment, industrial relations and pressures for social reform; communication, and propaganda; the determinants of morale; education, leisure and the arts; and so on. Some of the concepts he uses in building up his pesonal 'knowledge structure' wil be specific to the subject area, e.g., evacuation, rationing, conscien-tious objection; but they are likely to be fortified and illuminated by whatever more general concepts he is able to borrow (e.g., socialization, norms, the price mechanism, causation), along with the methodologies, from the several related disciplines.

In so far as the teacher has special knowledge of such a student's subject area and related disciplines, he may well be able to suggest possible content objectives. His chief concern, however, should be to help the student identify his own content objectives, appropriate to the thrust of the student's own inquiry. Unfortunately, the teacher is often more adept at manipulating students to achieve his objectives than he is at facilitating students in the achievement of their own. For insights into the social context of this phenomenon, see Keddie (1971) or Barnes (1971). The manipulative strategy is particularly evident among teachers who are under pressure to 'cover' a syllabus, but it occurs more widely. Frederick Macdonald (1971) gives an example of a teacher introducing a project on 'pioneer life' to a class of ten-year-olds:

> He asked the students what they wanted to study about 'Pioneer Life' and what kinds of questions they should raise concerning the subject. As the discussion proceeded, the children suggested the usual categories for studying a history unit – namely, the pioneer's food, shelter and clothing. One child mentioned that he had seen a Western movie in which a man accused of horse stealing was immediately hanged. This comment on the movie evoked considerable interest in the group and one of the children asked why the man was hanged right away. The teacher dismissed this question as irrelevant to a discussion of pioneer life. The decision not to utilize this question in effect set the stage for the kinds of things that the pupils would talk about. Had the teacher chosen to capitalize upon this question, topics concerning pioneer conceptions of justice and due process of law, the function of law-enforcing bodies, and the validity of citizens' arrest could have been developed. These topics did not emerge in the ensuing discussion, nor were they included as relevant points in the outline of topics to be studied under the heading of 'Pioneer Life'. The teacher's decision at this point, then, determined the character of what the children could learn.

The teacher himself needs a keen eye for priorities among objectives and how they relate to over-arching aims. He must recognize that many different methodological objectives can equally well support the most valued life-skills and that those methodological skills can equally well be exercised in attaining any of an endless variety of content objectives. Otherwise he will not be free to enter even into the kind of transaction described by Nicholas Farnes (1973):

> . . . 'trade-offs' can be made between the child's purposes and the teacher's purposes, so that some from both sources can be incorporated into an activity that has meaning for the child because it is rich in those things he is interested in doing and at the same time fulfils many of the teacher's own purposes. Activities that the teacher considers important and perhaps the

'real' purpose of education are best achieved when the child sees them as a means of achieving purposes that he considers important.

Interpreting the Model

So, in Figure 3.1, we see how, from different sources, three broad groups of objectives can be derived. The objectives identified in one group may influence the strategies we use in helping students attain objectives in other groups or may be seen as a means to the attainment (or practice, at least) of objectives in another group. It may be true to say that most Group I and Group II objectives are infinitely improvable – the learner will always be able to improve on each. Group III objectives, on the other hand, are less likely to allow for improvement beyond the point of attainment.

No doubt the model is over-simple. For instance, the division between groups may not be as clearly cut as the diagram suggests. As I have already hinted, I am not entirely convinced that methodological skills are fully separable from life-skills. Some writers (see Cole 1972) lump them both together under the name 'process objectives'. And if methodological skills are not also life-skills, how do we justify the compulsory presence of 'subjects' in the curriculum, considering how few people, apart from educators, continue to practise an academic discipline after leaving school? Again, I am not too happy about the division between method-ological objectives and content objectives. How realistic is it to divorce the content of the discipline from the characteristic modes of inquiry and perception by which that content is structured and extended? On the other hand, perhaps there should be more rather than fewer groups?

My reason for using this model is that curriculum-makers often do seem to postulate learning in each of the three groups I have described. For example, in his account of an Anglo-American conference on the teaching of English, John Dixon (1969) outlines three widely held models in the teaching of literature – the personal growth model, the skills model and the cultural heritage model – which chime in quite closely with my three groups. A similar three-fold division appears to be in the mind of Walter Elkan (1974) when he suggests that teachers of economics

> . . . really have to do three things. First, to teach people through the medium of economics to *reason*, to learn to be *critical*, to express themselves *lucidly* [life-skills?]. . . . Second, I see our task as teaching students the very

basic notions of economics, for example that there is a relationship between price and quantity demanded, the idea of choice and opportunity cost, the idea that consumption is ultimately determined by how much is produced [content objectives?]. . . . Third . . . some broad indication of *how* most of us would sub-divide and classify economics. . . . Students should also have some idea of what is meant by the *techniques* that are most commonly used by economists, like cost-benefit analysis . . . and national income accounting [methodological objectives?]. [My italics throughout.]

Unfortunately, few curriculum developers have done much to specify capabilities that might exemplify Group II and more particularly Group I. These groups are usually left as broad amorphous aims that are probably too vaguely articulated even to have the illuminating effect they should have on the teaching – which can squander its efforts on Group III, where objectives *do* get spelled out, in examination papers if nowhere else, though often at a low level of factual recall.

To my mind, this produces an upside-down curriculum. We could, and it is at least arguable that we often should, specify and teach Group I objectives without specifying much at all in Groups II and III. Yet we usually, and without argument, stake our all on an impoverished selection from Group III, with no more than lip-service paid to Groups I and II. As a result, we get the kind of malaise described by George Miller (1962) who evaluated teaching and learning in the medical school of the University of Illinois where 'critical thinking' was held to be an important aim (but was never spelled out as objectives). Miller found that students were given little opportunity to question and discuss and act 'critically'. When their overall course grades were compared with their scores on a standard test of critical thinking it turned out that the twenty-five 'most critical' students did worst on the course while the twenty-five 'least critical' did best.

Formulating Objectives

How might one actually set about planning and pinning-down some objectives? There is much to be said for beginning with a consideration of life-skills – obviously, perhaps, when planning courses and curricula, but often relevant no matter how short the duration of the learning experience being planned. Turn your life-skill aims into objectives, if you have not already done so, and decide which are relevant to the present planning. Don't over-emphasize cognitive to the neglect of affective and psychomotor objectives. Provided you are not committed to reaching those life-skill objectives through one particular subject discipline, you are then free to arrange or encourage whatever learning experiences seem appropriate. You may call on several established disciplines or on none, giving the student considerable scope for developing his own methodological and content objectives. (See Cole 1972, for guidance on 'process education'.) If you are committed to teaching a particular subject, you will need to go on to help students recognize essential methodological and content objectives, still bearing in mind whichever life-skill objectives are relevant.

Structure in Objectives

Try to 'unpack' each broad objective by asking: 'What *component* dispositions or capabilities go to make up this objective?' For example, suppose the student needs to learn to 'illustrate statistical data by means of an appropriate chart'. This has at least two component capabilities – 'choose an appropriate chart' and 'draw the chart'. We may even go on to identify *sub*-component abilities by instancing the various types of chart that might be appropriate to various data needs – pictogram, bar chart, pie chart and so on. Notice that, where component abilities fit together in some kind of task, the student must clearly attain all of them before he can be said to have mastered the broad objective. When, however, the component abilities represent 'instances' of the broad objective, it may not be necessary (even if possible) for the student to demonstrate them all in order to feel that he has 'sufficiently' or 'adequately' mastered the broad objective.

As well as the horizontal analysis into component capabilities, you can analyse objectives vertically – looking for contributory or *enabling* abilities. Try to develop your student's objectives into a hierarchy by asking of each one: 'What must the student *already* be able to do in order to achieve this?' For example, the student will not be able to illustrate statistical data with an appropriate chart unless he can already, among other things, decide on the purpose for which data is to be displayed. By tracking back through such prerequisites you may be able to uncover a string or network of enabling abilities, each contributing to the attainment of your student's higher-level objectives.

Figure 3.2 shows the beginnings of a horizontal and vertical analysis of the 'illustration of statistical data' objective. None of the strings of enabling objectives is complete and some have not even been started.

Furthermore, some of the enabling objectives themselves could usefully be unpacked to reveal their component abilities – e.g., what different abilities may constitute 'recall advantages and disadvantages of alternative chart types'? Nevertheless, even this partial analysis should be enough to suggest how a network may develop. The shape will vary, of course, according to the kind of objectives you are working with. Usually, you will find yourself analysing vertically and horizontally at the same time, as new objectives suggest themselves and you have to decide where they fit in the hierarchy. How far you take it depends on what you plan to do with it. This concept of an underlying network or hierarchy of component and enabling abilities certainly provides a useful way of generating and structuring all kinds of objectives, cognitive, affective and psychomotor, from life-skills to subject content.

Edgar Stones (1972) illustrates something of this hierarchy approach in the start he has made on a taxonomy of objectives in educational psychology for teachers. In fact, he deals rather scantily with life-skills, mentioning only that students should learn to 'weigh the evidence and exercise critical judgement in arriving at their own decisions'. Perhaps because he proclaims it is relevant 'to all education and its spirit should inform whatever teaching methods are employed', he leaves it as a broad aim and does not spell it out in behavioural objectives. However, he does go on to spell out Group II and III objectives (Figure 3.1) in ten different areas of his subject. Within each area he identifies a three-level hierarchy of broad objectives: the trainee teacher who is to *apply* certain principles in teaching must first be able to *identify* (and classify) new examples of those principles and in order to do that he must first be able to *recall* the principles. In the area of the 'Teaching of Cognitive Skills', for example, this produces three broad objectives for the trainee teacher:

A   Given a teaching objective involving cognitive learning, decide on the type(s) of pupil learning most appropriate to the objective and specify the teaching and learning activities most likely to optimize the pupils' learning.

B   Classify novel examples of teaching behaviour according to their appropriateness for different types of cognitive learning.

C   Recall the key principles for efficient cognitive learning.

Although these objectives are behavioural they are still very broad – several different behaviours would count as an instance of each. So Stones goes on to analyse out ten or more *component* behaviours for each

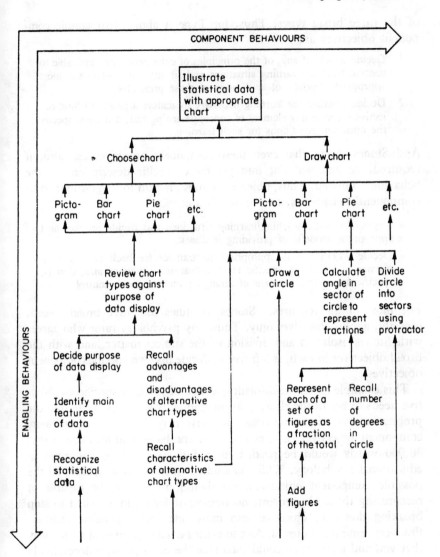

Figure 3.2 Partial analysis of a broad objective

of the three broad types. Thus, for Type A above, two sample component objectives are:

1   Decide which, if any, of the principles of cybernetics are applicable to specific teaching/learning situations and, if any are, specify the most appropriate mode(s) of application of those principles.
2   Decide whether the learning necessary to achieve a given teaching objective involves any element of concept learning and, if it does, specify the optimum conditions for such learning.

And Stones shows that even these component objectives can also, if required, be analysed out into yet more specific descriptions of the behaviours implied. Thus, objective 1 above is held to suggest four 'subcomponent' behaviours, two of which are:

– Appraise specific teaching/learning situations and decide on the most appropriate mode(s) of providing feedback.
– Decide whether it is appropriate to transfer feedback control from teacher to learner in specific teaching/learning situations and, if it is, specify the optimum means of arranging such feedback control.

For most of his ten areas, Stones identifies the three broad (recall, identify, apply) objectives only. Thus, any psychology tutor who agrees with Stones' isolation and division of the subject matter, and with the broad objectives in each, is left free to decide his own specific component objectives.

This example raises the difficult question of just how specific an objective needs to be. In the effort to avoid ambiguity we seem to run into the problem of prolixity. One broad objective may break down into many component objectives. Stones estimates (probably *under*estimates) that 30,000 words would be needed for a full taxonomy of objectives in educational psychology. While no student would need to achieve all the possible component objectives, we should presumably be capable of recognizing them. At present, no rules exist for deciding when to stop breaking down an objective into more and more specified abilities. Practical sense must prevail. Aim to describe the objectives in such a way that you and a colleague could each take the description, independently observe the performance of a given student, and be reasonably well agreed as to the extent to which he had reached his objectives. Clearly, the expected level of agreement between observers will vary accordingly to the type of abilities involved. For instance, one would expect a closer agreement in the case of what I have called 'masterable' objectives than one would with 'infinitely improvable' objectives. For any given type of capability, however, an *unexpected* amount of disagreement might suggest that the objectives still needed further explication. It is also the case that objectives for an individual lesson or module within a course will often need to be expressed more specifically than the broader objectives that may suffice for the course as a whole.

The Language of Objectives

One useful way to start specifying objectives is to begin the 'menu' with some such leading phrase as: 'The student will be able to . . .' or 'The student should improve in his ability to . . .' We can then attach however many objectives seem important, beginning each one with a verb to identify the nature of the expected response. Of course, not all verbs are equally useful here. Be sparing with verbs like 'understand' and 'know'. As Ruskin said: 'Education does not mean teaching people to know what they do not know. It means teaching them to behave as they do not behave.' Words like 'know' and 'understand' are more appropriate to aims than to objectives. They do not suggest what to look for in a student's behaviour. Even 'really know' or, as some teachers might say in a desperate attempt to raise the level of precision, 'really, really understand' tell us nothing more. If we use such expressions in our aims, we should expect to go on to spell out what we mean by them.

For instance, suppose a teacher wants his student to 'know and understand the internal combustion engine'. What sort of behaviours would demonstrate such knowledge and understanding? Should the student be able to recognize an internal combustion engine? distinguish it from other types? name it? draw a diagram of it from memory? explain how it works? detect faults in its running? correct such faults? dismantle it? assemble it? assess its effects on social history in the twentieth century? exhibit a faster heart beat at the mention of its name? argue the case for and against its continued use in a polluted world? invent an alternative? compose a song of protest about it? All of these behaviours, some of them, or none of them might be held appropriate by different teachers and students. There are no rules for adjudicating between proponents of conflicting objectives. Ultimately, the choice of objectives is a political or social transaction, dependent on interaction and debate between teachers and students, which cannot be realistic unless the variety of options is clearly spelled out.

Even practical-sounding words can prove unhelpfully vague. Suppose a teacher tells you that his students are learning to 'handle equations'. Apart from the fact that we don't know what kind of equation (linear? quadratic? cubic? exponential?, etc.), we are left to guess what is meant by 'handle'. Are the students learning merely how to recognize and name various types of equations? To draw graphs of them? To solve them? To solve word problems involving them? To think up their own word problems? Or what? All are quite different objectives requiring quite different types and amounts of learning. Two colleagues could easily disagree as to whether a student could 'really' handle equations simply because each interprets 'handle' differently.

So, unless you want to avoid examining the implications of what you are aiming for, probe behind the façade of words like 'know', 'understand' and even 'handle'. Such terms are acceptable in thinking and talking broadly about educational purposes, but in designing actual curriculum experiences we really do need to consider what kinds of observable behaviours they might imply. It is, of course, quite reasonable to *preface* a list of objectives with 'know' and 'understand', provided the objectives themselves are written in terms of how the student might be expected to *demonstrate* his knowledge or understanding.

Two columns of words and phrases are given below. Those on the left refer to hypothetical states of the student's mind. But since we have no direct access to his mind, we must infer what is going on there by observing what he says and does – his behaviour. So the words on the left are best avoided in favour of terms like those in the right-hand column. A useful check on any objective you write is always to ask: 'How would I assess the student's attainment of it?' If you can't think of a way, the objective is probably not yet behavioural enough. Clearly, objectives using words from the right-hand column are likely to be more directly observable, and therefore 'assessable', than any based on the left-hand column:

AVOID words like:	USE words like:
Know	Design
Understand	List
Really know	Describe
Fully understand	Evaluate
Be familiar with	Participate
Become acquainted with	State
Have a good grasp of	Assess

Obtain a working knowledge of	Explain
Appreciate	Select
Acquire a feeling for	Identify
Realize the significance of	Distinguish
Be aware of	Order
Have information about	Specify
Believe	Construct
Be interested in	Solve
etc. . . .	etc. . . .

Notice that either list could be added to indefinitely. The words shown here are merely samples. My point is that we may well use words like those on the left in sketching out our aims but must sharpen our focus to use words like those on the right when making clear the objectives. Thus, the student will be able to *design* an experiment, *list* the precautions to be taken, *describe* his results, *evaluate* conflicting interpretations, *participate* in out-of-class discussions and so on. Vernon Gerlach and Donald Ely (1971) suggest that all such behavioural infinitives have their roots in five basic types of capability:

Identify   Name   Describe   Order   Construct

They illustrate how cognitive objectives particularly can be built around these five categories, and suggest that they may also help in the description of affective objectives.

Newton Metfessel (1969) and his colleagues offer a scheme for generating objectives based on Bloom's taxonomy categories. They use a three-column layout in which the first column gives Bloom's category, the second gives a set of related infinitives from which possible behaviours can be chosen, and the third gives generalized 'direct objects' upon which the behaviour can operate. These direct objects can be made more specific in terms of subject matter and then linked with one or more of the infinitives to describe an ability students may need to attain. Here is just one section of the scheme, that dealing with Bloom's 'comprehension' category:

Taxonomy classification	KEY WORDS Examples of infinitives	Examples of direct objects
2.00 COMPREHENSION		
2.10 Translation	to translate, to transform, to give in own words, to illustrate, to prepare, to read, to represent, to change, to rephrase, to re-state	meaning(s), sample(s) definitions, abstractions, representations, words, phrases
2.20 Interpretation	to interpret, to reorder, to rearrange, to differentiate, to distinguish, to make, to draw, to explain, to demonstrate	relevancies, relationships, essentials, aspects, new view(s), qualifications, conclusions, methods, theories, abstractions
2.30 Extrapolation	to estimate, to infer, to conclude, to predict, to differentiate, to determine, to extend, to interpolate, to extra-polate, to fill in, to draw	consequences, implications, conclusions, factors, ramifications, meanings, corollaries, effects, probabilities

You may find it interesting to test the truth of Gerlach and Ely's assertion (that behavioural infinitives are of five basic types) by trying to apply it to the 'key words' in this section of Metfessel's scheme.

However, recognizing and formulating objectives is essentially a creative task which may certainly be started upon before the teacher and student get to know one another but which should be expected to take on new energies, *and* new directions, as their working relationship develops. How far such analytical approaches as those referred to above are really helpful is problematical. Although certain educators are reassured to know that such analyses can be made and are available for reference in difficult cases, I suspect that many would get more practical inspiration from studying models rather than mechanics. It is difficult to formulate workable objectives without having seen and thought about a variety of 'good examples' (see the references for this chapter). In any event, the analytical approach needs to be applied with caution and imagination lest, while helping elaborate the behaviours attainable by some abstract entity called 'the student', it causes you to lose sight of the phenomeno-logical needs of the person you are actually working with.

Robert Mager (1962) points out that an objective may need to specify not only the behaviour expected but also the *conditions* under which it is to occur (e.g., time restrictions) and the *standards* by which it is to be judged (e.g., percentage accuracy). Consequently, several sentences may sometimes be needed, especially where the objective demands high-level thought processes. For example:

> Given a poem he has not seen before, the student will be able to write an account of his developing perceptions of it, assessing the extent to which these are controlled by the poet and by his own previous experiences. He will define the central theme and attitude of the poem and outline his own considered interpretation (whether psychological, philosophical, religious, sociological, political, or whatever) contrasting it with the interpretation of at least one colleague. His interpretation will be assessed according to how amply it is supported by reference to the imagery, diction, rhythm, etc., of the poem and how well it manages to account for the poem as a whole. Students will need to consult with one another, they may consult any texts they wish, and they may take up to four hours to complete the exercise.

As we strive to describe an objective more and more precisely, we get closer and closer to suggesting examples of the operations that students might learn to perform. With the question: 'How would I assess the student's attainment of it?', we begin to consider possible test questions and assessment situations. Indeed for some areas of teaching, we may feel that our 'objectives' are best expressed by telling the students: 'You'll learn how to answer questions or tackle problems like the following . . .' and giving them a representative list of questions or problems.

Assessment and Testing

It is not customary in education for assessment to be considered in detail before the teaching has even been planned. Usually, assessment is an afterthought, and tests are engineered to produce statistics showing that while a few students have done very poorly and a few have done splendidly, the majority have done moderately well. Our problem-solving approach, however, demands that we try to indicate possible destinations before rather than after the journey. We are committed to suggesting in advance the kind of criteria by which the effectiveness of our teaching is to be judged. Thus, before we go on to design appropriate learning experiences, we must at least consider possible tests or situations wherein attainment of the objectives might be assessed later on. In doing so, we must recognize, as always, that we will surely wish to re-define some of our objectives once the processes of teaching and learning are under way – if not earlier.

Assessment ≠ Grading or Measurement

Let me remark here that assessment is not the same thing as grading or marking (or measurement). If you 'grade' or 'mark' a student (or his work – the distinction is not always made clear) you judge, value or ascribe worth to him (or it). Grading cannot take place without prior assessment, but assessment can and often does take place (e.g., in primary school) without being followed by grading. Unfortunately, 'assessment' is frequently taken to be just another word for 'grading'. Worse still, grading can so easily concentrate entirely on what the assessment reveals of the student's present educational status, giving no 'credit' for how much he may have *grown*. One of the unresolved problems of grading is how, and whether, to differentiate between the student who acquired most of the abilities you are looking for *prior* to coming on your course and the student who has acquired them since.

Another danger in identifying assessment with the awarding of grades and marks is that it attracts too much attention to student qualities that can be readily *measured*, ignoring those that can merely be observed and described. As teachers, we are often concerned with behavioural changes that lend themselves to appraisal but not to measurement. Joan Tough (1976) makes the point very well in relation to children's physical development:

> How does the child walk and run? What is the quality of his movement? What kind of control does the child have of fine and intricate manipulation and of movement that needs concentration of strength and effort? What is the child's general co-ordination of movements like? Is he awkward and ungainly or does he move easily and smoothly without apparent effort? Many of these qualities would defy measurement, and many would defy comparison with other children. But all could be appraised, i.e. described in terms which build up a picture of what the child is like.

As part of our work, we may often be called upon to quantify our assessments and record them as numbers or letters – sometimes in order to give students an indication of how *other* assessors (examiners) will quantify their work. As teachers, however, concerned with helping our students to their objectives, we should be choosing assessment methods on the grounds of whether they give us real understanding of our students' capabilities and dispositions, not of whether they will necessarily produce scores and percentages.

Relating Tests to Objectives

Planning assessment is a natural extension and check on the mapping out of objectives. There are many assessment methods to choose from and the problem is to decide which of them is appropriate to each individual objective. While developing the objectives we have probably had some general scheme in mind. Thus, for example, Stones (whose educational psychology objectives we looked at earlier) assumed that A-type objectives would be tested by practical teaching exercises (micro-teaching), B-type objectives by having students report their observations of classroom teaching and C-type objectives by paper-and-pencil tests. His only affective objective (that by the end of the course the student should be 'committed to an approach to teaching based on the principles of educational psychology') he would try to assess by attitude testing.

But, of course, we must look at each objective individually. Sometimes, we will have so framed an objective that it is virtually a test item already. For example, if one of our objectives is that the student should be able to 'sketch a contour map representing a conical hill' we could almost present him with this statement as a stimulus to the criterion performance. Similarly, the clay-handling objectives quoted earlier (page 41) need only very slight re-wording to turn them into a set of instructions for a practical test. On the other hand, objectives like those we suggested for study of D.H. Lawrence's novels (page 32) do not so immediately suggest specific test items. Nor do Carl Rogers' objectives (page 37). In general, of the three groups of objectives identified in Figure 3.1, Group III objectives are usually the easiest to translate into explicit and conclusive tests. Caution is therefore needed to make sure they do not have undue weight in the assessment.

This analysis of objectives with a view to testing sometimes reveals that certain objectives are less clear than we thought. For example, suppose the student is to be able to 'discuss the themes emerging in Act I, Scene 2 of *Hamlet*'. At first glance this may look almost like a test item. But what shall we be looking for in the student's 'discussion'? Presumably anyone who knows what 'themes' means, and can read the appropriate part of the play, can make some sort of attempt on the objective. But by what criteria shall we judge success? For example, what methodological skills in the use of evidence and canons of criticism, etc., are to be expected? What content knowledge is to be expected in comparing this scene with others and with the play as a whole?

Not surprisingly, many teachers new to educational technology find it easier, at first, to generate objectives *out of* a consideration of possible test items rather than vice versa. It is often not until they have worked out a few possible questions, and considered what sort of answers they would be looking for, that they can begin to grasp the underlying objectives. Once grasped, these objectives can then be used to sharpen further thinking on criteria for assessment. With all teachers, this is a stage at which previous objectives are likely to be dropped or redefined and new ones added.

However we set about assessing students' achievements of objectives, we must aim to find methods that are *valid, reliable* and *practicable*. That is, they must validly test the capability implied by the objective (and not some other behaviour instead); they must test this capability so reliably that two different testers would be reasonably in agreement as to the extent to which a given student had demonstrated it; they must be practicable in terms of cost and time and ease of application.

Ideally, we should be able to prove to students that assessment (like evaluation) is of potential value to them. Any assessment exercise should reward the student for his efforts by leaving him with a clearer personal insight into what he is and what he can do. The non-return of examination scripts, or their return without detailed comments or opportunity for discussion, represents a violation of this courtesy.

Assessment techniques and the pedagogical need for assessment should be discussed with students and their active, rather than passive, help enlisted. Whether or not they feel strongly about assessment, they can certainly contribute to its methodology. If we can encourage and pay proper respect to the student's *self*-assessment, we shall be giving him practice in a vital life-skill that is neither widely taught nor generally learned, even by students in higher education (Cowan 1975). Can we use assessment in such a way as to leave the student more capable of learning in order to satisfy his own criteria rather than someone else's?

A wealth of assessment methods exist and are described in detail in the references given for this chapter. (See, in particular, Satterly 1981, and, for an extended discussion of the rationale and ideology of assessment, Rowntree 1977.) Here, I have space only to sketch in the variety of techniques available and mention some of their distinguishing features.

Paper-and-pencil Assessment

The paper-and-pencil test is the most familiar assessment device. It may take the form of a so-called *objective test*, consisting, for example, of multiple-choice questioning, where the student has to choose the correct answer; or it may be a *constructed-response* test (short-answer, essay or problem) where the student has to construct his own answer, either in a few words or sentences or in several thousand words, or perhaps as a series of mathematical operations. End-of-course examinations are a particular form of paper-and-pencil test, and their role is discussed in Chapter 4.

Multiple-choice questions and their variants (matching, ordering, true/false questions and so on) are more useful than is often supposed (see Iliffe 1966, Bloom et al. 1971, Mehrens and Lehman 1978). Since, in a given period of time, students can answer far more multiple-choice questions than essay questions, objective tests can cover a far wider area of subject matter. They can also be reliably and accurately marked 'objectively' by someone unskilled in the subject matter, or even by a computer. Notice, however, that the description 'objective' refers only to the marking. The choice of questions, and the weight given to each question in arriving at a total 'score', remains entirely subjective. Furthermore, teachers may find it difficult to agree on just what abilities or mental processes are supposedly being tested by a particular set of multiple-choice questions (Fairbrother 1975).

Although multiple-choice questions may, on the face of things, call for high-level thought processes, the provision of alternative answers means that the student is, in the end, being asked to *recognize* (rather than 'think up') the correct answer. Thus there is always the danger he will guess, or at least choose, the right answer for the 'wrong' reason. There is also the danger that students of subtle and probing mentality may be penalized because they see good reasons why answers deemed wrong by the assessor are in fact right. You can, of course, ask the student to add an explanation or justification of his answer, but then it ceases to be an objective test. For a full critique of objective testing in the USA, where it has long been widely used, see Hoffman (1967).

Clearly, then, multiple-choice testing, while valuable, is of limited application. Where an objective involves the student in selecting from, deciding between, or in some way or other discriminating among given alternatives – whether the alternatives take the form of words, sounds, tastes, smells, pictures, objects or whatever, there you clearly cannot test his ability without presenting him with the appropriate alternatives. Some form of multiple-choice test may be valid for such an objective. But where an objective requires the student to recall, define, explain, invent or otherwise come up with his own answer, you will need to use a constructed-response ('own-answer') test.

An 'own-answer' test question or assignment may call for a one-word answer or for an extended essay or series of mathematical calculations, or even for a project report. At one extreme it can test objectives at the knowledge level while at the other it can validly test high-level problem-solving skills and creativity. Certainly it can test the student's ability to select and organize his ideas and to pursue an argument, verbal or mathematical, which the objective test cannot.

Whether such a question or assignment is to be answered by individual work or group work, with or without access to references, to a time-limit or not, will depend on the precise intention of your objectives. Because they take longer to answer, such questions are not always able to sample the student's grasp of so wide a range of subject matter. But the major weakness, at least of essay questions, is the subjectivity, and therefore unreliability, of the marking. Abundant research, from Edgeworth (1890) through Hartog and Rhodes (1935) to Edwards (1979), has shown that the same essay may be given wildly different grades by different 'experts', or even by the same marker on different occasions. Such unreliability in marking can be guarded against (for example, by making the question very specific and spelling out to the student the criteria that will be used in marking it, or by using more than one marker for each student). But uniformity of marking can never be automatic, especially in dealing with those complexes of high-level behaviour where 'experts' may legitimately differ as to which aspects of a student's performance they attach most value to. The basic paradox here is that for the majority of important cognitive objectives, the most valid test (own-answer) can be least reliable, and the most reliable test (multiple-choice) least valid.

Of course, affective objectives can also be assessed through paper-and-pencil tests and questionnaires, which may combine multiple-choice and own-answer questions. Even 'self-actualization' objectives like those of Carl Rogers are amenable to testing by existing personality inventories and attitude scales. But interviews and discussions will provide the most flexible context in which to assess affective, and many cognitive, developments in students.

Students can be asked to record, perhaps anonymously, their attitudes to the teaching and what they feel they have learned from it; they can help assess the developing personalities and cooperative work skills of individuals within their group, through direct appraisals of their colleagues' strengths and weaknesses, or indirectly through sociometric questionnaires requiring them to decide which of their colleagues best fits a number of given behaviour descriptions or which of their colleagues they would prefer to work with in various activities. Needless to say, in talking of self- and peer-assessment, I am not implying that such assessments should necessarily contribute to a student's marks or grades. Their possible contribution to any 'final report' on the student needs to be considered separately from their possible contribution to helping him learn. But, as I have suggested earlier, this is true of all assessment.

Situational Assessment

Cognitive, affective and psychomotor objectives will often be most validly and reliably tested by having the student carry out some practical task – giving a talk, making a film or sound recording, setting up an experiment, mixing and wedging clay, carrying out a social survey, engaging with others in sociodrama or whatever.

For the appraisal of complex decision-making skills, management education offers us a useful model in the 'in-tray exercise' (Lopez 1966). Here the trainee manager is presented with an 'in-tray' containing all the letters, memos, financial statements, committee agendas, etc., that might come to him in the course of a normal day; and he is expected to handle them by issuing orders, dictating letters, making telephone calls, planning meetings and so on, just as he would in the real job. With a little imagination we can equally well simulate the demands of the 'real-life' situation for historians working on primary source materials, for engineers faced with conflicting design specifications, for physicians interpreting a patient's symptoms and test results, and for a wide variety of 'problem solvers' working alone or in groups.

Usually, several objectives will be brought together in such a 'situational' test and, to ensure reliable assessment, it is vital to analyse them out in advance and perhaps produce some kind of checklist on which you can mark off and assess each objective as the student works through his task. (See Figure 3.3. for an example.) Clearly, in this sort of case, it would be more practicable (i.e., less consuming of time and materials) to have the student describe how he would perform the task: but such a description would *not* necessarily be a valid test of how he actually could perform it.

STRICTLY CONFIDENTIAL – Not to be shown to Apprentices   C. 198/17
NATIONAL COAL BOARD   COLLIERY APPRENTICE MECHANICS   FTY 6

Test Centre .... Name .... No. ....

                                                                        Date ....

Internal examination of a coal cutter gear head   80 mins.
Dismantle the gear head as far as requested by the examiner. Examine all parts that are accessible. Draw the
examiner's attention to the examinations and checks you are making, if necessary by exaggerating your movements
or by telling him what you are doing. Locate and, where possible, rectify all faults on the gear head. If not possible
to rectify them in the time available, note such faults in your report. Re-assemble the gear head. Write a planned
maintenance report on this examination.
NB – Two of the faults shown below must be prepared on the equipment prior to the test without the candidate's knowledge.
Show by X which of these faults the candidate was required to diagnose and rectify:
☐ Stress marks on spur gear wheels   ☐ Bevel wheel or pinion worn   ☐ Worn bearings
☐ Bevel wheel bolts not tight   ☐ The felt ring worn   ☐ Lack of lubricant

SECTION A. Did the candidate: *(Enter in each box a tick for YES, a cross for NO)*
    ☐ Complete the exercise in the time allowed
SECTION B. Did he:
    ☐ Locate and rectify or note in his report the main faults on the gearhead
    ☐ Re-assemble all parts in the right position and tighten all nuts and screws
    ☐ Keep the interior of the gearbox clean
SECTION C. Did he:
    ☐ Check his tools and equipment before starting the job
    ☐ Use the appropriate special tools and equipment
    ☐ Carry out the dismantling and examination systematically and skilfully
    ☐ Keep the dismantled parts tidy and in a safe and clean place
    ☐ Re-assemble all parts correctly and in the right sequence
    ☐ Examine all parts to make sure that they were clean before refitting them
    ☐ Use the tools skilfully and safely
    ☐ List in his report the faults he found
    ☐ Suggest in his report what action should be taken to rectify those faults which he had not been able to put right
    ☐ Describe the condition of the gearhead accurately
    ☐ Express himself clearly and concisely

GRADING. Enter in the box the grade awarded for this test
☐ Candidates should be graded as follows:
    Grade A – Where ALL items in Sections A and B and at least 8 items from Section C are ticked
    Grade B – Where ALL items in Sections A and B and at least 5 items from Section C are ticked
    Grade C – Where ALL items in Sections A and B and less than 5 items from Section C are ticked
    Grade D – Where ALL items in *either* Section A *or* Section B are ticked
    Grade E – Where both Sections (A & B) include at least one item marked with a cross

                                          Signed .... *Examiner*

Figure 3.3 Sample checklist for a practical test (Reproduced by
permission of the National Coal Board)

Unobtrusive Techniques

Assessment should also make some attempt to gauge the acquisition of 'will do' as well as 'can do' objectives. That is, we are surely interested not just in the student's ability to act in certain ways but also in his *disposition* to do so.

Most educational testing concentrates on what the student can do, and usually on what he can do immediately after the course and under threat of grading, rather than on what he can or will do some time after the course is over and of his own volition. Thus, examinations take place right after a course not simply for administrative convenience but in recognition of the fact that most of what students learn, at least in secondary school, may be so irrelevant to their interests that the learning will have evaporated through lack of practice if the assessment is delayed by more than a week or two.

Hence, unobtrusive techniques are also important in assessment. Some objectives, and especially their 'will do' aspects, can only be validly assessed when students are unaware that the assessment is taking place. Indeed, with certain psychosocial behaviours, obtrusive assessment might nip the learning in the bud. For instance, an adolescent who is gradually abandoning his previously hostile attitudes to children of another race may well assume them again, for fear of 'loss of face', if he is made aware that the change is being remarked upon. In such cases, systematic covert observation, backed-up by anecdotal records, rating scales and checklists, can, when properly handled, provide useful evidence about how strongly the behavioural changes really have 'taken' and give support to predictions about the likely longevity of such changes.

Eugene Webb et al. (1969) provide a fascinating compendium of unobtrusive measures. They make a useful distinction between:

- *observations* – e.g., noticing the aggression displayed by certain children in classroom discussions;
- *archives* – e.g., statistics showing a child's book-borrowing habits or how often he has appeared in the headteacher's 'punishment book'; and
- *physical traces* – e.g., the incidence of graffiti and desk-top carvings, or the condition in which a pupil maintains textbooks and other equipment.

Other such unobtrusive techniques include analysing the kind of question asked by students or the kind they choose to answer in tests and assignments, revealing aspects of the teaching that have puzzled or stimulated them; considering statistics on class attendance or numbers of students dropping out or signing-up for related courses; recording the views of other teachers about how far your students demonstrate the objectives (especially higher-level objectives) when in their classes; organizing observations by people whom students assume to have nothing to do with assessment. But are such surreptitious procedures justifiable? Perhaps this depends on whether the resulting data are to be used to the students' advantage or not.

Of course, unobtrusive assessment can run us into ethical problems. For example, James Popham and Eva Baker (1970) describe how a class of twelve-year-old children were secretly trained to be expert appraisers of the extent to which their teachers (students in training) were using a particular approach to teaching which they had been taught, knew well and had expressed positive attitudes to. Only one of the one hundred student teachers suspected that he was being assessed by his pupils. The reports of the accomplices established that, in this case, the attitudes to the teaching approach expressed by the student teachers in a question-naire tallied closely with their behaviour in the classroom.

Even when quite ethical, it is not always practicable or necessary to devise unobtrusive 'fly-on-the-wall' tests; but one must always remember that, in testing what students know and profess, one may not be getting a very reliable prediction of what they will actually do. Vance Packard (1957), in discussing the problems of market research, quotes many intriguing examples of discontinuity between the preferences people express in interviews or questionnaires and those they exhibit in their actions. He describes, for instance, how people waiting for a lecture, given two waiting-rooms to choose from, almost all sat in the room furnished in 'Scandinavian-modern' style, rather than in the 'period-ornate' waiting-room; yet in a questionnaire 84 percent expressed a preference for the 'period-ornate'. To allow anonymous questionnaire responses may help towards greater accuracy but, even then, students may incline to give the answers they think will protect the teacher's feelings, and it is sometimes difficult to interpret certain responses unless you know who made them.

Long-term Assessment

Rarely can we hope for long-term assessment of the kind reported by Bernard Asbel (1972). Here, two psychologists were able, after a gap of thirty years, to establish that a group of feeble-minded children, whose intelligence had become normal as a result of a few years intensive and affectionate attention from mentally retarded women in an institution, had indeed sustained their development and, without exception, become self-supporting, contributing members of society whose own children were of average intelligence or above.

Not enough longitudinal research has yet been done. We need, on the one hand, to follow up the students we are teaching now, to see what connection there is between their long-term, future behaviour and the performances they record during and on completion of their schooling. The current British study (Davie, Butler and Goldstein 1972, and Fogelman 1976), following the fortunes of a large sample of children from birth onwards, offers a useful research model. On the other hand we need also to investigate the backgrounds of a diversity of adults to establish what links exist between their early experiences and attainments and what they have become. For instance, Liam Hudson (1966) examined the degree class gained by each of a large sample of distinguished scientists, politicians and judges, concluding that 'there was evidence of some slight relation between eminence and degree class, but it was far from clear-cut and there were many striking exceptions.' Similarly, in the USA, Donald Hoyt (1965) reviewed forty-six studies of the relationship between college grades and subsequent achievement, only to conclude that 'present evidence strongly suggests that college grades bear little or no relationship to any measures of adult achievement.'

We must face the probability that education has not been the most potent factor in differentiating adults – a person's social connections are likely to have done more for him (or against him) than any specific learning he may have acquired. Or, as the popular wisdom puts it: 'It's not what you know, but who you know.' Nevertheless, longitudinal research may indicate how reliably we can predict future capabilities from tests that are applicable in the short term. Clearly, such research bristles with problems, and a methodology is yet to be found. In the meantime we take education on trust, in the cautious assumption that there is some positive correlation between short-term and long-term capabilities and dispositions.

Combining Techniques

Any assessment strategy is likely to combine a variety of methods, quantitative and qualitative, each chosen according to how it relates to a particular objective. As an example, look back at the ceramics objectives described on pages 40/41 and consider the possible assessment methods suggested for each below:

Ceramics
objective   *Possible Assessment Technique*

1 (a)   Records of class attendances.
   (b)   Teacher's recorded observations, self-report by student and appraisal by peers.

2 (a)   Short essay or oral discussion.
   (b)   Essay, or television programme or film.

3   Teacher's recorded observations and student's self-report.

4 (a/b) Teacher's observation (with checklist) of a practical exercise.

5 (a)   Essay or illustrated talk.
   (b)   Objective test plus essay (or oral discussion).

6 (a/b) Teacher's recorded observations, student's self-report and appraisal by peers.

7 (a)   Essay, talk, or group discussion based on given examples.
   (b)   Essay, discussions with other students.
   (c)   Teacher's recorded observations, student's self-report and appraisal by peers.

8 (a)   Teacher's recorded observations.
   (b)   Teacher's recorded observations and appraisal by peers.

Each form of assessment has its own limitations as well as its advantages. Taken together, the various techniques should help not only in appraising the developing capabilities and dispositions of individual students (assessment) but also in understanding the strengths and weaknesses of the teaching (evaluation). The *overall* evaluation of the ceramics course might require, in addition, such evidence as might be collected from, for example, attitude tests, reports from teachers of the students' other subjects, follow-up interviews with students some time after the course and so on.

Criteria v. Norms

As I said earlier, we have been concerned in this chapter with *assessment for teaching* (rather than for ranking and grading). That is, we are interested primarily in finding out what the individual student knows, is and can do – not least so that we can help him develop yet further. We are not setting out to compare students with one another, establishing that some have achieved more or less than certain others in the time available. Rather we are interested in how far we have helped students progress towards their objectives and how far each might still have to go. Comparisons, except with our idea of what might be reasonably expected from each particular student, are irrelevant. Indeed, if different students have *different* sets of objectives, as is often both feasible and desirable, then comparisons would also be illogical.

In technical terms, our assessment is criterion-referenced rather than norm-referenced. That is to say, it is meant to establish whether or not the student has attained or improved satisfactorily in each of the criterion capabilities – the objectives we agreed were appropriate for him. The tests are *not* meant to spread students out along a 'normal distribution' with a few doing very poorly, a few doing very well and the majority doing moderately well. Ideally, 100 percent of our students would attain 100 percent of their objectives or make 100 percent of the predicted improvement. In a norm-referenced test this indicates that the test was too easy; in a criterion-referenced test that the teaching and learning has been highly effective. Such a high standard is, of course, quite rare. Nevertheless, we would certainly expect the distribuition of attainment to look more like Y than X (the 'normal distribution') in Figure 3.4. Since we would hold ourselves responsible for the fact that many students in X had failed to reach the criterion level of attainment, it would suggest that we still had a lot of teaching to do – and our students a lot of learning.

In institutions that are geared to norm-based assessment, a department that produces grade-distributions like Y can be viewed as deviant by colleagues in other departments. I know of one course, in a science-based discipline too, where students have done so well (both on continuous assessment and in the examination) that the examiners have felt obliged, several years' running, to reduce the scores of the better students in order not to offend against the institutional expectations and find themselves accused of setting easy questions or being too soft on the marking.

Teachers' fatalistic deference to the 'normal distribution' too easily

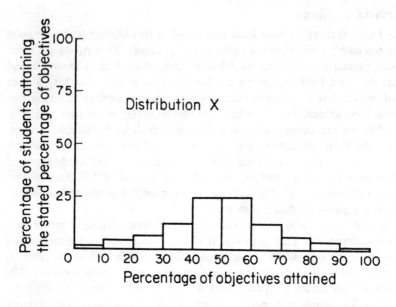

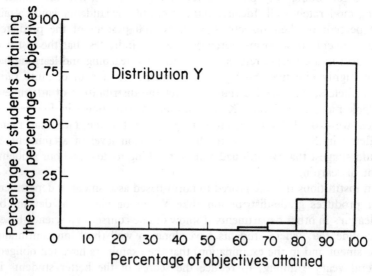

Figure 3.4   Norm-based (X) and criterion-based (Y) test distributions

becomes a self-fulfilling prophecy. 'We can't expect the majority of students to do very well, so don't blame us for the failures.' (See Insel and Jacobson 1975.) Thus, for example, it caused little public concern that, year after year, the General Nursing Council failed one-third of candidates taking the SRN examinations following three years of preparation (NT 1972). Fear of escaping the 'normal' failure rate is still preventing the Esperanto Teachers' Association from getting Esperanto established as a GCE 'O'-level subject. They are told the language is 'too easy' – too many students would reach the criterion. The difference between norm-based and criterion-based testing was brutally brought home to me several years ago, soon after I began work with programmed learning. In my innocent enthusiasm, I suggested to a GCE examiner that, with the help of programmes, all students would soon be able to pass 'O'-level mathematics. 'Oh no they won't,' he said, 'we'll just raise the standard.' (For a full comparison of criterion-referenced and norm-referencing testing, see Popham (1971 and) Rowntree★ (1977), pp. 178–188.)

Whether, and in what circumstances, we need to grade students on their attainment of objectives (rather than ourselves on the effectiveness of our teaching), and thereby label some as more and some as less successful than others, is an issue that will be taken up again later. Our immediate concern is to decide what tests will serve as the most valid, reliable and practicable criterion to judge the extent to which our students are individually attaining their objectives. Only when we have given this proper consideration can we be confident about designing appropriate and relevant learning experiences.

★ It was the realization that I was having to skate over so many troubling issues of assessment in this and other chapters of the first edition of this book that prompted me to devote the whole of my next book to the subject. So, for a more coherent analysis, based on the idea that 'the spirit and style of student assessment defines the *de facto* curriculum', see Rowntree (1977).

Questions on Chapter 3

1   Think of a course you have taught or studied. Can you identify life-skills, methodological objectives and content objectives that students might have been expected to achieve or enhance their ability in as a result? How realistic is the author's three-fold classification in your own subject area?

2   In the light of your answer to question 1, here is a question you could
    have considered earlier: Does the distinction between masterable
    objectives and infinitely improvable objectives make sense in your
    subject area? If not, why not? If so, give examples of each.

3   Make a list of at least six objectives for a course of your own,
    beginning the list with 'The student will learn (or improve in his
    ability) to . . .'. To what more general aims would these objectives
    relate?

4   Take one objective from your own course. Unpack it by sorting out
    its 'component abilities' and 'enabling abilities'.

5   Specify at least two different ways of testing what students have
    learned from your course. Did you find this easier or more difficult
    than specifying objectives? If easier, do you think it was made so by
    your having thought about objectives first? Or would you have pre-
    ferred to think about assessment first? How far do you think
    colleagues would agree with you that the tests you have in mind
    would provide a valid assessment of the objectives?

6   Would your assessment be chiefly norm-based or criterion-based?
    Why? If neither, what would it be based on? Why?

7   What would you see as the point of the quotation at the head of this
    chapter? Can you give an example illustrating the same point from
    your own (or anyone else's) experience?

CHAPTER 4

DESIGNING THE LEARNING:
CONTENT, SEQUENCE AND STRATEGY

We cannot teach another person directly; we can only facilitate his learning.
Carl Rogers

In this chapter and in Chapter 5 we shall consider the second phase of the problem-solving educational technology approach. We know the student's learning objectives, so we have provisionally defined our problem. But, how are we to solve it; what might we do to help the student attain those objectives?

The student will learn through interacting with his environment – an environment of people, things and ideas. Our task is to arrange a 'learning environment' that will encourage productive interactions and give him the 'learning experiences' he needs. To get him to his objectives, we must juggle with a complex equation whose terms include subject matter content, types of learning, learning styles, teaching styles, teaching strategies, learning sequences, stimulus modes and presentation media. Somehow we must come up with rational and effective answers that will be right, not just for a class of students as a whole but for each individual. Never an easy task, it would be all but impossible had we not already considered the capabilities and dispositions we might expect students to acquire or enhance as a result.

Considering Course Content

Before we can make firm decisions about how to teach, we need to do some thinking about the body of subject matter a student might encounter during the course. What are the main topics the student needs to deal with? Within those topics, what are the main ideas? How do those ideas fit in with conceptions that different students possess already? What routes might students take through the course content? Here is David Warren Piper (1969) discussing the development of a course in industrial design.

> Thus the study of Industrial Organization was included to enable the student to recognize what information different people would require from the designer, how they would use it, and thus what form it needed to be in. This was pertinent to the designers' decision of what to communicate and to whom. Perception Theory was not taught as a subject complete in itself, but as a means, among other things, of evaluating alternative methods of presenting information. Similarly the History of Design was not a separate, self-justifying subject assumed in itself to add virtue to the course; rather it was a study specifically aimed at giving the student information about other people's solutions to design problems and experience of other people's judgements of value and aesthetics. It was also an important source of analogy.

The above description suggests one way of deciding on course content – by relating it directly to the *objectives*, which in this case concerned students learning to recognize and solve design problems and to communicate and implement their solutions. Topics are not taught for their own sake, or as completely as they might be in other contexts. The criterion appears to have been how a topic and its constituent ideas might help the students towards better problem-solving and communication, e.g., by giving them a knowledge-base from which to think by analogy.

Perhaps this has been the kind of approach implied by the earlier chapters of this book. Perhaps I have tended to suggest that the concepts and principles of your subject – the definitions and relationships, the examples and counter-examples, the case-studies and the schools of thought – would all flow out of your thinking about objectives. So they may, indeed, especially if you are able to decide first what life-skills and/ or methodological objectives you are aiming for. You will then be in a position to select the most appropriate subject matter for students to work on in reaching towards those objectives.

But, as we know, not all teachers find it easy to begin by thinking about objectives, or to be so opportunistic in choosing subject matter. Some will begin by worrying about the syllabus they have been presented with and how they can hope to 'cover' it in the time available. Others will be concerned about what they see as the 'demands of the discipline', saying things like: 'you just can't call yourself any kind of physicist until you've had a good grounding in heat, light, sound, properties of matter

. . . and so on.' They will be discussing a content that must be taught for its own sake, not merely as material on which to practise skills. What help can we give such teachers in surveying the plethora of content on which they might draw, and in deciding what is most relevant and how it might all hang together?

At the end of Chapter 2, I mentioned a dozen 'intuitive' ways of beginning to think about content. If you look back through them now (page 59), you may agree with me that they seem to fall into two broad groups:

- Reviewing the subject, through your own and other people's experience; and
- Exploring what students might need from the course or could usefully involve themselves in.

As a result of such considerations, having talked to colleagues and students, read a range of relevant publications, taken a look at similar courses elsewhere, and come to some conclusions about what kinds of student activities seem most worthwhile, the teacher may feel knee-deep in potential content. He may then be ready to apply some more analytical approach to areas of content that look particularly promising. Two approaches, in particular, that he might consider are what I will describe below as *concept analysis* and as *diagramming*.

Concept Analysis

Concepts are the basic building-blocks of any subject – as they are, for that matter, of any interdisciplinary 'field of study'. Within the 'subject' of educational technology, we have already touched on such concepts as:

- Technology
- Systems
- Behaviourism
- Humanistic psychology
- Aims
- Objectives
- Assessment, and so on.

Students will begin on your courses with various sets of concepts already established in their minds. Each one's 'conceptual framework' may include some of the concepts your course needs to discuss. It may also include a number of 'commonsense' concepts that overlap or conflict with the course concepts. An example I often give concerns students of statistics who learn that a 'significant' result is one that is unlikely to have arisen by chance; however, they may also carry on assuming (erroneously) that the 'significance' of the result means also that it is big or important (as their everyday grasp of the word would imply). Likewise, in coming to this book, you no doubt already possessed some concepts that you would refer to by the words 'objectives' or 'evaluation'. But only you can tell how close they are to the concepts that I refer to by those words. Similarly, you may find your students happily using the same terms you use, but not necessarily with the same meanings attached – even at the end of your course. Thus, Ference Marton (1981) reports that about two-thirds of a class of economics undergraduates still saw 'price' as an inherent quality of a commodity (corresponding to its 'value') even though they had just been through a course based on the conception of price as a relation between supply and demand.

Just as we talked earlier about changing a student's behaviour, so we can talk now of changing his conceptual framework – of refurnishing his mind. How might you want to change his conceptual framework? At the very least, you will want to *extend* it. You will be wanting to hook new ideas into what the student already knows (or thinks he knows).

More challengingly, perhaps, you may be calling upon the student to *re-structure* his conceptual framework. That is, you will be leading him to see that some of the ideas he holds at present are superficial or mis-informed, or that they conflict with other, more powerful notions that are beginning to dawn upon him.

Old mental habits die hard. Fitting new ideas into one's conceptual framework can be an uncomfortable and time-consuming process. This will be especially so if they are at odds with ideas that we have regularly found useful in the past. Some of the old mental furniture usually has to be moved out to make room for the new; and even some of what is left may no longer seem quite so comfortable as it once did. My colleague Andy Northedge (1976) reminds us of how students (all of us) are inclined to resist the refurnishing:

> I recall, for example, when first presented, at school, with the idea that 'seeing' involved light being reflected from objects towards my eyes, feeling very awkward and unhappy about it. It had always seemed so obvious that something went outwards from my eyes to the object (as depicted by dotted

lines from people's eyes in comics). At first the new notion was so different that it was virtually incomprehensible and I simply felt like ignoring it. Eventually under pressures from adults and with growing awareness of the inadequacy of my system for accounting for some aspects of the 'real' world, I grudgingly replaced my old, comfortable and familiar way of understanding sight.

Perhaps you have felt yourself fighting against new ideas in reading this book. I know I have done between writing the first and second editions. Be sure your students will too from time to time.

We need to be alert to the kinds of difficulties and confusions that can attach to the concepts we plan to teach. We should also be at pains to acquaint ourselves with all the connotations that can impel or impede our students' understanding of a new concept. Accordingly, many teachers may be interested in analysing the concepts they are exploring with students. In Rowntree (1981) I illustrate the use of some useful analysis techniques based on the ideas of John Wilson (1974). Here I have space to do little more than list them, but I think the list will be reasonably suggestive:

- *Isolate the concepts* – from the facts, principles, examples, etc. of our subject matter.

- *Define each concept* – dictionary-type definitions to begin with, perhaps.

- *Examine model examples* – to sharpen the definition by deciding which features of the examples are essential to the concept and which are incidental.

- *Examine counter-examples* – to further establish the essential character of the concept by identifying features that would negate it.

- *Examine border-line examples* – to clarify our understanding of the crucial features of the concept by considering cases where it 'almost' applies or applies only 'in a way'.

- *Consider invented examples* – testing the concept by inventing imaginary cases that might really stretch the features we have identified for the concept.

- *Compare social contexts* – to consider the extent to which people from different places and/or times might disagree with our examples and non-examples.

- *Compare personal contexts* – in recognition that the concept will have different connotations for different individuals (which may or may not hinder communication).

- *Examine related concepts* – studying one concept leads us into seeing how it fits into the surrounding network of concepts.
- *Elucidate the principles* – concepts are related to other concepts in principles (rules, theorems, axioms, generalizations, statements) which constitute the 'message(s)' of the subject matter, and the key principles need to be identified and classified (e.g., as empirical, evaluative, definitional or semantic statements).

There is, of course, no need to work through all of these techniques with every concept in your course. Life is too short. Usually a concept will be clarified sufficiently after you have been through three or four of them. But all are at hand for the key concepts of your course – the central ideas, like 'objectives' and 'evaluation' in educational technology.

Sometimes you may decide that the most effective way of *teaching* the concepts is to work carefully through all the techniques *together with* your students. That is to say, the analysis of concepts (and principles) may be used not merely as part of your course planning but as part of the course itself.

Diagramming the Subject Matter

Many teachers find they can best get to grips with their course content by drawing a picture of it. One popular method is the 'spray diagram' promoted by Tony Buzan (1973). He recommended it to students for making 'patterned notes' about what they are getting out of a course; but it can equally well be used by teachers deciding what to put in. Here we start by writing the name of a key topic (say 'Reading Skills') at the centre of a piece of paper (or chalkboard). Then we spray out lines from the centre, one for each major aspect of the topic that occurs to us. These lines will then be branched to indicate sub-aspects, and so on. Figure 4.1 (page 109) is a spray diagram showing relationships among the ideas in one chapter of my programmed book *Learn How to Study* (Rowntree 1970. (Compare this with Figure 4.13, page 134.)

A looser form of diagram, a kind of concept-association chart, is formed when we simply start with the name of a key topic or concept (e.g., 'educational technology') and draw lines from it to a number of related concepts. Then we write in the names of concepts related to these and join them up with lines also. Figure 4.2 is such a concept map of the field of educational technology as seen by my colleague David Hawkridge (1981). In this kind of diagram, as he says 'lines connect words, reflecting connections of some kind without revealing exactly what. Moreover, many other lines could be added to show additional connections.'

Furthermore, he points out that the map of educational technology 'could be drawn differently . . . by other educational technologists'. I bring attention to this perhaps obvious remark because many people setting out to draw a concept map seem to get obsessed with uncovering the 'true, underlying structure' of the subject. Even if such a structure exists, there is no need for that degree of dedication. Drawing such diagrams is a personal and subjective activity whose purpose is simply to help you externalize your own understanding about how the concepts within your field connect up. So long as you find it helpful in your own course planning, there is no need to worry that others might have mapped the territory differently. To emphasize the point, Figure 4.3 shows a similar type of chart for a similar field – 'instructional systems design' – drawn by David Mitchell (1981). The arrows in this diagram, a type sometimes called an 'entailment structure', indicate that the idea mentioned at the 'blunt end' of the arrow is somehow important to an understanding of the idea mentioned at its tip. How similar is David Mitchell's conception of 'instructional systems design' to David Hawkridge's conception of 'educational technology'? Comparison of the two diagrams should help you decide.

Figure 4.4. shows the first sketch of a concept map I drew up for a course on diet and nutrition. I started with 'Food' in the middle and then began by identifying chains of connected concepts. I put down the ideas more or less as they came to mind, without wondering too much about whether all would be needed in the eventual course, or what else might be needed in addition. Again, I drew lines wherever there seemed to be a connection, of whatever kind; the broken lines suggest links I was less sure about than others. I would admit, of course, that other people would map the field differently, but so might I on another occasion. The fact is, the diagramming served its purpose, at the time, as a course-planning device enabling me to see my way around the field *as I conceived it*.

Sometimes a much more structured diagram may emerge from this kind of process. Figure 4.5 is a well-developed network (re-drawn from Fritts 1966), illustrating the relationships between climatic factors and the growth of trees. In this case, arrows link causes with effects. The column of double arrows down the centre indicates the primary chain of causation, with the factors affecting food storage to the right of it and the direct effects of growing-season climate upon growth on the left. This chart can be seen to incorporate principles – that is, statements involving the concepts – as well as the concepts themselves. For example, 'Less root growth causes less water absorption' or 'Rapid evaporation and low soil moisture lead to increased water stress in the tree.'

Another form of chart in which the arrows express very definite kinds of connection is the *algorithm*. Such a diagram can be invaluable in sorting out a subject area in which the emphasis is on classifying cases or examples, or deciding what action to take, on the basis of a number of yes/no decisions as to whether each of a limited range of characteristics applies in a particular case. For example, classifying a soil specimen as loam, clay, sand, etc. depends on noting what combination it exhibits from among such qualities as grittiness, silkiness and resistance to deformation. Similarly, diagnosing a patient's disease may depend on which combination he presents from a range of physical signs and symptoms. Working out an algorithm is a useful way of investigating the relationships between the factors that need to be taken into account and the decisions that may emerge as a result. Figure 4.6 shows part of a medical algorithm concerned with the diagnosis of peripheral vascular disorders in patients presenting with colour changes in their limbs. Such charts are useful not only as course planning devices; they may also be discussed with students, or worked out with them, as part of the teaching (or even instead of teaching). For further guidance on algorithms and how to develop them, together with a wide range of examples, see Lewis and Woolfenden (1970).

Algorithms are interesting in that, like the tree-ring diagram, they go beyond merely showing that certain topics are linked. They actually indicate the *nature* of the links – a network of 'if this . . . then that' statements. Other forms of diagram may also enable one to explore statements about the relationships between concepts. My colleague Bob Zimmer has provided me with Figure 4.7 which might be called a 'noun-verb diagram'. With the phrases along its arrows linking the concepts in the circles, it is clearly making a number of statements about thermodynamics.

How might sketching out such a concept diagram help us in deciding on course content? It might suggest to us a number of things we might need to explain to students or have them undertake themselves. For example:

– Define energy.

– Measure energy in its various forms.

– Give examples of different forms of energy and energy convertors.

– Calculate the efficiency of particular energy convertors.

– Explain the basis of the calculation, e.g., by drawing a concept map.

Finally, let me mention a form of visual representation that is often useful when we have a body of knowledge that can be classified and talked about with more than one set of categories in mind. For example, we might set out to classify house plants according to whether their foliage is grassy, bushy, palm-like, rosette, etc.; or we could go by whether or not they bear fruit and if so, the nature of the fruits; or we might attempt to classify them by the colour of their flowers, if any. In such cases, we may try drawing a table or *matrix* where the vertical columns will represent one way of classifying the subject content and the horizontal rows another way. (A third way of classifying can just about be managed by turning the matrix into a three-dimensional block.)

As an example, I have recently been involved in developing a course for school governors. Figure 4.8 shows part of a matrix that was produced at one point in discussions about what content might need to go into the course. Earlier consultations had revealed that governors would need to consider not only matters pertaining to their individual school but also matters relevant to many schools in their local area and even matters of national concern. At the same time, the kinds of matter involved seemed to be divided among six main categories: curriculum, staffing, pupils, organization, resources and finance, and community. For instance, governors are clearly concerned with how resources and finance are allocated within their own school; but the amount available may be determined by the influence they can have on their local education authority; and the amount available within the local area is largely determined at the national level by government policy which governors need to keep abreast of and take into account.

Hence the matrix emerged as a possible way of coping with the cross-classification of knowledge in this field. It enabled us to be systematic about asking what are the school aspects of, say, 'curriculum' with which governors must concern themselves; what are the local aspects; what are the national aspects? In actual fact, we also had a third classification system that cut across the other two – how do governors of voluntary schools differ from county school governors in their concerns? – but I have not complicated the matrix in Figure 4.8 by drawing in this third dimension. Such a matrix, then, is a device for systematically asking questions about possible course content.

My purpose in showing these various ways of diagramming knowledge has not been to urge any one of them upon you. There are many other kinds of diagram I could have shown, and indeed there is one more we must look at later in the chapter. Furthermore, you may well have your own ways of diagramming that are more suited to your particular purposes. Like any tool in educational technology (like behavioural objectives, for instance), concept diagrams can be a useful servant or a dangerous master. Their purpose is to help you generate ideas. If some form of diagramming seems helpful on a particular course, then use it. If different forms seem suitable for different parts or phases (e.g., matrix followed by concept maps) then use more than one. But don't let the diagrams dictate to you. For example, the matrix in Figure 4.8 gives eighteen possible categories of course content to think about. It would be dangerous, however, to assume that every cell of the matrix must necessarily have something in it. Some cells may be empty and some may be considerably fuller than others. Nor should we allow the matrix to blind us to the possibility that some important topics may fall outside its boundaries or even be obscured by this quite powerful way of carving up the conceptual territory.

Finally, remember that it is the *process* of drawing such diagrams that is recommended as potentially helpful, not the resulting product. It may be, on occasion, that your diagrams will be so revealing of the structure of your subject that you will wish to share them with your students. On the other hand, you may think it more to the point to help your students develop *their own* maps.

Sequence in Learning

By whatever means we identify the main topics, concepts and principles that need to be studied by our students, we come next to questions of how they might be ordered within the course. Can we identify possible sequences through the subject matter content? The aim is to ensure that, where practicable, the ideas our students encounter early in the course are those that will facilitate, or at least not interfere with, their later learning.

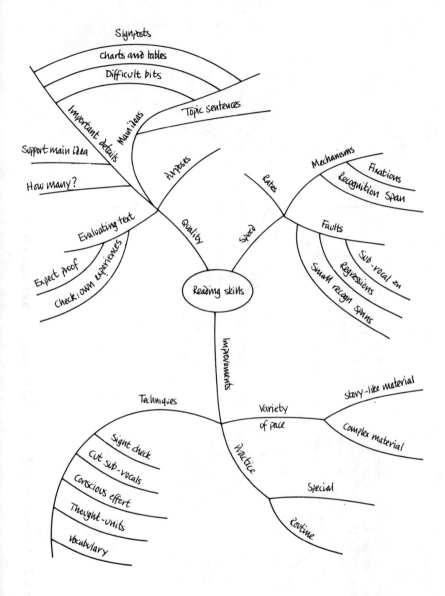

Figure 4.1   A spray diagram (based on Rowntree 1976)

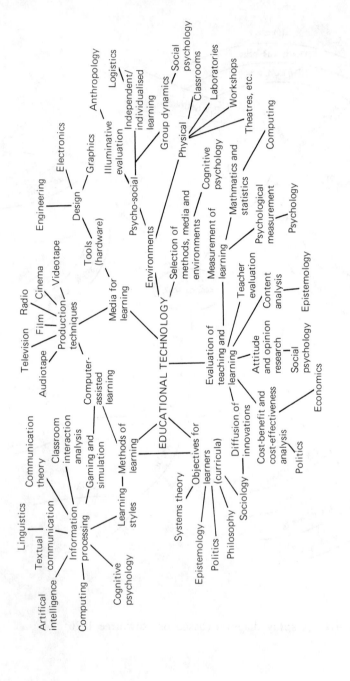

Figure 4.2   A concept map of educational technology (Hawkridge 1981)

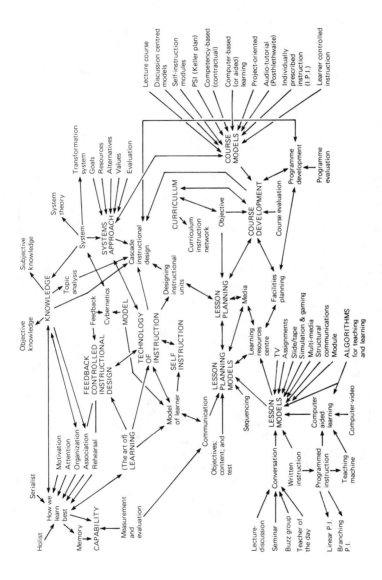

Figure 4.3 An entailment structure for 'Instructional Systems Design' (Mitchell 1981)

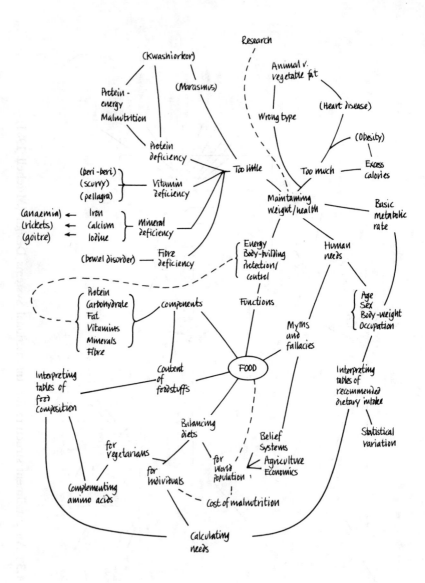

Figure 4.4   Initial concept map for a course on diet and nutrition

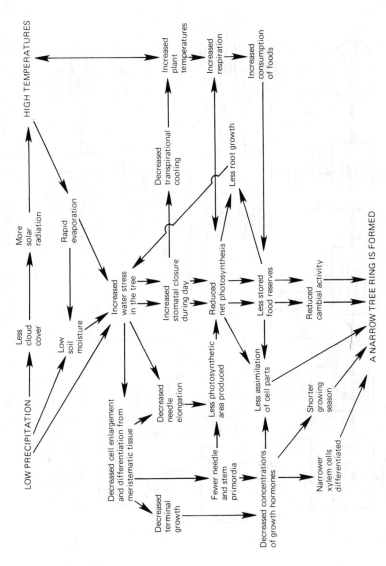

Figure 4.5 A cause-effect network for tree-ring growth (after Fritts 1966)

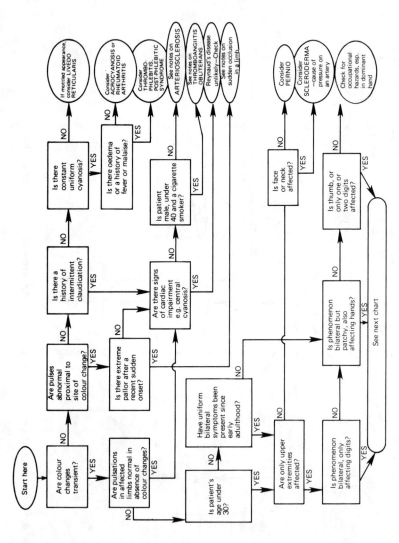

Figure 4.6 Part of an algorithm for medical diagnosis (re-drawn from Lewis and Woolfenden 1969)

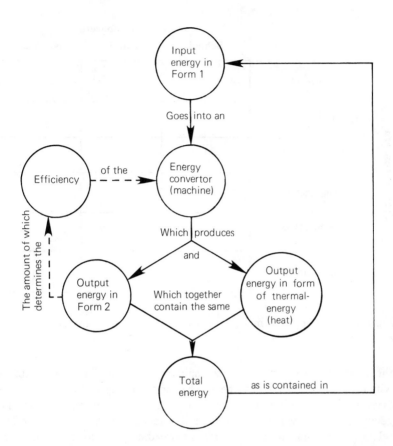

Figure 4.7   A noun-verb diagram for thermodynamics (Zimmer 1981)

Varieties of Sequence

When planning a course or a lesson, we may identify many types of sequence. For instance, the subject matter may lend itself to *chronological* treatment, pursuing events over a period of time in the order in which they happened. This kind of sequence will obviously suggest itself when you are dealing with the historical development of institutions, scientific discoveries and the like. Closely related is the causal sequence, in which

	Level of concern		
	School	**Local**	**National**
Curriculum			
Staffing			
Pupils			
Organization			
Resources & Finance			
Community			

Type of concern

Figure 4.8   Part of a matrix for a course for school governors

the student works through the chain of causation for some event in which he is interested until he reaches and can explain the effect – the event itself. This kind of sequence might be relevant in meteorology and geomorphology, where the student is establishing the cause-and-effect relationships that result in different weather patterns and landscape formations.

Sometimes, the *structural logic* of the subject matter will dictate a sequence. Perhaps it is obvious that a certain topic just has to be explored before a certain other one and that the second cannot be understood without prior understanding of the first. In teaching languages, for example, it may be obvious that discrimination of sounds must be learned before imitative articulation; in statistics, it may seem clear that probability must precede statistical inference as a topic in the course; before a student can comment usefully on critics' reactions to a certain dramatist's work, he must already have read (seen?) some of his plays.

Within a course, some units may be *problem-centred*. That is, problems suggested to the students, or arising out of their experience, may be used to generate the sequence of ideas. Thus, a course on urban development might pose the problem: 'Why did Liverpool grow to be a more important port than Hull?'; an integrated humanities course might deploy a variety of approaches to the problem: 'Is man free?'; a problem such as: 'Why are people the same but different?', might, if posed within a biology course, lead to a genetics sequence like that described by Jim Eggleston (1971):

> The attention of pupils may first be directed to variation in animals and plants by collecting, observing, measuring and attempting to devise systems of classification; thus, students become familiar with the fact of variation. This may include the classification of human beings in terms either of such bizarre qualities as their ability to taste phenylthiocarbamide or the presence or absence of earlobes, such interesting properties as their fingerprints, or such socially relevant properties as their intelligence or blood group.
>
> The problems of measuring and systematizing continuous variations are defined and solutions sought. Students may now be invited to speculate on possible causes of variation and conversely similarity. The students may at this point achieve some perspective of the nature and nurture problem to which Charles Darwin once addressed himself.
>
> Patterns of inheritance may be studied by systematically breeding such convenient organisms as fruit flies. Physical and mathematical models may be constructed to account for the results observed and their variation. Attention may also be drawn to the implications of these models and the possibility of a material, particulate theory of inheritance.
>
> The physical links between generations, sperms and eggs are observed. With the aid of staining techniques and microscopes the behaviour and structure of chromosomes are studied and found to be consistent with the physical models which furnish the hypotheses which accounted for the observed patterns of inheritance.
>
> Anomalous results of certain breeding experiments then lead to a refining of the initial hypotheses, to the concepts of gene and locus. At a later point in this sequence of inquiry, the ways in which genes might work, the origin of variations and the conditions for the spread of genes in populations, are investigated.
>
> The facts and principles so discovered can be applied to evolutionary studies, to agricultural practice, to the proposals of the Eugenic Society; to the problems of racial differences and selection in education.

Clearly, casual and structural elements are also entering into the sample sequence quoted above. It is to be expected, in any sizeable learning structure, that several kinds of sequence will mingle and interact.

Often you will want to arrange for a *spiral* sequence (Bruner 1960).

This kind of structure may be called for in those subject areas where, at first glance, it appears the student cannot get deeply into any topic until he already knows something about all the others. Thus, he may be taken on a brief tour of all the main conceptual landmarks in, say, economics, at GCE 'O' level, coming back to examine them more closely at 'A' level, and analysing them in still greater depth at university. The mutability of the concepts so acquired is well caught by Eraut et al. (1975):

> Even the mastery of a single concept is partly illusory because it cannot be isolated from the cluster of concepts of which it is part. The rich understanding of the expert can never be mistaken for the relatively poor understanding of the novice. Nor is it fixed in time. The understanding of 'inflation' possessed by a first year student will be different from that of a third year student, and different again for a member of faculty; and how many members of faculty will understand inflation today in exactly the same way as they did five years ago?

At each new level of the spiral, the student treats the concepts in more sophisticated ways, relating them to a wider and wider network of more recently acquired understandings. Bruner gives the example of 'force' in physics being introduced first as a 'push or pull', then in terms of acceleration – using graphs, and then represented algebraically. This spiralling ties in with Piaget's suggestion that we need experience with concrete realities before we can cope with visual representations of reality and with the visual images before we can handle abstract representations. It also ensures that the student always has some kind of grasp, however superficial, of the *whole field* of inquiry. Charles Reigeluth et al. (1980) use the analogy of a 'zoom-lens' to describe what they call an 'elaboration' approach to sequencing subject-matter content, which seems similar in intention, being meant to keep the overall structure of the subject always in the student's view, as well as the fine detail.

> A student starts with a wide-angle view of the subject-matter and proceeds to zoom in for more detail on each part of that wide-angle view, zooming back out for context and synthesis. In some cases, it may be best for a learner to pan across the entire subject-matter on one level before zooming in for more detail on any part, whereas in other contexts it may be best for the learner to continue to zoom in all the way on one area before zooming in at all on any of the other areas. In still other contexts, it may be best to let the student follow his/her interests, as long as he/she uses a zoom-in pattern rather than a zoom-out pattern.

Finally, one form of sequencing might almost be called 'no necessary sequence at all'. This I refer to as the *parallel themes* approach. A course so structured would involve the study of a number of related themes or topics, each of which could, after an initial introduction to the overall ethos and purposes of the course, be tackled in *any order*. That is, none of them need depend on any of the others having been studied first; they are 'in parallel' rather than in a necessary series. Thus, a course on modern poetry might have the following topics:

– Introduction: poetry today

– English Poets

– American Poets

– European Poets

After studying the introduction, students might then choose their own sequences through the three parallel topics. Notice, however, that there might well be other kinds of sequence *within* any of the topics (chronological, structural logic, etc.) – e.g., from 'easier' poets to less accessible ones.

The parallel themes approach can be quite useful – especially in subject areas where it makes sense to establish a method of analysis or framework of debate in an initial lesson (or set of lessons) and then offer the student a series of 'case studies' or topics for investigation to which he can apply the new methodology or scholarly criteria.

Logic v. Psychologic

When considering the topics and ideas to be dealt with in a course or lesson, it is natural to look for some kind of 'logical order'. But the logic we should look for is that which will ensure learning, and this may not be the same logic that would appear tidy to someone who knows the subject already. We need student's logic rather than teacher's logic. A much-quoted report by Robert Mager (1961) describes how he encouraged students to generate their own learning sequences in a course on electronics. Traditionally, electronics teaching begins with the simple (electron theory) and builds up to the complex (actual electronic devices). But every one of Mager's students, free to investigate the subject in his own way, wanted to begin with the fairly complex. Specifically, every student within the first forty minutes of tuition wanted to know about vacuum tubes (radio valves). For these students, vacuum tubes somehow symbolized electronics and that is where they wanted to begin. If the project were repeated now, such students would probably hook on to 'the chip' instead. Apart from vacuum tubes, students also wanted to know about how television pictures are formed, how a radio works and about hi-fi and stereo sound reproduction, asking always about things before theory, concrete before abstract, function before structure, *how* rather than *why*.

In fact, there is often a conflict between logical and psychological order. The psychologically satisfying order is often from complex to simple, from the whole to the part, rather than the 'logical' reverse. It may be more productive, for example, for a piano teacher to let her pupil compose and play a simple tune in the first lesson rather than start with scales and chords and finger exercises. The student who is learning to fly may well benefit from taking the controls of an aircraft before he learns the theory of flight. Psychological considerations may outweigh the chronological even in historical studies, where students may prefer to work backwards from where they are, examining, say, the current and recent state of affairs in Northern Ireland before they search for earlier and yet earlier influences. One is reminded of how Alexander Graham Bell was not motivated to learn about electricity until he had *already* conceived the idea of the telephone.

Again, Eraut et al. (1976) have an example to offer from their study of undergraduate economics teaching:

> Previously it had been assumed that the most difficult aspects of learning economics were the concepts and techniques, and that their application [*to real-life economic problems*] would arise naturally. Now it seemed that the reverse might be true. The process of analysing economic problems and deciding which techniques were relevant was the most difficult thing to acquire. Once that had begun to take root the learning of concepts and techniques became less difficult.

Backward Chaining

The work of Thomas Gilbert (1962), pioneer of a form of behavioural analysis known as mathetics, has interesting implications for the sequencing of learning. Wherever objectives involve the learning of sequences (or chains) of behaviour – whether simple chains (like tying a shoelace) or complex (like applying 'scientific method') – Gilbert urges the motivational value of 'backward chaining'. By this he means that the *final* step in the chain should be taught first. Suppose your student is to learn a chain involving these main steps in scientific problem-solving:

- A   Recognize and state a problem.
- B   Form a hypothesis.
- C   Devise a test of the hypothesis.
- D   Carry out the test.
- E   Interpret the results of the test.

Gilbert might recommend starting with Step E. That is, you could present the student with data on Steps A to D for a particular problem and teach him to do the interpretation. Then, taking another problem, you would present him with data on Steps A to C and have him carry out the test before going on to interpret the results. Next, you could give him the results of Steps A and B for a fresh problem and get him to devise a test, carry it out and interpret. Next time, given a problem, he should be able to form a hypothesis, devise the test, carry it out and interpret the results. After this experience the student should learn to recognize and state a problem for himself (Step A) before running through the chain from start to finish. Backward chaining is held to be more effective than forward chaining because, in the course of it, the student *completes* the sequence several times over instead of once only. Thus, he gets more frequent (and earlier) satisfaction and can always see the relevance of each new step in the learning.

In each 'run', Gilbert says that the teacher should teach a new step, remind the student of the last step he learned and then expect him to finish the chain unaided. Thus a five-step chain like the one mentioned above might need seven runs for complete mastery and we can represent them as in Figure 4.9.

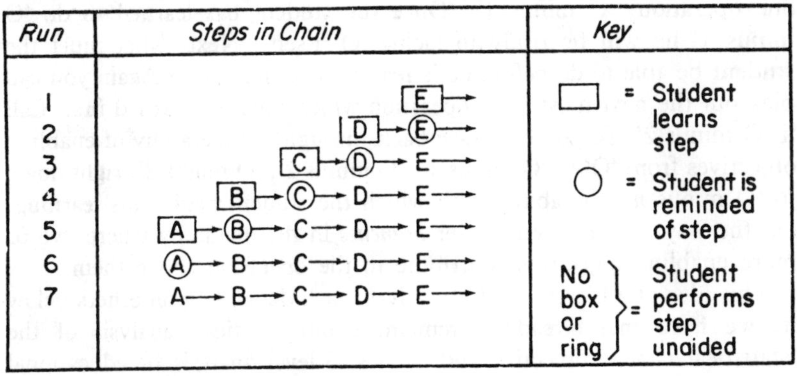

Figure 4.9   Backward chaining

Subsequent research has, of course, demonstrated that not all chains are best taught backwards. Nevertheless, the concept dramatically reminds us that the obvious way is not always the only way to sequence teaching. Like certain other mathetics concepts which have helped in the abandonment of the painfully small steps in programmed learning materials and in making them more challenging, backward chaining is now quite widely, and sometimes unexpectedly, encountered. It can be clearly recognized, for example, across the four-year structure of the industrial design course described by Warren Piper (1969) in which the student might 'be told the [design] problem and how it was derived during the first year, would identify his own problems according to a specified procedure in the second year, would use a variety of procedures in the third year, and be able to justify a choice between procedures in the fourth year'.

Hierarchies in Learning

One of the most thought-provoking approaches to sequencing is based on the work of Robert Gagné (1965). Again we are asked to think (though not necessarily teach) backwards. Gagné suggests that we analyse each of the student's major learning objectives and look for a *hierarchy* of 'enabling objectives' leading up to it. Each objective represents some operation that the student will be able to perform by the end of the course. So we must ask: 'What must the student be able to do before he can attain this final performance?'

If we call the final operation 'O', we are now asking about the last but one operation, 'O minus 1'. (Once the student has learned to do 'O minus 1' he will be ready to tackle 'O' itself.) Next, what must the student be able to do before he is ready for 'O minus 1'? Again you can pick out the next most basic operation which must be learned first. Call it 'O minus 2'. So you can trace back through the hierarchy of enabling objectives from 'O' to 'O minus 1', 'O minus 2', 'O minus 3', right down to 'O minus n', the ability with which the student begins his learning. On the way, you may encounter *branches* in the hierarchy where two or more enabling objectives contribute to the operation above them.

This idea of a hierarchy of objectives, each depending on others below it, we have met already – remember our 'vertical' analysis of the 'statistical charts' objective and Stones' 3-level analysis of educational psychology objectives, discussed in Chapter 3. Let's look now at another example. Suppose we have as our objective that the student should be able to:

State the time as so many hours o'clock or in terms of hours and minutes (e.g., '8 o'clock' or '4.37') reading from a conventional 12-hour clock.
(Needless to say, there is no intrinsic value in this objective; if all clock-faces were replaced tomorrow by digital indicators it would then be of antiquarian interest only.)

Once we start analysing back through the behaviours that lead up to this performance (Figure 4.10), we find that two streams of enabling objectives immediately begin to form and that these in turn have several tributaries. Thus, we can trace back, discovering the succession of objectives the student needs to have achieved prior to being able to decide on the hour, or the number of minutes or whether the time is exactly 'something o'clock'. Eventually we get down to quite lowly abilities (e.g., 'say the number represented by the numerals 1 to 12' or 'recognize that clocks show the time') which may or may not already be in his repertoire.

Certainly, the analysis shows *essential* enabling objectives only. There are many other time-related activities (e.g., making water-clocks and hour-glasses, experimenting with colleagues' perception of elapsed time, discussing the meaningfulness of such questions as 'what time is it now on the moon?') that do not belong in this particular hierarchy. Such activities might be essential to other valuable objectives but have no apparent role here except, arguably, as representatives of a very wide range of activities that might offer relief, encouragement or enrichment to students working through the hierarchy. Perhaps this is the distinction being made by teachers when they dichotomize ideas in terms of 'must know' *v.* 'nice to know' and by experienced students when they 'scan, skim and skip' in their reading.

If Figure 4.10 already looks so complex that you wonder how anyone ever learns to tell the time at all, remember that even now the analysis is incomplete, or at least the objective is fairly limited. For example, should the student also learn to say 'minutes to' and 'minutes past', 'quarter past', 'half past' and 'quarter to'? If so, when (and how)? Of course, we could take any student who had mastered this hierarchy and teach him to distinguish between 'minutes past' and 'minutes to' (the latter leading him to 'count backwards from 12') and also to associate 3 with 'quarter past', 6 with 'half past' and 9 with 'quarter to', and so on. But, if we had started out with this wider objective of stating the time, we might have preferred to build in these distinctions and associations further *down* the hierarchy. You might find it an interesting exercise to develop a hierarchy for the following objective:

> The student should be able to state the time to the nearest minute, in each of the following forms: 8 o'clock; quarter past 8; half past 8; quarter to 8; 8:35; 25 minutes past 8; reading from a conventional clock face.
>
> (Notice that neither this objective nor the one represented in Figure 4.10 includes the ability to 'State the time represented by the *written* expression' or to 'Write the time'.)

If an apparently simple task like learning to tell the time depends on such a massive network of previously acquired behaviours, imagine the richness of the hierarchies underpinning such performances as reading, carrying out an historical investigation, designing an experiment, performing a medical diagnosis, analysing a film or play. In fact, the more complex the objective, for example, the further it gets from being a matter of simple recall and the closer it gets to the upper end of Bloom's taxonomy, the deeper and perhaps more personal to the student is the hierarchy likely to be.

If one of your student's objectives, say in literary studies, is 'to develop a tolerance for ambiguity', you may feel that he must first be able to recognize ambiguities, classify them, analyse their purposes or effects, compare them with related examples and so on. But equally important would be affective traits that the student may or may not already possess, like open-mindedness, willingness to take risks and a distrust of the superficial. The teacher and student exploring together for possible hierarchical connections among such abilities and attitudes might learn much both about what they mean by 'tolerance' and about one another's prejudices and predilections.

One can sympathize with teachers who feel somewhat reluctant to start unravelling the hierarchy (or perhaps I should say *a* hierarchy, for many alternative structures might equally effectively 'enable' a given objective). But, whether they recognize it or not, the hierarchical principle does enter into their students' learning; and difficulties in learning may well be attributable to neglected steps in a hierarchy that has not been recognized. Preece (1976) has shown that, at least in physics, proficient

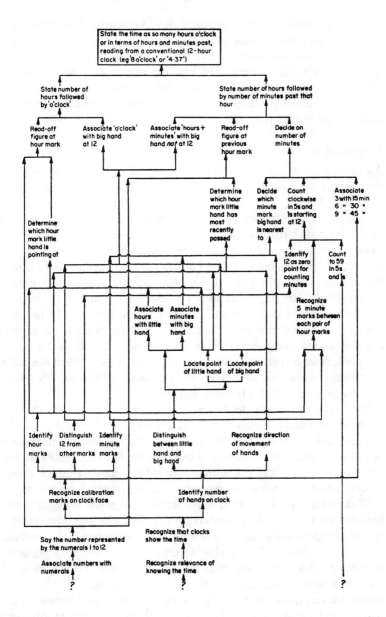

Figure 4.10 A learning hierarchy

students do tend to have organized their knowledge hierarchically.

In practice, the development of a hierarchy is often fairly straight-forward; for you are likely to find that, in thinking about objectives, you have come up with a number of enabling objectives as well as 'terminal objectives'. Thus, the task becomes largely one of arranging them in attainable order and filling in gaps, rather than of thinking up enabling abilities absolutely from scratch.

Prerequisites

Analysis *à la* Gagné can be enormously productive, whether applied to the wider objectives of a course or to the objectives of a smaller unit of learning. Firstly, it clarifies our thinking on *prerequisites* (or entry behaviour) – the abilities with which the student should (or does) come to the learning situation. Gagné suggests that we take our hierarchy and draw a line across at the point below which lie the abilities students are assumed to possess before embarking on the learning and above which lie the abilities they will learn. If we are writing a textbook or a unit of programmed learning, or teaching a lesson, we can state at the beginning what prerequisite skills we are expecting of the students. In fact this is not done as frequently as it should be – perhaps because the necessary analysis seems too complex. Too often, the author of, say, a statistics textbook soon forgets his initial promise that all the student needed was the ability to use the 'four rules' of arithmetic, and he rapidly loses his readers in a welter of advanced algebraics.

Whatever media are to be used, we need to recognize that some students who embark on a unit of learning will not have achieved all the 'prerequisites', while others will have achieved not only the prerequisites but also a number of objectives above the line. We must take care not to omit experiences that the former individuals need. But we must be equally careful to bypass experiences that the latter do not need.

What we need is some kind of preliminary *diagnostic testing* to establish how far each student has climbed up the hierarchy and how far he still has to go. Only then can we make the learning system fit the individual rather than attempt the ignoble reverse. This is not an argument for streaming – teaching students as groups whose members are assumed to have a general similarity of aptitude across a range of subjects. Not unless we can think of streaming for each major objective *within* a given subject and recognize that the student will be in different streams for different objectives, sometimes perhaps being in a stream of one. What it implies is *individualization*, and not necessarily the kind of 'individual-ization' that merely allows the student to go at his own speed towards someone else's goals.

Also, if we need to explain a student's failure to learn, it is more help-ful to look for specific deficiencies in 'entry behaviour' than to blame the failure on a lack either of intelligence or of maturational readiness. Rosenthal and Jacobson (1968) have shown how teachers' information (and misinformation) about students' relative intelligence exerts on classroom interaction a self-fulfilling prophecy whereby the supposedly 'bright' become brighter and, obligingly, the supposedly 'dim' become relatively dimmer (see also Insel and Jacobson 1975, and Nash 1976). Perhaps this is why Brian Jackson (1964) found that, after a few months in the bottom streams of primary schools, children were duller than they had been on entry. Thankfully, the concept of a fixed IQ has by now lost all credibility. Teachers are coming to regard a child's 'intelligence' as a complex of skills they should be helping him to enhance, rather than as an immutable constraint, and hence a convenient scapegoat for poor attainment. However, lack of 'maturity' is still offered quite frequently as a reason why certain children appear not to be 'ready' to learn. David Ausubel (1959) advises us not to accept this explanation too lightly:

> To equate the principles of readiness and maturation not only muddies the conceptual waters but also makes it difficult for the school to appreciate that insufficient readiness may reflect inadequate prior learning on the part of the pupils because of inappropriate or ineffective instructional methods. . . . the school, which is thereby automatically absolved of all responsibility in the matter, consequently fails to subject its institutional practices to the degree of self-critical scrutiny necessary for continued educational progress.

For a fuller examination of the concept of 'readiness', see Tyler (1964).

Types of Learning

In addition to helping clarify our thinking about prerequisites, the idea of a hierarchy reminds us that learning is not all of the same type. In fact, it suggests that the higher one climbs up a hierarchy of objectives, the more complex does the type of learning become. Gagné (1965) identifies eight types of learning, each of which results in different kinds of behaviour and each of which needs different conditions to produce it:

1   *Signal learning:* involuntary, conditioned behaviour, e.g., blinking at a sudden movement near the eyes, withdrawal of hand from hot objects.

2   *Stimulus-response learning:* voluntary, selective responses to stimuli,
    e.g., making pencil marks on paper, imitating the pronunciation of
    a new word.

3   *Motor-chain learning:* a sequence of physical acts carried out in a
    fixed order, e.g., tying a shoelace, writing with a pencil, starting a
    motor car engine.

4   *Verbal association* (Verbal chaining): verbal responses often useful in
    more complex learning, e.g., saying the alphabet, naming an object,
    giving English equivalents of foreign words.

5   *Multiple discrimination:* responding differently to similar stimuli,
    e.g., naming each member of a group of people, giving an appro-
    priate English equivalent for each of a set of similar foreign words
    (say, *fin, femme* and *faim*).

6   *Concept learning:* responding to new stimuli according to the abstract
    properties they share with previously encountered stimuli, e.g., say-
    ing which of two objects is nearer or further away, bigger or smaller,
    lighter or heavier, saying which of a group of numbers are primes,
    saying which of a group of animals are dogs and which are cats.

7   *Principle learning:* putting two or more concepts together in a
    relationship, e.g., using (without necessarily being able to state) a
    rule like: 'hot air rises', or 'area = length × width', or 'ontogeny
    recapitulates phyllogeny'.

8   *Problem-solving:* recalling previously learned principles and perhaps
    generating new higher-order principles, to achieve some goal, e.g.,
    writing an essay, planning a diet, making a medical diagnosis,
    tracking down the fault in a motor car's electrical system, con-
    versing in a foreign language, making a ceramic jug, refereeing a
    football match.

Both Gagné and John De Cecco (1968) give many examples of these
different learning types and suggest how each can be brought about. (See
also Stones 1979.) Although most school learning aspires to the higher-
numbered categories, Gagné points out that 8 depends on 7 which
depends on 6 which depends on 5 and so on; he also demonstrates the
hierarchy at work in typical school subjects. If you feel there may be
more than these eight types of learning (especially around categories 6, 7
and 8), Gagné would not disagree with you.

Structures and Sequences

The third benefit to be had from a Gagné-type 'hunt the hierarchy' is, of course, the help it gives us in sequencing learning. Notice, though, that the analysis is unlikely to produce just one cut-and-dried, take-it-or-leave-it sequence. Apart from the fact that more than one hierarchy is usually possible, any given hierarchy, because of branches within it (and possible branches to topics *outside* it), may well show several possible routes. For example, in Figure 4.10, the student could follow first the route dealing with deciding on the hour, or with counting the minutes. Then, if he follows the 'hour-route' first, he has a choice of tackling 'minutes past' or 'o'clock'; or should you try to advance him up all routes at once?

In short, the analysis does not generate *the* sequence but rather reveals a *variety of pathways*. One of these will sometimes be identifiable as 'best', but often the variety is best used to accommodate the variety of learning styles among the students – more individualization. For instance, Pask and Scott (1972) show how quite different routes may be taken by students they distinguish as *serialists* (who are content to string ideas together step by step) and *holists* (who search for pattern and structure).

Detailed examination of the concept map I drew for diet and nutrition (Figure 4.4, page 112) revealed that it contained a hierarchy of topics. This I show in Figure 4.11 where the arrows indicate the direction of the hierarchical flow, with knowledge of the 'components of food' as the cornerstone of understanding in this field. I have then taken the analysis further in Figure 4.12 by looking for linear routes through the topics. There are at least two possible sequences. After studying 'components of food', the student may work down the left-hand side of the diagram first, as far as 'analysing sample diets', and then down the right-hand side as far as 'interpreting RDI tables'; or he may take the right-hand path first. Either way, he must have followed both chains before going on to 'evaluating diets'.

Teaching Point Outlines

If we were planning a course to be presented to all students in the same sequence, e.g., as a series of lessons or as pre-packaged materials, we might need, sooner or later, to write down an ordered list of *teaching points*. These would constitute the main statements we wished to make

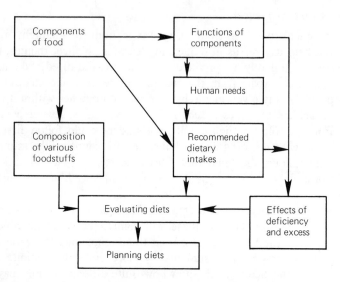

Figure 4.11   A hierarchy in the diet and nutrition course

about the subject matter. Such a teaching point outline can be drawn from our concept maps, hierarchies and flow diagrams. Based on the diet and nutrition flow diagram, such a teaching point outline might begin: 'Food has six main components; these components are . . .; they can be divided into the following categories . . .', and so on. Teaching points might also be drawn from an extended prose overview such as that for genetics on page 117.

For a completed example of a teaching point outline, see Figure 4.13 which formed the basis for a chapter in my programmed book *Learn How to Study* (Rowntree 1976). Compare it with the spray diagram in Figure 4.1 (page 109). If you have not already diagrammed your subject area, this kind of teaching point outline can be produced (as can a concept diagram, for that matter) by starting out with a number of topics, e.g., 'speed of reading', 'quality of reading', 'improving reading' – and dividing them into subtopics. Then look for sub-subtopics within your subtopics, and so on. Keep going until you have teased out all the important concepts down to an appropriate level of detail; then decide on a sensible sequence (Mechner 1967).

But if we want to keep our options as to teaching/learning sequence

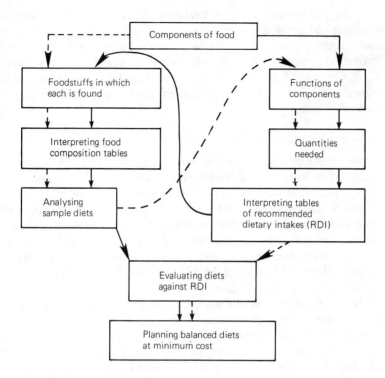

Figure 4.12 A flow diagram for the diet and nutrition course

open for as long as possible – so as to allow for individualization perhaps – prose outlines and lists may seem too prescriptive a way of displaying teaching points (or objectives). Unavoidably, they suggest 'preferred' sequences and, even more basically, they encourage a linear approach to the subject matter. Non-linear structures, like concept networks and hierarchies, can more powerfully illustrate the multiplicity of inter-connections between ideas.

Looking back, for instance, at the tree-ring diagram (Figure 4.5 on page 113), we can see how several different teaching point outlines – different in substance as well as sequence – might be drawn from the same concept map. We might want to start by defining the concepts: 'solar radiation', 'xylem cells', 'water stress', etc. Or we might begin by discussing the primary chain of causation. Yet again we might start by examining the cause-and-effect clusters on either side of the primary chain. Another approach might be to work backwards from the final outcome, the narrow tree-ring, uncovering the causes in reverse order, i.e., if z is caused by y, what causes y? The different teaching point outlines and their differing sequences might appeal differently to different students.

Students' Own Sequencing

Let me emphasize this as the final point about sequencing. Our concern should not be to find some ideal sequence which we will then prescribe for all students. Rather we should try to identify a number of possible alternative sequences (without necessarily being exhaustive) that will enable us to help the individual student, wherever possible, to choose or construct one that suits him best. Of course, where an area of the subject matter is truly hierarchical, the student cannot miss out steps or transpose them; but he may be able to include additional stages or branch out into a related hierarchy.

It is worth noting, by the way, that even when we do present our students with a standard sequence of teaching points, they may re-order the sequence to suit themselves. For instance, students who are given a set of self-teaching modules (e.g., Open University correspondence texts) may choose not to read them in the numbered sequence and/or, within any one text, they may study later sections before earlier ones or have a go at the end-of-unit test questions before reading the unit itself. Even within a classroom lesson, students may be processing ideas in a different order from that in which the teacher is presenting them. Whether or not they believe they can or should do anything about it, teachers should at least be alert to the possibility that different students are finding different ways through the subject matter.

Ideally, the student should be encouraged to construct and justify his own hierarchies, networks and learning sequences, just as he should learn to formulate his own objectives. For example, Harrison and Hopkins (1967), whose course for Peace Corps volunteers I mentioned in Chapter 2, numbered among their objectives that the students should be weaned of their dependence on expert, authoritative advice and should learn to take responsibility for solving problems on their own, often in the light of uncertainty and inadequate information, and always having to deal constructively with the strong feelings generated by confront-

1 Despite 'experience' few college students read as well as they might. (Too slow, can't concentrate, forget.)

2 For *better* reading (improved comprehension):
   (a) Apply SQ3R to get sense of purpose.
   (b) Look for topic sentence in each paragraph:
        (i) Usually first or last sentence, and
        (ii) Contains the *main idea* of the paragraph.
   (c) Look for important *details:*
        (i) e.g., proof, example, or support for main idea.
        (ii) Usually at least one to each main idea.
   (d) In hunt for main ideas and important details:
        (i) Watch out for signposts: visual (Layout and typestyles), verbal (Clue words and phrases).
        (ii) Study all charts and tables.
        (iii) Don't skip difficulties.
   (e) *Evaluate* the text:
        (i) Be sceptical (expect author to prove).
        (ii) Look for applications in your own experience.

3 Towards *faster* reading: (most people could read half as fast again and still understand just as well).
   (a) During reading:
        (i) Eyes jerk left to right in series of *fixations.*
        (ii) At each fixation, brain decodes group of words, making up its *recognition span.*
   (b) Poor readers:
        (i) Have small recognition spans, therefore make many fixations.
        (ii) Regress frequently (backward glances).
        (iii) Read aloud (or make sub-vocal noises).

4 Can improve reading (speed *and* understanding).
   (a) Five basic steps:
        (i) Check whether you need specs.
        (ii) Stop saying words aloud.
        (iii) Consciously try to read faster.
        (iv) Read in thought-units (2 or 3 words at a time).
        (v) Build up vocabulary (reading, speaking, writing) by reading widely, learning Greek and Latin roots, noting new words, using dictionary, making glossaries.
   (b) Practise (absolutely essential) by:
        (i) Nightly sessions (15 to 30 min.): read articles of known length, time yourself (w.p.m.) (Progress chart?), test your comprehension.
        (ii) Reading *all* study material faster.
   (c) Vary your reading pace:
        (i) Faster for 'story-like' material and main ideas.
        (ii) Slower for complex argument and for important detail.

Figure 4.13 A teaching point outline (from Rowntree 1970)

ations of value and attitude. Thus, when trainees arrived expecting a traditional university classroom course (which would clearly have been inappropriate), they found that they had to design and sequence large parts of the course for themselves.

> From their arrival, the trainees would be encouraged to participate actively in the planning of their program. In fact, in a sense, there wouldn't be a program unless they planned it through determining what kind of a training program they needed in order to reach the objectives they had formulated.
>
> The program would be 'experience-based'. There would be ample opportunities furnished for 'doing things', such as organizing and operating co-ops, raising chickens and pigs, planting and tending gardens, approaching 'academic' subjects through research projects, etc. Trainees with needed skills would be urged to teach them to others, formally or informally. The emphasis, in short, was to be on trainee activity, not passivity.

Colin and Mog Ball (1973), in urging a curriculum based around community involvement, give many similar examples of how enterprising schools have enabled students to generate their own sequences of learning out of the problems they identify in the locality. Perhaps it is fair to say that the more non-directive we plan to be about sequencing, the more versatile and opportunist we have to be at recognizing worthwhile learning objectives and keeping them in view, and at helping students obtain access to suitable learning resources.

Strategies in Teaching

It is difficult to think seriously about content and sequencing without at the same time making some assumptions about the broad strategies one will use in the subsequent teaching. For example, the statement of sequence in genetics (page 117) can be seen to imply a strategy of *guided discovery*. Students are to be 'stage-managed' into deriving the structure of the subject for themselves, while at the same time practising the investigative techniques of the biologist. Such a strategy is chosen as the means most likely to achieve the higher-level (and Group II) objectives (see Figure 3.1).

Constraints

Relating the means to the desired ends will, of course, be tempered by the ever-present constraints – time and facilities, people and ideologies – of the system within which we work:

- Do we operate within an educational 'closed shop' – acting as though all the student's education happens in school? Or can we recognize and build upon his extra-mural learning and community life?
- Are our students timetabled and expected to switch their interest from one subject to the next every forty minutes or so? Or are we free to schedule and reschedule throughout the day, enabling each student to develop his own working rhythm, crossing and re-crossing subject matter boundaries?
- Do we have to operate in bleak ancient premises with inadequate facilities for storage, display and practical work? Or do we work in a modern building whose architects had some conception of the variety of learning activities that might take place within it?
- Are our students accustomed to formal, authoritarian class teaching, with the emphasis on remembering what the teacher says? Or are they prepared for independent learning and thinking, as individuals and small groups, with the teacher acting as guide and counsellor rather than as instructor and inquisitor?
- Are we cut off from contact with parents and others who might be interested in our students' learning? Or are parents and other members of the community encouraged to concern themselves actively, even to the extent of working with children in or out of the classroom?
- Are the students regarded as naturally lazy and potentially disruptive creatures who need to be made to learn and who must be kept in check by means of a strict code of discipline, enforced if necessary by physical assault? Or are they treated as reasonable and inquiring beings who naturally want to learn and who are capable of responsible self-discipline?

Few educational institutions lie at either extreme of the continuum implied in the above questions. Few are entirely teacher-centred; fewer still entirely learner-centred. I believe, however, that the spread of educational technology ideas (among students as well as teachers) will result in teaching becoming more closely related (both in ends and in means) to the needs of individual learners. I believe also that it will foster such learner-centred concepts as flexible scheduling, integrated studies, non-graded schooling, multi-media resources and independent study. Before we follow such an educational technology, we must be realistic about the constraints. Although inadequate architecture and lack of resources can often be overcome by enterprising teachers, it is much more difficult to develop learner-centred innovations in an environment where staff and students have become habituated to teaching rather than learning. Difficult but not impossible, and such environments are usually those in greatest need.

Without losing sight of the constraints, let us consider some of the decisions about strategy that we need to take:

Exposition v. Discovery

The balance between expository, predigested teaching ('telling them all they need to know') and discovery or inquiry learning ('helping them to find out for themselves') is one of the major strategic decisions to be made in teaching. It reverberates around so many subsequent choices. The controversy has rumbled on for some time (see Shulman and Keislar 1966, for a useful review of the issues). But it has become muted since discovery and inquiry methods of a kind were embraced by curriculum development groups like Nuffield and the Schools Council, gaining them recognition by more and more teachers (in primary schools at least).

Much of the controversy has always centred around confusion of terms. 'Discovery learning' has proved an ambiguous term in many ways, not least in its implications for objectives. Are we concerned with learning *by* discovery or with learning *to* discover? If we are aiming merely at limited content objectives, it may be difficult to justify discovery methods. (See Ausubel and Robinson 1969, for a spirited defence of expository teaching which results in what they call 'reception learning'.) A discovery approach may be no more effective than simply expounding the principles and then engaging the student in suitable practice. And the discovery approach is certainly likely to take more time. Ernest Coulson (1971) tells how students took between four and five hours to 'discover' the effects of heat on calcium carbonate compared with the thirty minutes it had taken him to 'teach' it to previous classes. But during the four or five hours, the discovery group had also gained experience of planning and carrying out experiments, making mistakes, rethinking their assumptions, and so on. In fact, they had also been attaining higher-level (life-skill or methodological) objectives that were denied to the passive 'receivers' of the thirty-minute demonstration. They were learning the *processes* of investigation as well as the products.

It can be very difficult for teachers to refrain from over-explaining things to students. Rarely do we realize how ineffective it can be to take our own experience or that of some third party, transmute it into a flow of words, and thrust it on to the student in the hope that he can reconstitute from it a similar experience (as opposed to a similar verbal comment or conclusion) in his own mind. (Note the quotation from Sanders on page 173.) As Froebel pointed out:

> To have found one-fourth of the answer by his own effort is of more value and importance to the child than it is to half-hear and half-understand it in the words of another.

We should know from our own endeavours as learners that understanding is impossible unless we can somehow re-create for ourselves the experience that gave rise to the ideas at issue. Ideas that we struggle to establish out of our personal fumblings and strivings are generally both more meaningful and more memorable than those we have merely been told about by someone else. As teachers, we should do all we can to respect and support the student's own fumblings and strivings, introducing him to whatever resources and experiences seem likely to help him towards the insights he is reaching out for.

One of the resources our student will be most in need of is *time*. Learning to live with new insights and new ways of looking at the world, e.g., as in learning elementary algebra or a new language, may be neither a smooth nor a rapid process – especially if comfortable old ideas have to be forced out to make room for the new.

Ideally, you will vary the balance between discovery and exposition from one part of your teaching to another. In doing so, you may take into account not only the objectives being dealt with but also the differences among students in their preferred ways of learning. For a useful insight into some of the underlying factors that may be at work, see the account by Tallmadge and Shearer (1969) of how different kinds of student – e.g., non-anxious introverts with a technological bent *v.* anxious extroverts with humanistic interests – benefited differentially according to whether they were learning logical or arbitrary subject matters from discovery or expository approaches.

Expository teaching will often be useful, for example, where you want students to grasp a few basic ideas or guiding principles as preparation for launching into a more open-ended inquiry of their own. Generally, discovery should predominate where your objectives relate to the 'how' of learning rather than to the 'what' – where students are learning how to learn and perhaps acquiring the affective strength that will enable them to adopt the inquiry approach as part of their life-style. Hirst and Peters (1970) ask:

. . . how the interest of children is awakened and stimulated in the appraisals and achievements that are characteristic of the different modes of experience. How, for instance, in the case of science do children come to care about getting their facts right, being clear and precise? How do they come to abhor what is irrelevant, inconsistent and false? How, in the moral sphere, does the sense of justice develop? How does sporadic sympathy develop into respect for persons and animal caution into a more reflective prudence?

Such 'rational passions' are presumably acquired not through the reception of meticulous 'explanations' but through structured experience, involvement and self-discovery.

You may also find it necessary, especially when working with students unused to such freedom, to vary the balance of 'reception learning' and 'learning by discovery' from one individual to another. Not everyone is initially able to tolerate the ambiguity and uncertainty inherent in open-ended inquiry. Consider the difference between two American visitors, one of whom is quite content to watch rugby on television and work out such 'explanations' as he needs by observation as the game proceeds, while his colleague feels uneasy until he has first cross-examined you for several minutes on all the game's rules and stratagems. Compare also the new student of a foreign language who is happy to plunge into a conversational situation, aware of but unconcerned at the many phrases not understood, while his colleague is reluctant to converse at all until he has built up considerable grammatical competence. Students who are over-dependent on correct answers and infallible teachers can learn to be self-confident inquirers, but their introduction to discovery will need to be gentler and well supported.

The kind of discovery learning identified with Bruner (1960) would be regarded by many radicals as a rather bogus form of inquiry, in that it does not produce new knowledge or knowledge of particular significance to the inquirer. Postman and Weingartner (1969), one of whose suggestions is that we 'prohibit teachers from asking any questions they already know the answers to', chide Bruner and his followers for paying too little attention to the questions students want to inquire into and concentrating instead on what is of interest to Bruner, i.e., the structures of established subject disciplines. Clearly, there is little motivation to fearless, personal inquiry if students feel the only meanings they are allowed to discover are those already perceived and codified by outside authorities. Herbert Thelen (1972) suggests that 'we have ground out students who can solve problems but who will for ever have to be guided by someone else.' Admittedly, even ritual, 'let's pretend' discovery can be more interesting than passive, 'reception learning'. But it can also be helping students towards a most unfortunate affective outcome if it encourages the belief that 'others' must be relied on both to sanction the problems and to ratify the solutions. We are back to objectives, and the need for students to learn how to formulate their own.

The ultimate in discovery learning is the kind of self-directed *project* mentioned in Chapter 3. Here the learner is exploring a subject area of his own choice and he may well emerge more knowledgeable than his teacher. Unlike 'guided discovery', the teacher cannot know in advance just what is to be discovered. He needs to abandon his role of subject matter expert and guide in favour of being a vastly more experienced student and a critical friend. That is, being broadly familiar with the area his student is tackling, he will be able to discuss the student's approach and help him evaluate and extend his results, even though the specific insights gained by the student may be new to teacher and student alike.

Other aspects of strategy closely related to the balance of discovery and reception learning are the grouping of students, the pacing of learning, the assessment of students, and the teacher's role and style in the classroom.

Groups and Individuals

Discovery learning tends to imply children working individually and in small groups rather than as an homogeneous class. An illusion of discovery can take place in a large group; but the 'discoveries' of the faster children are immediately made known to the slower ones, thereby preempting any discoveries they might have made. Even assuming a whole class will be interested in the *same* discoveries at any one time, will the watchers get as much out of it as the maker? Research does not tell us.

If he conceives of his class as a unity which must be advanced in lockstep through the subject matter, the teacher will tend to adopt the role of performer, lecturer and fount of all wisdom. If he prefers his students to work as individuals or in small groups, he will find himself acting more as an adviser on resources and as learning counsellor. The latter teacher will work with individuals and cooperating groups to help them sense and define their problems, to seek out people or materials providing relevant data, and to help his students widen and make meaning out of their researches. Each time the teacher goes from group to group, he needs to adjust to a new problem and new learning difficulties. He will be aware of the differing demands of what Galton et al. (1980) call 'the attention-seekers, the intermittent workers, the solitary workers, and the quiet collaborators'. He is left in no doubt that he is working for his students rather than they for him. Needless to say, not all teachers find it easy to change from class teaching to individualized learning (even if they, their students and the school recognize the need). Teachers who have introduced 'resource-based', individualized learning systems describe the psychological strains of adjustment as well as the rewards (see Butler and Cavanagh 1969, Gray and Sare 1970, Caton 1972, Buswell 1981).

Learning environments built around 'packages' and 'multi-media resources' permit individualization without absolutely requiring it. Taylor (1971) describes the variety of ways in which packages may be used, perhaps suggesting to many teachers how they might progressively make the transition from teacher-centred to student-centred learning:

> We can discern, then, an ascending order of ways in which a package may be used. First, a package may be used by a teacher under close supervision; all the children then do the same thing at much the same time – a near lock-step but with less verbal teaching. Second, a package may be used part-time, the teacher covering certain topics in the conventional way and the materials the rest. Third, a package may be phased, the [students] working independently at varying materials but all within the same general topic. Fourth, when packages in a range of subjects are available they can be used in the Dalton manner. In this, although the work to be done by a class in any subject is phased over, say, a month a [student] is allowed for part of each day (or for a day or so each week) to choose how he distributes his time between subjects. Provided minimum requirements are satisfied in all his subjects, he is free to put his emphasis where he likes and may, when his stint is finished, work beyond normal school subjects and requirements. Fifth, a teacher or team of teachers may allow all [students] or certain individuals, to work freely through the packages at unrestricted, individual speed – what is called continuous progress.

Individualized learning does not mean that the student is necessarily working on his own, though no doubt he will be for at least part of the time. It should mean that the objectives pursued by a student and the means and materials he uses are related to his personal needs and interests (and those of any small group of like-minded peers) rather than to the convenience of the class as a whole. Sometimes these ends and means will be suggested by the teacher, sometimes they will come from the student, but always they must be relevant to that student.

Equally clearly, the fact that the student is working on a 'package', alone or with a couple of friends, is no guarantee that the work is individualized. Resource materials are sometimes so pre-selected, pre-structured and virtually pre-digested – what Edgar Friedenberg calls the 'TV-dinner approach' to educational packaging – that the student is left no freedom to use the package in his own way and take from it just what he needs. We should be suspicious of monolithic packages that assume all students have the same objectives and the same learning style – even if they are promoted as 'individualized learning'.

The term (or slogan) 'independent learning' is sometimes used instead of, or as well as, 'individualized learning'. When it is, one might usefully ask: '*Of what* is the students' learning meant to be independent?' Of objectives imposed by the teacher? Of learning methods imposed by the teacher? Or simply of the obligation to keep pace with other students? Usually only the latter is implied. (Students may actually decline to exercise this form of independence, as I shall illustrate below.) In practice, though it might not officially be part of the scheme, students may also be expected to be independent of the frequent advice and encouragement that only a good teacher can give.

Clearly, there are dangers as well as benefits in packaged learning, especially if the package has not been produced by the teacher who is working with it or, of course, if it is seen as a way of minimizing contact with students. One teacher, in a secondary school where pupils used packaged materials throughout the week in some subjects, told Carol Buswell (1981) that: 'I don't like teaching other people's work. I got more satisfaction when I class taught. I'm just a glorified clerk now.' Other teachers were enthusiastic, however, and felt that opposition came only from 'the ones with traditional educational ideas . . . they're nostalgic for the past.' There is also the danger that pupils may not be progressing through the material as fast as might have been expected. Carol Buswell collected pupil remarks like: 'I like to be the same as everyone else – if I get ahead in maths I slow down a bit'; 'I like to keep the same speed as me friends'; and 'If you're two books ahead of the others, they call you a swot'. Pupils' use of packaged learning needs to be carefully monitored, especially where the teacher operating it has thereby surrendered some of his control over curriculum content, teaching method and assessment to other professionals, even if only to other teachers in the same school.

Perhaps the best approach to packaging is 'modular' – implying a multiplicity of smaller packages, or units, or sets of learning materials.

They may be open-ended and non-prescriptive, or they may be quite specific about the objectives they are most useful for; either way they should impose minimum constraints on teachers and students who wish to choose from among them and combine them with other resources and experiences in personally meaningful ways. Better maybe to hack out a path to your own destination than to ride the royal road to someone else's. Nathaniel Cantor (1972) saw more clearly than most what is entailed by a truly individualized use of learning resources:

> No two students learn the same way. Every individual will take out of the course what he feels he wants or needs and will put into it whatever efforts his capacities and willingness to learn allow. The [teacher] who is aware of these differences in learning will permit different students to use him, and the material of the course, in their own unique ways. As long as the student is sincerely trying to do something with himself and struggling to learn, he should be permitted to move at his own speed and on his own level.

In post-secondary education, resource-based learning is increasing in popularity. The Open University has made 'distance learning' respectable at university level and the 'Open Tech' scheme may help establish it more widely in further education also. Students in many institutions are also learning on campus from packaged teaching (e.g., Hills 1976, Morton et al. 1974, Pronay 1979, and Roach and Hammond 1976). Keller Plan courses are widespread both in the UK and in the USA (e.g., Allen 1978, and Bridge and Elton 1977). For a review of resource-based learning in post-secondary education, see Noble (1981) though, like many of the references mentioned in this paragraph, it has many useful ideas to offer school teachers also. Clarke and Leedham (1976) is devoted to papers about individualized learning at all levels of education; and I will leave you to judge how far and in what ways the learning described is truly individualized.

Individualizing Objectives

If for no other reason than to harness the motivation generated by 'doing one's own thing', teachers would be wise to help students choose or preferably formulate their own objectives for at least some part of the school day. If students need help in formulating their own objectives, one way is to ask them what *questions* they would like the course to help them answer. Probing the implications of their questions, you can help them generate yet more. The resulting list of questions often suggests quite different objectives from those the course might otherwise have had. By this means, students can often generate objectives even in a 'technical' area which they might claim to be quite ignorant of, as apparent in Robert Mager's interesting experiment in teaching electronics which I mentioned earlier (page 119). Neil Postman and Charles Weingartner (1971) give many examples of how a 'curriculum' can be shaped out of questions raised by students – what they call the 'What's-Worth-Knowing Questions Curriculum'.

How well the teacher is able to encourage and tolerate a variety of objectives among students depends to a very large extent on how far he feels free to relinquish some of his power to impose his own meaning on the learning situation and unilaterally decide what is to count as worthwhile learning (see Rowntree 1975). It depends also on how clearly he can recognize his students as individuals. Does he know, and respect, each one's strengths and weaknesses, fears and fantasies, interests and aversions? Can he at least recognize, for any desired objective, whether or not a student has achieved all the prerequisite or 'enabling' objectives. Essential this, whether the teacher is thinking of a life-skill objective to be attained by all students or of a methodological or a content objective perhaps of relevance to one student only. How far has the individual student grown? How far can he grow now and in what directions?

As far as possible, we should work with the student to diagnose his needs and balance his menu of objectives, from all three 'groups', accordingly. As a broad example, consider a college of education taking in 'mature' trainee teachers. It finds that, since leaving school, some of them have gained a great deal of teaching experience but have not furthered their own academic education, while others will have pursued advanced academic studies but have no teaching experience. Consequently, the college may assume that the balance of academic study and teaching practice thought appropriate for the more homogeneous students coming straight from school will not necessarily be appropriate for all 'matures'. Hence, in order to satisfy their differing objectives, it will arrange for some to spend a higher proportion of their time in contact with children and others a higher proportion on academic work. By such adjustments, pursued in its day-to-day detail as well as in its overall structure, the course can be made to serve the student's objectives rather than expecting the student to serve those of the course.

That last example assumes all students are to end up equally balanced in capabilities. The fact that they are pursuing different objectives is merely a necessary means to bring about their approximate equivalence by the end of the course. However, in some circumstances, we may not wish to aim for such equivalence. Students may be allowed to pursue different objectives with a view to emerging from the course each with a rather different (possibly very different) repertoire of capabilities. At present, for example, I am involved in discussions about a possible one-year course on health and disease, which would look at the issues from a variety of perspectives: biological, technological, sociological, economic, political, historical, psychological, philosophical. Students would come to the course from a variety of backgrounds, some from the arts and social science, others from science and technology. So, the question arises of whether we ideally want them all to emerge from the course at approximately the same level of knowledge and skills in applying each of the contributory disciplines to questions of health and disease? Or, given perhaps a *common core* of knowledge and skills in all the disciplines which all students will be expected to achieve, can we in the rest of the course allow those with a biological bent to specialize to some extent on biological questions while the politically minded develop politically oriented objectives, and so on? Can we enable and justify diversity rather than uniformity within such a course? The debate continues.

The Pacing of Learning

If the ends and means are individualized, who controls the pace and the time available for learning? Will the student be able to go at his own pace in reaching his objectives? Will there be an overall limit on the amount of time he can take? This raises the concept of 'mastery learning' (see Block 1971) and the idea that, for 90 percent of students, their spread of attainment in any given course is more due to shortage of learning-time available than to difference in potential. Benjamin Bloom (1971) argues that the 'normal distribution of scores' on such a course arises because, at each successive level, a percentage of the students who have so far coped find that they cannot achieve the new criterion capability in the time available and are thus inadequately prepared to attain subsequent criteria. His recommendation is: 'Make time the variable and let students take as long as they need to master each objective.' The slower learners may take five or six times as long as the faster to achieve mastery. With extra attention, and special help from the teacher and other learning resources, Bloom suggests that at least 90 percent of any group should be able to attain the standard currently achieved by the *top* 10 percent.

We are entitled to be sceptical about the kinds of learning implied in

Bloom's suggestion. For instance, how compatible is it with what I have called 'infinitely improvable' objectives? Yet we can hardly help being stimulated by the implicit challenge to traditional assumptions about learning speeds. The institution of 'continuing education' for adults can be seen as the same phenomenon writ large.

Of course the ramifications of 'own pacing' are extremely wide, as the first large-scale applications of programmed learning soon showed (see Butler and Cavanagh 1969, Reid and Booth 1969). Within a 'class', some children can get on faster in some areas, some in others, with all having occasional slow downs, blockages and regressions. The tradition of annually elevating the whole class to a new level of the broad curriculum, on the grounds of their more-or-less common age and disregarding their individual diversity of attainment levels, begins to look more and more suspect. Hence, the increasing interest in 'continuous progressing' (where the second-year student may still be working on what had hitherto been first-year science, while working also on 'third-year' maths and 'fourth-year' German) and in the 'non-graded school' (Goodlad 1966).

Assessment of Students

'Own pacing' and 'mastery learning' also call for new attitudes to student assessment. In particular, the roles of examinations and of grading – neither of which is a logically necessary part of assessment or of teaching – need to be thought about.

In Chapter 3, I stressed the need, in choosing assessment instruments, to look for *valid* measures of the objectives being aimed at. Even when the appropriate test of a particular objective might be to have the student organize an exhibition, carry out a research project or engage in a disputation with colleagues, too often he is asked to write an essay about it instead. Often indeed the only assessment data given any weight are that collected from an essay examination at the end of the course. Whatever the other purported objectives of the course, one of the chief abilities being tested in the examination is that of being able to write at abnormal speed, under unusual stress, on a topic suggested by someone else, and without reference to one's usual sources of information.

In so far as examinations are to be used in assessment, Joseph Schwab (1969), a biologist, suggests a procedure that is more 'life-related' and 'cooperative'; it is applicable to both arts and science subjects. He suggests that a couple of weeks before the end of a course, students should be given a 'set work' (e.g., a new novel or engineering design problem) which they are to tackle in the examination. It should be typical of those the student has worked with during the course, and accessible to the methodological skills he has learned, but one that is quite new to him and should not have been discussed by the teacher. Students may then choose their own ways of coming to grips with the new work, consulting whatever resources they please and working alone or in groups. They may bring their books and notes to the examination and will be at liberty to exchange words with colleagues. As Schwab recognizes:

> This runs counter, of course, to the tradition of examinations. Students are collaborating; they are cheating in fact; borrowing ideas from each other, criticisms, tips and caveats, which is exactly what we have taught them to do. They are doing exactly what we do – unless we are poets or egomaniacs – when we undertake a similar work, for we too borrow ideas from colleagues and predecessors (and it matters very little whether we seek their help face-to-face or by way of their publications), and seek from colleagues charitable enough to give it, criticisms of our thoughts and formulations. The examination, in short, is a continuation of the curriculum as well as a certifying device.

One might wonder why even so enlightened an examination should be needed at all if it is meant simply to assess capabilities already observable during the course itself. The fear still lingers among many institutions that they would lose academico-political prestige if they abandoned altogether the purgative ritual of a three-hour essay examination. However, 'end-of-course' assessment may very well be needed to check that certain crucial capabilities which students acquired and demonstrated earlier in the learning process have been maintained. Thus, the success of a hospital programme to 're-educate' drug addicts cannot ultimately be judged by how patients behave during therapy but only by how they behave after passing through the critical period of 're-entry' into society.

Furthermore, where earlier behaviours represent component objectives, we may need to assess whether students can now *combine* them in order to achieve some overall objective or *transfer* their skills to novel situations. Often this assessment may need to utilize media and methods different from those used during the earlier learning. Thus, the trainee teacher may have made written responses while learning certain principles of teaching but is now called upon to use those principles on a small group of students in a micro-teaching situation. The student who has been learning to tell the time by a classroom clock is taken out into the town to tackle clocks of all shapes and sizes. The Peace Corps volunteer who has been learning to cooperate on projects with colleagues in training camp is observed in the jungles of Latin America to see how effectively he cooperates with locals in the real-life situation. Whether we gain or lose by habitually conceiving of this end-of-course assessment as an 'examination', rather than as the culminating learning experience, is problematical.

Wherever possible, we should be at pains to use assessment as a teaching rather than a policing device. The assessment tail can so easily wag (and even strangle) the education dog, as we are so forcibly reminded by a student quoted in Bishop (1971):

> I'm so sick of grades I'm ready to quit. I can no longer enjoy a good book. If it's not a book required for a course I'm taking, I don't have time to more than skim through it. If it's required reading I can't enjoy it because the back of my mind keeps trying to figure out what the instructor will ask in order to grade me.

Of course, a student does need frequent appraisal of his progress and attainments. But grades, marks and scores are not essential in this, and will often be counter-productive, especially if made public. The more we encourage our student to abandon the regurgitation of facts (impersonal and safe) in favour of striving to create and express his own personal images and interpretations, the greater the vulgarity and irrelevance of labelling his work with a B– or a 65%. What he deserves from us is a human response, critical but sympathetic, hopefully affording insights into his strengths and weaknesses and helping him towards further growth. He is not helped by normative comments implying he is in competition with anyone other than himself, or by crisp, pseudo-objective grades with little function other than to make him feel better or worse than his peers. As Ralph Tyler remarks (in Tyler and Wolf 1974), if we're learning golf we would not expect our instructor, after a few practice sessions, to say '"You are getting a D in your work. I may have to fail you if you don't improve." Instead, we expect him to say, "You are making progress on your drive, but you need to bring your full body into the swing. A little later I'll give you further practice on your putting to increase accuracy and decrease power."' (See page 178 for further discussion and examples of teaching through assessment.)

Sooner or later, however, we face the demands of certification. As seems unavoidable in our complex, interdependent society, other people – parents, teachers and eventually employers – will want to know about our student. Often, they will hope to learn about the person through studying what we have said about him on paper. They will not actually learn much if all we give them is the too frequent but easily assimilable gross valuation, purporting to capture the totality of our student in a single cipher – whether it be 'C', 'pass', '70 percent', 'lower second' or whatever. The reflections of Bel Kaufman (1964) on a student's grades remind us of how much information about the person is *lost* in such totalizations:

> His IQ is 133; his marks last term: 65, 20, F, 94, 45. The 94 is in Social Studies. The 20 is in English. I marvel: why 20? Why not 18? or 33? or 92? Is it based on his thinking, feeling, punctuation, absence, self-expression, memory, insolence? . . . What mark does Eddie get for the way the white world has treated him? Or Alice for the fantasies the movies have fed her? Or I – or even I?

John Hajnal (1972), criticizing the arbitrary and uninformative 'labelling' of university graduates simply by class of degree, points out that:

> . . . graduates who have gained a degree in the same subject from the same university in the same year may have followed somewhat different curricula or may have shown strength in different aspects of the course. Even if they have the same class of degree and would thus appear to have exactly the same educational qualification, a closer examination of their studies and of their performances in them might suggest they would be suited to rather different jobs.

He goes on to call for a more informative statement, something along the lines of that envisaged by Warren Piper (1969) for his course on industrial design:

> . . . each student would be provided with a document on which were recorded all the objectives, with an indication against each of how the student had fared. This would give a succinct record of the student's attainments and weaknesses, and would be more meaningful than a grade on a diploma.

Such explicitness is surely not too much to ask for? If I am expected to trust my life to a newly trained physician or pilot who is, in effect, labelled as '80 percent successful', I think it not unreasonable to inquire whether he is 80 percent (whatever that may mean) on everything, or perhaps 100 percent on some things (e.g., bedside manner or take-off) and 0 percent on others (e.g., diagnosis or landing). In short, I'd prefer to be able to check the extent to which the student has attained each of the capabilities and dispositions that are critical to his vocation or field of interest.

Marking in terms of simple 'pass/fail' is sometimes suggested as an alternative to grading. This may be justifiable in vocational training *if* it is established that some particular level of attainment indicates a clear boundary between students who will be able to perform well professionally and those who will not. Even then, however, it might be more encouraging to mark in terms of 'pass/further training needed'. But such crude categorization throws away much valuable information about what the markers have judged to be the individual differences in skills and capacities among the students. Consequently, it cannot be justified in educational assessment.

Perhaps we should aim to provide 'interested parties' with a detailed, multi-faceted *profile* describing what the student can and cannot do, which objectives he has achieved and which not, what we see as his strengths and limitations, how his work has improved, deteriorated or fluctuated (and why), what he is becoming as well as what he is. Such a profile, building up over a period of time, could be contributed to by students and parents as well as by teachers. It might even, like the art student's portfolio, contain significant specimens or personal records of his work. The 'profile' would provide a resource whereby anyone sufficiently interested to give it proper attention could, vicariously, get to know our student. Ideally, potential employers and institutions of further education would reciprocate with equal honesty and detail about the nature of the work they are offering and what 'entry behaviours' it realistically requires of the recruit. However, so long as education is content to act as a ritual sieve for industry and the professions, few organizations will see the need to develop more relevant selection procedures of their own. (For further discussions of profiles in assessment, see Klug 1974, Rowntree 1977, pages 228–240, and Mansell, 1981.)

The more explicit the records we keep, the more opportunity we have to reflect on our effectiveness as teachers. In general, education has always been more proficient in selecting and certifying students who were already talented than in developing talents among the handicapped majority it eventually rejects. Nevertheless, some teachers believe that education should aim to remedy rather than reinforce the unequal chances with which children start in life. They are likely to be suspicious of assessment systems that constantly tell certain students they are inadequate, undesirable and of little worth. As William Glasser (1968) puts it:

> Very few children come to school failures, none come labelled failures; it is school and school alone which pins the label of failure on children.

The wasteful and enduring effects of such conditioning is distressingly evident among the numerous adults who, while merely uneducated, regard themselves as being fundamentally 'brainless'. The teacher who learns to use assessment as a teaching device rather than an instrument of competitive grading (and ultimately of social stratification) may overcome the 'cops and robbers' role-ambivalence that so often taints the relations of students and teachers above primary school level. That is, he may be able to convince his student that he truly is a guide and mentor – *not* a judge and executioner. He may even leave all his students, even the slowest, with an enhanced confidence in their ability to learn.

Teacher Style

Strategic innovations of the kind we have been discussing are, of course, closely bound up with the teacher's personality and classroom style. Although little is done in a student teacher's training to affect his personality, or help in what Abraham Maslow (1954) called 'self-actualization', there is evidence that the teachers who most effectively bring about desirable learning outcomes are those who can develop flexibility of approach, and *warmth* towards their students – accepting, approving, trusting, encouraging (see Irvine 1979). Typical of such evidence is that of Stephen Wiseman (1964) who found that attainment in reading and arithmetic were higher in 'progressive' (learner-centred) schools than in others (especially at secondary level). Again, Haddon and Lytton (1968) found children from 'informal' schools better at divergent thinking than those from 'formal' schools. Morrison and McIntyre (1969) sum up the research on strategy and style:

> Most pupils prefer classroom situations where teachers use 'discovery' methods and where they establish relatively democratic relationships. Teacher-centred situations, in which there is a great deal of expository teaching, tend to produce more learning where the tasks are all actively straightforward and emphasize the acquisition of routine information and skills. Learner-centred teaching, where more attention is given to group work, where pupils are encouraged under guidance to seek solutions to problems, and where they are stimulated to produce and develop their own ideas, often seem preferable where the tasks are more complex, and where insightful and cooperative behaviours are primary objectives.

On the face of things, this might seem at odds with the college-level findings of Robert Dubin and Thomas Taveggia (1968) who examined the results of some ninety studies comparing many different teaching strategies (with special reference to closeness of teacher–student contact, e.g., class lectures *v.* small-group discussion) only to conclude that there were *no measurable differences* between them in their effects on student learning. However, Dubin and Taveggia unequivocally assert that 'students are in institutions of higher education to learn content' and it emerges that the criteria used to evaluate teaching effectiveness were those relevant to information-giving strategies and not to interactive strategies (e.g., group work) whose outcomes we'd expect to assess in terms of developing life-skills (especially the affective) and methodological skills – in brief, not content but process objectives. Thus, because only content learning was deemed relevant, very real differences between the outcomes of the strategies may have been not so much 'not measurable' as merely 'not measured'.

The same narrowness of criteria may also explain why the well-publicized findings of Bennett (1976), gathered from research in a dozen primary school classrooms, seemed in conflict with the Morrison and McIntyre summary above. That is, Bennett found that pupils in classes taught by 'formal' teachers were, in general, making more progress than those taught by 'informal' teachers. However, progress was judged only by easily measured capabilities like reading age and numerical competence, taking no account of quality of learning. Even on those variables, as Bennett admitted, the pupils making best progress of all were those taught by a teacher who *combined* the best of both formal and informal methods, varying her strategy according to circumstances.

The respective merits of formal and informal approaches will not be easily decided, not least because critics differ in how they value the means as well as in what they see as the outcome. The same is true of many other dichotomies or continua of style and strategy that might be investigated in classroom teaching. Nevertheless, the reflective teacher can gain many insights into his own interactions with pupils by considering the literature produced by researchers who have observed classroom activities in various systematic ways. (See McIntyre 1980, for a review.) For example, the teacher may begin to wonder whether, as Barnes (1971) noticed among so many teachers, he does most of the talking, asks only questions he knows the answer to, allows only brief responses, squashes digressions, and fails to build on children's out-of-school interests and experience. Again, on reading that section of the literature concerned with teacher-expectations and the self-fulfilling prophecy (Brophy and Good 1974), he may wonder whether he could possibly be expressing attitudes to pupils of certain social classes or ethnic groups that hinder them in developing as they might. Such self-questioning may yield even greater benefits if he and a trusted colleague can arrange to observe and comment on one another's teaching, using whatever criteria they see as most important to them.

Personally, and idiosyncratically, I incline more and more to what I might dub 'the charismatic theory of curriculum'. Briefly, this is the proposition that, when all is said and done, what makes a person what he is, what gives him the impetus to believe in himself and make something worthwhile of himself is not what he is taught in school but (in so far as it is anything to do with education at all) *by whom he is taught*. How much do any of us remember of the content of our schooling compared with what we remember of the general social ambience and especially our feelings in relation to learning from the people who taught us? All our educational yesterdays seem to resolve into that succession of personalities who variously mortified us, lit something like the divine spark, or left us cold. Hence, for a child of mine, I would be more concerned that he should be taught by one or two men or women charismatic enough to light that spark than that he should be thoroughly grounded in a wide and well-balanced range of curriculum subjects. Even more basically, I would hope for him to fall in with teachers whose relationships with pupils were like those in a congenial and *nurturing family* rather than, as so often is the case, like those in a factory.

One thing is certain. Our styles and strategies in teaching will strongly determine the nature and quality of our students' learning, especially in the affective domain. As Charity James (1972) says: 'It is not true that provided you learn it does not matter how you feel about what and how you learn, since in large measure it is those feelings which determine what kind of person you become.' Hence, as with the media and methods we discuss in Chapter 5, our choice of strategies should be made in the light of careful and continuing thought about our educational purposes and priorities. What we do must depend on what we are trying to achieve.

Questions on Chapter 4

1   Identify some concepts in a course you are familiar with (either as teacher or student) that give students difficulty? Why is this? Might any of the analysis techniques mentioned on pages 103–4 offer any help in overcoming such difficulties? How?

2 Try drawing a concept map and/or a matrix for your course, or for a topic within it. If possible, compare it with ones drawn by other people who are familiar with that subject area.

3 Think of a course or topic you have taught or studied in which logical and psychological considerations might seem to suggest competing or contradictory teaching/learning sequences. How would you decide which one to use? Could they be combined?

4 Within the course you have in mind, could you use all of the types of sequence mentioned in this chapter? If so, how? If not, why not? What kinds of sequence(s) has the author used in *this book*?

5 Try drawing up a hierarchy for one of the chief objectives of your course (if you have not already done so in tackling question 4 for Chapter 3). Stop when you reach the prerequisite abilities! Identify at least two possible routes that students might take.

6 Which of Gagné's eight types of learning predominate in your course? Why? If any *other* type of learning is of even greater importance, how would you describe it?

7 Make a list of at least six sequential teaching points from your course.

8 Give examples of areas within your course in which 'discovery learning' and 'reception learning' might prove most relevant. How would you decide?

9 Where, within your course, might students best be working in groups and where as individuals? Why?

10 To what extent, and in what areas, might students within your course be pursuing different objectives, even objectives of their own choice or devising? If this would not be possible, why not?

11 Would assessment on your course be directed chiefly towards developing the students' learning or towards recording a judgement of how much they have learned already? How would you justify this?

12 Would you expect the style of teaching on the course you have in mind to be described as formal/teacher-centred or as informal/learner-centred? Why? How would the style be justified?

CHAPTER 5

DESIGNING THE LEARNING: MODES AND MEDIA

> I hear, and I forget,
> I see, and I remember;
> I do, and I understand.
> Old Chinese proverb

Decisions about stimulus modes and the media of teaching and learning
are, in fact, intertwined with those about sequence and strategy.
Sometimes, plans will be finalized first in one area, sometimes in
another; but the decisions interact and help limit one another. Thus, the
decision to put strong emphasis on a discovery strategy might make the
lecture an unlikely presentation medium, while the need to teach mainly
through the printed word (e.g., in a distance learning course) might
increase the need to predetermine a clear learning sequence. And the
major factor determining rational choices in all these areas is the nature
of the objectives: what kinds of knowledge, skills and attitudes might the
media be expected to help the students acquire? Conversely, the known
availability of certain media may influence the choice of objectives, e.g.,
the spread of low cost audio playback equipment can help shift the
objectives of language teaching from writing towards speech.
Non-rational factors enter into our designs also, as we shall notice later.

Sometimes we'll be designing 'in the large' – planning the success of
learning experiences we call a 'course'. At other times, we'll be designing
the component learning experiences – selecting or producing
programmed learning materials or films, planning lectures or
demonstrations or group discussions – directed at a subset of the
objectives of the course. At all levels of operation we shall be faced with a
wealth of pedagogic possibilities and the urgings of enthusiasts, all of
whom think they've found the answer, be it team-teaching, programmed
learning, discovery, group dynamics, community involvement, love,
discipline, audio-visual aids, computer-assisted learning, transcendental
meditation or what you will. Each of these, and other techniques, may

have a place in our scheme of things, though not necessarily the place claimed by panacea-mongers. The problem is to decide when and how to use what. Some teachers solve it by shutting their eyes and ears to new thinking in education: they stick to the methods they themselves were taught by and use only the technique (chalk and talk, probably) they feel most at home with. The seriousness of this situation is well pointed by an analogy of Mager and Beach (1967):

> We would be in a fine fix if the surgeon only performed those operations he is 'comfortable' with, or if the carpenter refused to use any tool but the hammer because he likes the 'feel' of it.

Since it is true that a teacher is unlikely to work effectively unless he does feel comfortable with a method, he should, as a professional, be constantly at pains to extend his repertoire and *learn* to like the feel of an ever-widening range of media and techniques.

Unfortunately, many factors combine to inhibit such exploration. Often, in terms of job-survival, it is functionally unnecessary; the teacher can get by without it. Even if he is willing, he may not get the necessary support from his colleagues. He may also be frustrated in his attempts to familiarize himself with what may be a promising method but which is described and appraised in impenetrable research reports. Then again, the bulk of media research has been directed to investigating the nature of a single approach or medium, e.g., discovery learning or television, rather than to establishing how various approaches and media might best be combined in the kind of multi-media environment needed in schools. (See Campeau 1972 and Heidt 1980 for reviews of research.) Educational technology is now helping through the action research of teachers who can spread both the word and the will among their colleagues.

Before discussing modes and media we must cut our way through another terminological tangle. Different writers have used terms like 'medium', 'mode', learning resource', 'hardware', software' and so on, without always making clear what they were referring to but nevertheless contradicting one another's usages. Without wishing to pretend my usage is better than anyone else's, let me at least distinguish between the meanings I attach to the terms.

Modes *v.* Media

By mode I mean the kind of stimulus presented to the student. Thus, written symbols represent one mode, pictures another. The vehicle carrying this stimulus mode is the medium. There will usually be a variety of media available for presenting any given stimulus mode, e.g., books, posters and film can all present written symbols. When we transmit a message using a mode that requires a tangible medium of presentation (e.g., film) the result is a piece of *software* (e.g., a piece of film containing moving pictures). Not every piece of software needs *hardware* to display it but film does – a projector or viewing device. A *learning resource* is any combination of stimulus mode and presentation medium with a message for some student. Potentially, everything and everybody can be a learning resource. A piece of hardware is a learning resource only if accompanied by related software. Many people remember the early days of programmed learning in which so-called teaching machines were often produced without programmes to accompany them. Thus, a tape-player complete with a programmed foreign language tape is a learning resource. The tape-player is hardware, the programmed tape a piece of software. In this case, audio-tape is the medium, and the stimulus mode used is recorded sound – mainly speech, perhaps with some background noises.

I am not suggesting that stimulus modes are the only influences on learning. Clearly, general environmental factors like adequacy of diet, sleep, fresh air, exercise and affection help determine *how much* a student learns, but they do not usually carry a specific message affecting what he learns. Such factors facilitate rather than shape the learning. In passing, however, we should perhaps acknowledge the possible emergence of one facilitator that may turn out to be more specific than most – psychopharmacology. It has long been known that certain drugs affect learning (see Claridge 1970); for example, by reducing interference from stress or anxiety. Thanks to experiments on animals and therapy with brain-damaged or prematurely senile human patients, it is now becoming apparent that, as David Krech (1967) puts it:

> . . .these drugs do not work in a monolithic manner on something called 'learning' or 'memory'. In some instances, the drugs seem to act on 'attentiveness'; in some, on the ability to vary one's attack on a problem; in some, on persistence; in some, on immediate memory; in some, on long-term memory.

Krech implies that the learner from an impoverished environment which has failed to stimulate the necessary chemical resources in his brain and who therefore suffers from suboptimal learning ability, may be able to use such drugs to help make up the deficit. As with any technology promising effectiveness, the attendant possibilities of misuse should prompt us to sharper debate about the aims, objectives and ethics of education. Who is entitled to which drugs in what circumstances towards which objectives and under whose supervision? In view of the already substantial public concern about the use of tranquillisers and hypnotics to control people's mental states, we must hope that, this time, our answers are ready before the technology.

Five Stimulus Modes

Now, let us return to the immediate present and identify five stimulus modes:

- Human interaction (verbal and non-verbal).
- Realia (real things, people and events).
- Pictorial representation (still and moving images).
- Written symbols (words, figures, etc.).
- Recorded sound (speech, music, 'natural noises').

Human Interaction

By 'human interaction' I mean the mode that becomes available for communication whenever two or more people are aware of one another's presence, and begin responding consciously or unconsciously to one another's messages. The spoken word will often be the dominant element and the message communicated will often be cognitive, as when you ask someone for information or discuss alternative routes to a destination. But sometimes non-verbal elements are dominant – postures, physical gestures, bodily contact, eye contact, facial expressions, non-linguistic utterances. Here the message is largely affective and emotional, as when you comfort an anxious child or try to conciliate in a dispute.

The intensity of the interaction — the degree to which each person modulates his behaviour in the light of responses from others — will vary from one presentation medium to another. Using the lecture medium, little interaction can take place, especially if the audience is large. The responses of the listeners are usually either hidden from the lecturer or are ambiguous; and so he has little opportunity to adapt his manner or material to satisfy their individual needs. If the lecturer encourages questions from his audience then, of course, the level of interaction is raised. For a high level of human interaction we could look at the tutorial medium, especially the one-to-one dialogue where both tutor and student respond directly to one another's verbal and non-verbal signals. A similarly responsive group situation is found in the T-group medium, sensitivity training, encounter groups and the like, where the overall objectives might be for the individual to recognize how other members of the group regard his behaviour, to evaluate the relationships between the others, and to respond appropriately to them (see Whitaker 1965). When Jules Henry (1971) suggests that deprived children and their teachers sit down to breakfast together, he sees 'school breakfast' not just as a means of feeding hungry children but also as a medium through which friendly interactions can calm and encourage them. Discussion groups, seminars, project teams, demonstrations and telephone conversations are other media utilizing the mode of human interaction. The intensity varies according to such factors as the number of people involved, the social and geographical distances between them and how far they perceive the work they are doing to be worthwhile. But all such media combine cognitive and affective, verbal and non-verbal elements.

Perhaps one of the most promising of interaction media developed in recent years is that of role-playing and 'simulation' games. In such simulation games, students act out a working model of some real-world human situation. They are provided with background data and roles to play, together with constraints that may change due to 'outside intervention' or 'chance factors' as the game proceeds and they work in interacting groups with some kind of realistic problem to solve. They may find themselves, in different games, coping with vandalism in a country village, or running the nation's economy, or surviving a period of unemployment, or negotiating the siting of a new airport, or conducting an industrial dispute, or simulating a local election, or whatever. Games based on community problems can be invaluable to students as a prelude to, or reflective respite from, 'real' community involvement. The 'in-tray exercise', discussed as an assessment technique on page 89, can equally well be considered as such a learning situation, if the student has to work with colleagues as well as with materials.

Certainly, games appear to be an effective teaching medium, both cognitively and affectively. To use the terminology of Piaget, a game is a 'concrete operation' through which a student can experience a new concept before he can recognize it formally. In fact, the essential concepts and structures of the real-life situation are built into the structure of the game and, like the decision-making processes involved, the student learns them by having to operate with them. In addition, he may well learn a considerable amount of factual information because he needs and uses it in a memorable context. Games are particularly noted for the high-level of motivation they generate among students, especially among those who don't respond so well to formal methods. There are many explanations for this: Students are hooked by the relevance of the problem at issue; they are involved as producers rather than consumers of the subject matter; they are freed from dependence on the teacher and are able to learn from one another; they are able to experiment safely with feelings as well as rational processes; they get a powerful and immediate response to their decisions and are aware of having an effect on the human environment. Human interaction is intense. (For fuller details about simulation and gaming in education, see Boocock and Schild 1968, Tansey and Unwin 1969, McAleese 1978 and Megarry 1978 and 1979.)

Simulation, however, does not necessarily demand human interaction. A computer, for example, may be used to simulate the systemic responses of a 'patient' on whom a medical student is practising diagnosis and treatment; or it may help students test out genetic principles by generating simulated 'populations' of fruit flies in seconds instead of the weeks they would take to breed experimentally.

Clearly, media employing human interaction are not necessarily dependent on the presence of a professionally certified 'teacher'. Students will learn from parents, classroom 'helpers' and other supposedly unqualified people in the community. Above all, students will learn from one another. This was demonstrated, in a sense, in the nineteenth-century schools operated on the Lancastrian or monitorial system, where the teacher taught the older pupils only (the monitors) and they passed on this instruction to the younger pupils (see Lancaster 1803). Similarly, universities frequently employ graduate students to act as 'demonstrators' in laboratory subjects for the benefit of undergraduates.

But children have rarely been considered seriously as teachers of their peers, except in the field of sex education where their age-old pre-eminence is generally held (though possibly unfairly and certainly without serious evaluation) to have had a baleful influence. Nevertheless, students are perhaps one of education's most under-utilized learning resources (see Thelen 1969). They can provide one another with special information, enthusiasm, collaboration, encouragement, alternative viewpoints, additional insights, audience feedback and evaluation.

Trainee teachers have been heard to say that they can learn some things, maths for instance, more easily from the children they meet in school visits than from their college lecturers. And experienced teachers recognize that their students often have ways of making one another understand even when more 'professional' approaches have failed. (For a review of 'peer teaching' in higher education, see Goldschmid and Goldschmid 1976.)

The personal growth experienced by adolescents acting as peer counsellors, as primary school teachers, or as nursery school helpers is well described by the authors of a symposium on 'deliberate psychological education' compiled by Ralph Mosher and Norman Sprinthall (1970). Colin and Mog Ball (1973) sum up the many advantages of enabling children to teach others (disadvantaged adults as well as younger children):

> First, it develops a sense of 'community' in a school, by cross-age grouping and providing an activity in which even non-academic kids can participate as tutors. Second, it avoids the cultural and generation gaps, which a teacher of forty experiences with a twelve-year-old child. Third, it encourages co-operation between tutors and tutees. Fourth, it gives the tutors a feeling that they are needed, it gives them valuable self-esteem. Fifth, it shows that knowledge has a real use: it is to be shared, to be used to form relationships. Sixth, it increases many times the amount of teaching that actually goes on in a school. Seventh, it offers some children a leadership role which doesn't require Outward Bound courses but exists in their own schools. Eight, it makes individual instruction – a cherished goal of many teachers – possible. Nine, it provides an 'army' to combat the remedial problems which confront so many schools.

As a tenth advantage, the children who are teaching will be testing and consolidating *their own* knowledge.

I have dealt with human interaction first because it is, in several senses, the primary mode. Obviously, it was about the first one we ever had. Again, it appears to satisfy a primary need – students need a human response to their efforts. The high drop-out rates on correspondence courses is often attributed to lack of human interaction; if the Open University continues to maintain its relatively low drop-out rates it may well be partly due to the attempts made to facilitate encounters between students, and between students and tutors. Also, partly for this latter reason but also perhaps because of its low cost and flexibility, human interaction is often used in conjunction with other modes to smooth their path; its associated media are often chosen as the setting in which other modes and media are deployed. Hence, students can usually get more out of a television broadcast – using the modes of pictures and recorded sound – if it has been briefly introduced by a live human being and is followed by discussion.

Notice that media such as radio, television and film can *demonstrate* human interaction to the student but they cannot involve him, except vicariously. This vicarious involvement can be very valuable, especially for the student who has to work on his own, but seeing and hearing human interaction does not provide the same stimulus as being a part of it. It is important to distinguish between a medium being used to provide access to a stimulus mode more relevant than human interaction and one that is merely being used as a *substitute* for such interaction.

Realia

My second mode of stimulus is 'realia'. This is a word coined to include real *things*, real *events*, real *animals* and, where the student merely observes them rather than interacting with them, real *people*. (I find the term ugly, but confess myself unable to think of a better one – realities, actualities? – that would be properly suggestive of all four kinds of reality just mentioned. I pronounce it 'ray-arlia', by the way.)

The child learns from realia about as early as from human interaction. The textures of nappies and cot blankets, the swaying and bouncing of prams, the smell and taste of his food, the brightness of overhead lights, the sound of slamming doors, the painfulness of fire, all these and others are building up what Gagné calls signal learning and stimulus-response learning from the moment of birth. Then, as the child becomes more mobile, he begins to respond to a wider range of realia – plants in the garden, complex toys, the postman and shopkeepers and people passing in the street, cats and dogs and birds, events like the dropping of an egg or the arrival of visitors – developing motor chains, verbal associations and multiple discriminations, leading him, especially when stimulated also by human interaction, to more and more complex learning. All this he attains, of course, without 'professional' help from teachers, but he is largely dependent for its richness on the cultural background of his parents (see Chazan et al. 1971). Research by Rosenzweig et al. (1972) indicates that an unstimulating early environment results not just in 'mental' damage but also in physical, measurable deterioration in the anatomy and chemistry of the brain. (See also Krech 1967.)

When he gets to school the child meets yet more realia, but now they are systematically organized and deployed – sand and water, clay and paint, headteachers and caretakers, Cuisenaire rods and counting frames and Montessori materials, visits to farms and seaside and factories and railway stations, flowers, shells, rocks and fossils, drums and recorders, insects, mammals, fish and birds — things he can see, feel, hear, smell, taste and touch, experiencing them in a sensory totality. As he gets older, the realia become more sophisticated – cadavers for dissection, antique documents, esoteric chemicals, complex laboratory equipment, visits to concerts and the professional theatre, field-trips to archaeological sites and scenes of geographical or historical interest.

The significance of realia as a stimulus mode is epitomized in the rich learning from real things and events that can take place when working in the laboratory and, especially, 'in the field'. Here, for example, is Keith Wheeler (1971) telling how 'geographical imagination':

> . . . can only grow out of the first-hand experience of landscape and environment which can be had from fieldwork, because the child who has studied his own river, for instance, has a greater chance of imagining accurately the development of a river like the Mississippi which he may never see. Or the 15-year old who makes a land-use map of a farm during a field-study is more able to appreciate the agricultural land utilisation in other parts of the world.

Of course, field work does not necessarily have to take students far from home. Nor does it need to operate in an exploitative way, using the environment simply as a walk-in visual aid. Colin and Mog Ball (1972) quote many examples of schools whose pupils contribute to the local 'field' through such activities as renovating an old windmill and maintaining it as a museum, acting as pollution watchdogs, undertaking public opinion surveys, landscaping derelict areas and planting trees, preserving a sphagnum moss bog in danger of drying out, and, in all these activities, themselves *learning* and practising a very full range of methodological skills and life-skills.

Both laboratory work and field studies are likely to use the mode of human interaction as well as realia. Indeed, realia can be used along with any other mode in a variety of media, from lectures and tutorials to the programmed learning package.

It is worth noting that students not infrequently come back from a field-trip or out of a laboratory with only the haziest notion of what they were supposed to be learning. The context in which realia are to be encountered may need to be thoughtfully structured; and the encounter will probably need to be followed up in some way. Otherwise, the expected learning may not materialize.

Direct observation of things and people and events is the source and sustenance of all understanding; but, as he gains in experience, the student is expected to work less with the realia and more and more with the symbolism (chiefly pictures and words) that represents it. The ability to manipulate this symbolism is a vital part of the individual's cognitive growth and gives him a powerful tool for communication. Unfortunately, teachers often forget the need for preliminary experience with the realia of a new area of study and continued human interaction. Thus, they hurry the student on to a verbal facility before he can, quite literally, know what he is talking about. Harrison and Hopkins (1971) guarded against this in their training of Peace Corps volunteers for Latin America by running the course at a primitive camp in Puerto Rico rather than at Yale University.

Pictorial Representation

The third stimulus mode, pictorial representation, comprises pictures and diagrams, realistic or symbolic, still or moving. Photographs, 'artist's impressions', drawings, diagrams, graphs, charts, maps, all are representations of reality. Sometimes reality is too big for the classroom – e.g., the solar system, or too small – e.g., the heartbeats of a water flea; or too slow – e.g., the sequence of cloud-types during the passage of an occluded depression; or too fast – e.g., the wing movements of a humming bird; or too inaccessible – e.g., peristalsis in the small intestine; or too dangerous – e.g., defusing a bomb; or too cluttered up with confusing distractions – e.g., classroom interactions between pupils and a trainee-teacher; or it may be invisible – e.g., the pattern of sound waves from an underwater echo location device; or even extinct – e.g., dinosaurs. In all such cases, pictures may be able to overcome the disadvantages or non-availability of the real thing.

With pictures we can control reality. We can make it smaller or bigger; we can speed it up (with time-lapse photography); we can slow it down (by slow-motion techniques); we can take cameras and the artist's imagination where the human eye cannot go; we can picture what could not be safely observed in reality; we can emphasize (using diagrams, editing or selective photography) and can eliminate confusing detail; we can picture the invisible (using diagrams, animated or still) and, of course, we can picture scenes that never were, things and people and events that are no longer here to be looked at or have not yet come into being. Replicas and 'table-top' models (e.g., of the development of a river delta, or the structure of a molecule, or the relative motions of planets in the solar system) can have many of the advantages mentioned above and are best regarded, perhaps, as three-dimensional 'pictures'.

The 'editing' of reality has its dangers, of course. We may be getting rid of 'extraneous' detail if we present a student with a diagram or photograph or plastic model instead of actual specimens of, say, a fruit he is studying. We can thus get him to concentrate on what we regard as 'essential' features. But how far is the student's experience *impoverished* by denying him contact with the three-dimensionality, colour, smell, taste, feel and particularity of a real specimen? Again, this may depend on how much prior experience he has had with the realia. Perhaps we should be teaching students, as a vital life-skill, how to 'read' pictures, and especially how to evaluate them and allow for the often subtle differences between pictures and reality (see Gombrich 1962 and Evans 1978).

A great many media are capable of presenting the mode of pictorial representation. Still photographs, paintings, maps, diagrams, graphs and the like can be made available as individual prints to be handled by students. They can be made large enough to display separately on a wall, or incorporated into a poster or chart. They may be presented on film – as slides or a filmstrip. They may be used along with other modes – in the pages of a book, on the visual display unit of a computer terminal, on a work card, on the sleeve of a gramophone record, or on an overhead projection transparency for use during a lecturer or seminar.

If we want moving pictures or animated diagrams we may, if the sequence is sufficiently clear cut, e.g., the 'dance of the molecules', get away with presenting our pictures in a booklet so designed that its pages can be flicked through fast enough to give the illusion of continuous motion. For presentation to groups, a similar effect can be obtained using specially prepared transparencies on an overhead projector. Quite complex animated diagrams can be presented by the visual display unit to a student learning from computer-assisted instruction. The most frequently used medium for presenting moving pictures, however, is television or cine-film, usually in association with other modes, especially recorded sound and written symbols.

Written Symbols

This brings us to the fourth mode of stimulus – written symbols. The use of written symbols, and especially printed (or written) words, developed out of human interactions, realia and pictorial representation. Writing was a late starter and, from some diehards, received as chilly a reception as more recent innovations have done:

> . . .this discovery of yours will create forgetfulness in the learners' souls, because they will not use their memories; they will trust to the external characters and not remember themselves. . .they will be the hearers of many things and will have learned nothing.
> (Socrates to Phaedrus – from Jowett, B. (trans.) *The Dialogues of Plato* Encyclopedia Britannica 1952, Chicago.)

But now the written word assails us from breakfast-time to bedtime and the conditioned response to any piece of print is to read it, whether or not we feel in want of a message. Despite Marshall McLuhan's contention that electric wizardry is disrupting the long domination of print and the frequently heard prediction that audio-visual communications are making reading less and less necessary as a life-skill, the written word is still the most respected medium. Chiefly this is because of its relative accessibility as a versatile generator, organizer, store and disseminator of ideas.

Plato was right that we forget much of what we read, but the spoken word, with which he was comparing it (let alone pictorial representation and human interaction) is not necessarily more memorable and may not even be properly 'understood' in the first place. Research indicates, for example, that hospital out-patients tend to forget the vital details of treatment explained to them by the doctor, even though they may remember what was said to be wrong with them; and fears have been expressed that members of juries may reach their verdicts on the basis of a less than perfect recollection of the legal points raised by the judge in his summing up. In such cases, print media may be needed to *supplement* the spoken word. At least with print you can make it stay still while you chew over a point; you can go back to the beginning and start again, see the whole shape of the argument 'in black and white' and, above all, re-read it whenever you like, either considerably faster or more slowly than it was spoken. Thus, print affords us control over the 'reality' of spoken words.

All that does, of course, presuppose the ability to read. There is abundant evidence to suggest that most students (even at college and university level) do not read as effectively as they should (Melnick and Merritt 1972). From Harvard, William Perry (1959) writes of what he calls the 'obedient purposelessness' demonstrated by nearly 1500 undergraduates, all highly competent readers, of whom, although all were able to answer detailed questions about a chapter they had been set to read, only one in a hundred was able to sum up what the chapter was about.

Students without plan or purpose tend to work their way laboriously from word to word, making little attempt to challenge the ideas presented or relate them to their own experience. Consequently, they find difficulty both in concentrating and in remembering what they've been reading about. Linked with this reading style is a tendency to use reading as an authorized escape from thinking. We all know the temptation, in planning an essay, to keep on reading 'just one more book', supposedly in search of inspiration but actually to put off the moment when we have to wrestle with our thoughts and turn them into written words of our own. Something can be done to improve students' reading techniques (see Rowntree 1970 and Gibbs 1981) and we should aim to expose them to printed materials that call for active responses from the reader.

Written symbols – mathematical and technical symbols as well as words – are presented by a variety of media. The 'purest' medium of presentation is, of course, the book, whether in programmed or conventional prose. Even here the stimulus of pictures may be used as well. Print may also be presented by 'automatic page-turners' – teaching machines or computer-controlled devices – which may be able to claim the advantage of 'adapting' material to different students in some way. Again, slides and filmstrips may present written symbols, perhaps along with pictures and diagrams; and when written symbols are used in television programmes and cine-films, they may be linked with recorded sound as well as pictures. The teacher generates his own written symbols, along with human interaction and other modes, when using the chalkboard, flip-chart or overhead projector. He may also prepare written material and present it to students through such media as flash cards, name labels, lecture handouts, data sheets, work cards and booklets, posters, charts, programmed texts and test exercises. Students may also produce such written materials for one another's use and, of course, they use the mode extensively in making their own responses, filling exercise books and loose-leaf binders with short stories and poems, test answers and geometrical 'proofs', letters and reports, notes and essays and PhD theses.

Recorded Sound

Finally, the fifth stimulus mode, 'recorded sound'. Here again, the stimulus mode helps us control reality. Sound is ever-moving and we cannot persuade it to stand still for inspection. But we can capture it on tape, amplify it, slow it down, edit out confusing noise or extraneous detail and, above all, repeat it when, where and as often as we like. The sounds we are interested in may be physiological, e.g., heartbeats; mechanical, e.g., the knocking of a worn 'big end'; musical, e.g., a concert; conversational, e.g., foreign language sounds; dramatic, e.g., a poetry reading; instructional, e.g., a lecture; or environmental, e.g., birdsong.

Again, several presentation media are available. Recorded sound can be presented on audio-tapes and gramophone records and 'talking pages'. It can be presented on radio or as the sound track of a television programme or cine–film. On television and film, the stimulus of recorded sound can be combined with pictures and diagrams and with written symbols, but not with realia or human interaction. The 'missing' modes may, of course, be available in the teaching situation in which the sound recording is used: For example, students working in pairs may discuss the taped instructions they receive while learning to handle a machine.

Multi-modal Learning

Clearly then, most of our stimulus modes can be used, separately or together, in a variety of presentation media. When two or more modes are used together within the same medium (e.g., sound and pictures within a film) we must make sure they complement each other, or at least do not interfere with one another's message. Most of our media can be used by individual students as well as by small and large groups. Most can operate without the need of a continuous performance from a 'live' teacher. The kind of 'multi-media/multi-mode', individualized learning system that can be developed is illustrated in the first-year botany course at Purdue University (USA) described by Samuel Postlethwait et al. (1971):

> Most of the factual information is acquired through independent study in a specially-designed learning center containing thirty booths. Each is

equipped with a tape player, an 8mm movie projector, a microscope, live plants, test tubes, diagrams and other materials pertinent to the week's study. Learning activities may include listening to short lectures, performing experiments, reading from texts and journals, studying demonstrations, viewing short films, discussions with the instructor and/or other students, microscope study, dissection of specimens and any other study activity deemed helpful by the senior instructor or the student. Since the independent study is unscheduled, experiments do not have to be designed to fit into a three-hour time interval, and some experiments can take the form of miniature research projects.

Similar learning environments are to be found in Britain also, from university level (see Tribe 1973) to primary school (see Kefford 1970). The question is: In setting up such a learning environment, how do you decide when to use what? And before we can answer the question we'd better consider the several functions that sequence, strategy and stimulus mode must fulfil through whatever media are used in the learning situation.

Functions of Media

What do media actually have to do to help the student learn? Basically, they must present him with a *stimulus* and evoke a *response*. But if we carry the analysis a little further, the basic stimulus and response requirement might seem to imply a number of functions like the following:

- Engage the student's motivation.
- Recall earlier learning.
- Provide new learning stimuli.
- Activate the student's response.
- Give speedy feedback.
- Encourage appropriate practice.

Of course, these are not the only functions that might be picked out. Gagné (1965) and Dressel (1971) have rather different lists. But I think these six are the most crucial functions. They are listed here in the order perhaps in which they enter the learning situation, though at certain times several of them may be going on simultaneously. Let us examine the functions now, bearing in mind the variety of media available and how they might fulfil each one.

Engage the Student's Motivation

Somehow the student must be persuaded to involve himself in the learning. The necessary motivation must come from within him, though it may be stimulated, activated and encouraged by others. Here the teacher is constrained by the wider social context. His efforts to engage the student's motivation need to take into account what the student believes to be important in the light of influences from family and friends and classmates, mass communications media, and so on.

The student is motivated when he identifies with the objectives to which his learning leads, or when he enjoys the related activities as ends in themselves. If the objectives are developed by the student himself, or if he is 'turned on' by what the teacher suggests, there need be little difficulty. Problems with motivation really arise only when we try to teach people things they don't want to know or that seem inappropriate to them. Then there is a temptation to rely on negative motivators like fear of failure or of punishment. Although one has to admit that, especially with older students, even learning objectives that seem to them both relevant and interesting may find competition from stronger, non-educational objectives – like the desire to be economically self-supporting. Extrinsic motivators, like cash payment, may then be required.

Hansen and Jensen (1971) warn the student against external 'motivation' applied as 'bait', to persuade him to work on things that are basically of no use or interest to him. They advise the student that

> To learn anything useful it's important
>
> that you should want to;
> that you find the subject interesting;
> that you understand why you have to learn it;
> that you get a chance to say something yourself;
> that you are allowed to work on the subject in your own way;
> that you are allowed to co-operate with your friends.

To suggest this list of desiderata (echoed in our six functions above) is not to imply that the student should always be sole judge of what is good for him. Sometimes you will recognize objectives whose certain benefits the student will simply be unable to appreciate until he is well on the way to achieving them. If much effort and sacrifice are called for, he may, like most of us, need some initial persuasion to get him started. Such motivation will flow most easily, of course, where the relationship is one of mutual trust and respect between teacher and student.

Certainly, one of the first functions of media is to ensure that the student knows the objectives and appreciates their relevance. This cannot be done by exhortation and bland assurances. It is not enough to say: 'Electronics plays a very important role in modern life (so it must be worth spending forty hours of your life on).' Say: 'By the end of this course, you'll be able to build your own amplifier, electric guitar and moog synthesizer', or refer similarly to whatever outcomes of the course are likely to appeal to different students. Michael Eraut et al. (1980) describe their experience with economics students:

> . . .Faculty tend to assume that students make their own links between theory and socio-economic problems. But we found that even the more able students experienced great difficulty in discovering the connection between economic theory and its practical application. Moreover, this connection cannot be regarded as just a desirable extra. It seems to be a crucial source of student motivation. When assessment is still a long way off, relevance is probably a major influence on student morale and work-rate.

Especially if the objectives are generated by the teacher, he must take the trouble to explicate them, give examples of how they apply and show how they relate to other interests, aims and experiences of the student. In doing so, he may well be not only engaging the student's motivation but also helping orientate him, providing what David Ausubel (see Ausubel and Robinson 1969) calls 'advance organizers' – a kind of mental scaffolding on which the student can construct his learning.

Motivation can perhaps be engaged most flexibly by human interaction media, yet the effort needs to be made when using other media also. Thus, the first few pages of a book or minutes of a film may be aimed at motivation. But motivation should be kept in view throughout the learning experience and 'topped up' from time to time, especially when approaching a new topic or new level of difficulty. Between whiles, successful learning should be self-motivating. Indeed, many students will happily continue learning, even in a subject that has no intrinsic interest for them, so long as they find its demands neither insultingly trivial nor impossibly taxing. The fact that our students seem to be pursuing their studies with diligence should not always be taken as evidence that we are engaging them in relevant learning.

Sometimes the initial motivation can be engaged by moving pictures in the form of a television programme or film. Often, contact with the real world will be possible, as in the multi-media environmental studies packages described by Colin Kefford (1970): 'A visit to a local building site may provide the stimulus which will encourage some children to study the programme *Building a House* while others pursue the topic *Houses and their History*.' Human interaction with teacher and fellow students will usually flow abundantly in such a motivational contact with realia. For a general review of student motivation, relating particularly but not exclusively to post-secondary education, see Beard and Senior (1980).

Recall Earlier Learning

Reminding the student of what he has already learned may well be part of engaging his motivation. Certainly he may need at least a review of the main ideas before he begins on new learning. If there is anything like a Gagné hierarchy involved – where further learning is impossible without mastery of some prerequisites – it may even be necessary to test him and give special 'remedial' instruction for any prerequisite skills in which he is lacking. Again, whatever media are used, such reviewing, and maybe testing and remedial teaching also, may need to be done not just at the beginning but also perhaps *during* any lengthy sequence of learning.

Provide New Learning Stimuli

Many sub-functions can be identified under this heading. For instance, the media must provide the student with a meaningful message, explain things from his point of view, give illuminating examples (and non-examples), emphasize the vital issues, control interference between competing ideas, draw the student's attention to important discriminations and generalizations, 'show the student what to look for without telling him what to see', provide a varied repetition of the main ideas, encourage transfer of learning to new situations, adjust the intensity of learning so that the individual student is neither bored nor overwhelmed, but is always challenged, persuade the student to aspire to 'mastery,' and so on.

In pursuing these functions we consider such questions as: What kinds of vocabulary or sentence length will ensure readability in a printed text? Which models, metaphors and analogies will make most sense to the student? Can we find examples from the student's own experience – to avoid explaining something he doesn't understand by reference to something else he doesn't understand? What language of gesture, intonation, graphic design or typography shall we use to give special emphasis? Shall we use a simplified line drawing, rather than a photograph or the real thing? Shall we present a variety of viewpoints, some conflicting? Can we avoid telling the student things (in the manner of the 'cut and dried' textbook) and, reasonably efficiently, enable him to find out for himself? Can we re-state, paraphrase and find new applications for the ideas being developed? Can we enable the student to speed up or slow down the teaching, obtaining more or less help according to how well he is coping from minute to minute in the learning situation? Can we get the student to identify with the 'master performance' and come to expect success and satisfaction in learning?

The extent to which these functions are fulfilled depends largely on what the student is called upon to do. Whether he is having a conversation, listening to a lecture, engaging in free group discussion, watching a film, or visiting a railway station, it is not enough to let the 'message' wash over him – somehow he must respond actively to it. Hence the importance of the next function.

Activate the Student's Response

If the learning is to mean anything to the student, and if he is to make it his own, he must be led to respond to it – to be an active producer and user rather than a passive recipient of knowledge. So the media must provoke him into the appropriate activity. This does not necessarily mean physical, observable activity like the filling of notebooks, which can so easily degenerate into 'busy work'. 'Appropriate' activity may involve some writing, and possibly some discussion, but it will certainly involve a good deal of *feeling* and *thinking*. Essentially, the media must enable the student to shape and use the ideas being developed in the learning situation – contributing to them, applying them, testing, confuting, modifying, and combining them – in general, *constructing* his learning rather than taking it 'off-the-peg'.

Unfortunately, the media are often used to present expositions so 'perfect' as to inhibit all real thinking (or feeling) activity. Sometimes, there is nothing for the student to do but nod in agreement and commit the message to memory. Here is Norris Sanders (1966) saying about textbooks what is often equally true of the way other media have been used – films, television programmes, lectures, classroom interactons and all:

> Although many are attractive, accurate, readable, and understandable, they are also one of the biggest deterrents to thinking in the classroom, because

the writers assume that students learn best by studying a polished product. The key function of the writer is to explain, and a good explanation is interesting, orderly, accurate, and complete. The vocabulary suits the level of the student and complex ideas are clarified by dissection, integration, example, and visual images. *Thus, the textbook is weak in that it offers little opportunity for any mental activity except remembering.* If there is an inference to be drawn, the author draws it, and if there is a significant relationship to be noted, the author points it out. There are no loose ends or incomplete analyses. The textbook is highly refined and as near perfection as a human mind is capable of making it – but the author does the thinking. The book never gives a clue that the author pondered (maybe even agonized) over hundreds of decisions. The result is that the creative process and the controversy of competing ideas are hidden from the students.

Sanders' comments are no doubt somewhat over-stated. There is a place for perfect exposition, not least by way of setting students an example to emulate in their own communications. But too much of it is likely to be inhibiting and stultifying. Such instruction, in whatever medium, resembles what my colleague, Brian Lewis, calls a 'mention list' where we mention a number of things to the student in the hope that, later on, he will be able to mention some of them back to us. The resulting 'reception learning' is sterile and for ever alien, because the student has had no part in its formation. He is forced into the role of passive receiver rather than active creator of knowledge.

Sanders' paragraph above, however, suggests the kind of response that the medium should call forth from the students: they should be dissecting, integrating, exemplifying and picturing ideas, drawing inferences, and pointing out significant relationships themselves rather than leaving it all to the medium.

Perhaps it is easiest to involve the student's active participation when the medium embodies human interaction. Face to face, teachers and students (and others) can bring together diverse and conflicting viewpoints and, by challenge and questioning, provoke the individual to feel and think, helping him assimilate his experience through communication with others. There is little of this in the lecture situation, as a rule, for the line of communication is virtually one-way (see Figure 5.1). Two-way communication becomes possible in a tutorial situation (Figure 5.2) and this can be opened out into a group discussion (Figure 5.3) where each participant can call for responses from any other participant. Whether highly structured (see Hill 1969), or 'free' (see Abercrombie 1969 and

1970), or 'non-directed' (see Chapter 15 of Rogers 1961), group activity can be a powerful means of bringing together the cognitive and the affective involvement of the student. Lewis Elton (1977) suggests that educational technology has only recently become concerned with small group learning – having worked its way from mass instruction to individualized learning – and has little yet to say about it. However, Bligh et al. (1975) do offer guidance on several different ways of organizing small groups for teaching and learning.

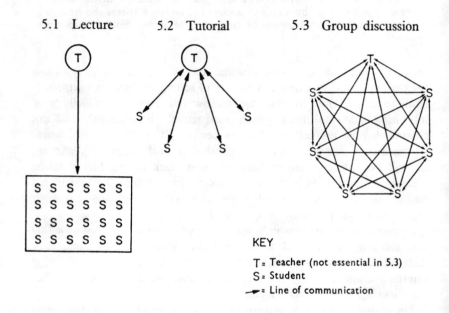

5.1   Lecture   5.2   Tutorial   5.3   Group discussion

KEY

T = Teacher (not essential in 5.3)
S = Student
⟶ = Line of communication

Figures 5.1, 5.2, 5.3   Patterns of communication

Yet it is also possible to encourage active participation using the written word and other modes not involving human interaction, as has been shown so clearly by programmed learning. In a programmed text or tape-recording, each new step forward in the argument is followed by a question requiring the student to solve problems, make predictions, come to decisions, anticipate the development of the argument; in short, when done well, it requires the student to grapple purposefully with the ideas being developed. Thus, every few minutes during the learning session, the student must pause and apply his understanding before going on to see what the programme says about his response and how it links with the next step in the argument. Using a programme, a student can be making an individual response far more frequently than he would in any human interaction situation other than a one-to-one tutorial or conversation. But of course the programme may be more limited in its ability to react differently to different responses.

This 'programmed approach' can be seen also, for example, in the correspondence texts on philosophy, history, musicology, literature, religion and art history produced by the Arts Faculty of the Open University (1972), and by other faculties since then. These 'tutorials in print' stimulate a dialogue between tutor and student, with frequent requests for the student to make a personal response and the author then continuing with a discussion of possible answers and where they might lead to. Ernest Rothkopf (1968) has found that questions embedded in a text can enhance the student's understanding and retention even of those portions of the material about which questions are not asked. Such questions appear to help the student to read questioningly. See Figure 5.4 for a sample page from a 'tutorial in print'.

Again, films and television programmes and even excursions into the outside world can be 'programmed'. Not just in the crude sense of inserting occasional questions but also, less disruptively perhaps, by presenting the student with a few key questions or advance organizers beforehand, asking him to look out for answers (and more questions of his own) and giving opportunity for discussion of them afterwards. This approach can also be used to encourage thinking activity and student participation during a lecture. With lectures it is also possible to issue students with a worksheet, stopping the lecture at certain points so that students can complete some exercise that will help them try out their understanding of the argument so far. The lecturer may then pick up some specimen responses from students and weave them into the next stage of his presentation. This procedure can be systematized (with or without hardware) to establish what has become known as the 'feedback classroom' (see Holling 1969 and Glynn et al. 1970). Alternatively, the lecturer may provide activity breaks that engage students in a brief discussion with neighbours, and the ideas that emerge may be picked up as the lecture develops. (See Bligh et al. 1975.)

Fanny has long been an upholder of Mansfield virtues; but there is nothing in the play-episode as explicit as this. *Then* her most prominent feeling was that to make any changes to the settled order of things would be wrong. *Now* she knows precisely what it is that she values.

Portsmouth is deficient in the qualities of Mansfield Park that apparently are not to be bought with money. And yet what is it that enables Fanny to introduce 'Mansfield' qualities of order and repose into certain areas of her Portsmouth life?

Her uncle's gift of £10. With this she buys the knife that removes one particularly noisy and distasteful area of contention. And with this money too she subscribes to a library, and begins the reclamation of Susan—repeating the invaluable service that Edmund had once done for her. Just as Sir Thomas's worries about how he is to provide for Fanny are not to be discounted, so here we are given this neatly defined reminder that money is not to be despised, nor can it be separated from immaterial values. It is a detail which can serve as a reminder of that confidence in her society's basic values that we have already noted in Jane Austen. Materialism like Maria's is wrong, but Jane Austen has certainly no wish to suggest that there is anything wrong with money.

At the end of Chapter 39 Fanny feels that 'If tenderness could be ever supposed wanting [at Mansfield], good sense and good breeding supplied its place'— surely a very generous understatement of what is missing from Mansfield. Her not unironic conclusion is that 'though Mansfield Park might have some pains, Portsmouth could have no pleasures'. But do you think too much is too readily forgiven at Mansfield, and that everything is condemned at Portsmouth?

I ask this question because I used to think this was the case: that Fanny forgets all her miseries and idealizes Mansfield simply because Portsmouth is worse. It may be that you have not missed the point, as I did, but it's important enough to be worth emphasizing.

Of course we're not meant to forget all that Jane Austen has been at pains to criticize in Mansfield Park. Its people are no better than those at Portsmouth. Sam, Tom and Charles are noisy and unruly: Tom Bertram is a gambler—an upper-crust rowdy. Betsey is spoilt: so are the Bertram girls. If Betsey and Susan squabble over a silver knife, Maria and Julia fall out over Henry

Figure 5.4 Sample page from a 'tutorial in print'. (Unit 3, on Jane Austen's *Mansfield Park*, by Cicely Havely from Course A302, The Nineteenth-century Novel and its Legacy, Open University Press, Milton Keynes, 1973)

Give Speedy Feedback

As should be apparent in the above discussion, response must be followed by feedback – by knowledge of results. Somehow or other the media must provide comment on the student's response. Otherwise the student will have no spur to modify his performance or improve. If no one ever corrects your German pronunciation you can go on practising the same mistakes for years, and you will never learn to swing a golf club properly if you are prevented from seeing what happens to the ball. Knowledge of results is the life-blood of learning and it must be kept flowing. The time-lapse – hours, days, weeks – between the student thinking out his answers and his getting to know his teacher's reaction is the great weakness of much of the 'marking' that is done in schools.

If we can quickly tell the student that his response is correct or reasonable, he is reinforced or rewarded. Consequently, he is more likely to tackle similar problems appropriately when next he is faced with them. Even if we have to tell him he is wrong, or only partially correct, the experience can still be rewarding – provided we can show him how his mistake arose and how he might overcome it.

Even if there is no right or wrong answer, perhaps especially here, the student needs some kind of response to his efforts, e.g., one that might enable him to re-appraise his answer for himself, either in his own terms or from alternative viewpoints that had not occurred to him. Just how soon he needs the feedback usually depends on how long he took over the piece of work. A five-minute exercise may need feedback within a few minutes. Having spent five weeks on a project, however, the student will probably be able to bear a couple of weeks delay in getting the teacher's considered appraisal of it. Indeed, he might *need* the delay in order to distance himself from the work and so be able to consider the feedback fairly dispassionately. Ultimately, of course, especially if he is learning to work for his own satisfaction rather than the approval of his teacher, the student should become more and more capable of providing his own feedback.

Feedback can be provided very speedily and flexibly by human interaction, especially when the participants are few and in close contact. In lectures, both feedback and interaction are normally sparce because of the infrequency of student response. In programmed learning, where the necessity of rapid feedback first became apparent, or in a 'tutorial in print', the student gets immediate knowledge of results by checking his response (e.g., a written phrase or calculation) against the author's comments.

The nature of the feedback is also important, if the student is to learn much from it. To be useful it should enable the student to take some kind of action towards identified objectives. For example, it might indicate 'facts' he needs to check, or suggest an alternative line of argument. There is evidence (see Page 1958) to suggest that students who are given individualized verbal comments on their work incorporating suggestions for improvement tend to 'improve' significantly more than students who are simply given standard comments or marks and grades.

The *tone* of such comments, whether written or spoken, should also be carefully conceived, if they are not to be counter-productive. In the survey of secondary schools by HM Inspectors (DES 1979), the authors quote written remarks like these:

> Comment on the results, Duncan – why is there, do you think, such a difference between the least and the greatest? Should these be taken into the average?

> An excellent visual and written description of — Abbey. Your essay would have been neatly tied up with a historical introduction of the Abbey's rise and a conclusion alluding to its dissolution and later history.

And they contrast them with these comments earned over a series of English essays by a girl whose teachers had selected her work as representing that of a very able pupil (which it was):

> Not thought out – Full stops and caps not clearly written – Errors of fact – You write a letter as briefly as possible – Needs more careful thought – Not developed – Padding – You have not thought this out sufficiently – Is this all? – Weak – Not what you were told to do – Keep it clear, concise and simple – Spoilt by carelessness – Tenses – Keep it clear, concise and simple – Argument poor – Repetition – Poorly expressed – Meaningless – Rubbish – Last paragraph muddled.

Clearly there is an art in commenting and giving feedback to students. In Rowntree (1981) I discuss it as a vital aspect of the *teaching* process. Notice, for instance, that the earlier pair of comments quoted above are both trying to provoke the pupil to *carry on his thinking* about the piece of work, asking him questions or, after offering credit where it is due, suggesting a possible improvement. By contrast, the series of comments on the girl's essays sound nagging, peevish and ineffectual. They are devoid of suggestions as to how the hapless pupil might think more carefully; argue less poorly; be clearer, more concise and simpler, etc., as exhorted repeatedly by the teacher. Thus, unless their censorious vagueness were to be counter-balanced by warm personal tutoring from the teacher, their effect would be to make the pupil feel bad, but not to encourage, let alone help her to get better. Teachers are often under considerable time-pressure in checking written work but, if we cannot be constructive in our comments, it is perhaps better to offer none at all (or else get the students to comment on one another's work).

Not all feedback uses symbols, words and numbers, spoken or written. Non-verbal human feedback – the teacher's smile or scowl, the colleague's mirth or hushed silence – has a strong influence, especially on learning in the affective area. Often the appropriate feedback will be musical sound or foreign language speech-rhythms. Sometimes we get our feedback from 'still' pictures, e.g., when drawing graphs or 'realizing' blueprints; or from moving pictures, e.g., when our teaching foibles are brought home to us in a video-taped 'micro-teaching' exercise. Realia too can provide salutory feedback, e.g., when the screaming of our gears tells us that we haven't yet got the feel of the clutch, or when the smell from the test tube indicates that we've applied too much heat. Such is the power of immediate knowledge of results that people can even learn to lower their own blood pressure or, with the help of feedback from an oscilloscope, control their own brain waves (see Barber et al. 1971).

Encourage Appropriate Practice

The media must enable a student to make his response not just once but many times. In learning chains and verbal associations, like typing and pronunciations, spelling and technical vocabulary, practice is obviously necessary, supported by appropriate feedback. But the constant repetitions and drilling (or 'over learning') suitable for rote-instruction are of no help in the development of concept- and principle-learning or problem-solving. Misapplied rote-instruction – 'hammering home the fundamentals' through practice and repetition – has been responsible for generations of dismal results, both cognitive and affective, especially in mathematics and science. We have all met students who have picked up sufficient verbal chaining to answer stock questions but who have no grasp at all of the concepts and principles involved. Typical is the group of fifteen-year-olds I saw asked to multiply three-sevenths by five-ninths. Almost all of them got the correct product, yet scarcely any of them had been able to say in advance whether the product would be bigger or smaller than either of the two fractions they started with. Practice obviously does not help a student understand if all it produces are verbal chains where there should be concepts.

That said, practice can help consolidate understanding once it has been achieved. The student must be led in some measure to discover for himself the concepts, principles and strategies – e.g, democracy, plant succession, scientific method – but, once he has grasped them, practice may help him use them more confidently and transfer them to a variety of new situations. Especially if he finds his newly acquired skills, e.g., critical thinking or group problem-solving, are not initially the most 'natural' way of doing things, practice may be the only means of building up such a fund of satisfying the experience that the ability becomes habitual. In other words, successful practice may help turn 'can do' capabilities into 'will do' dispositions.

However, there is no reason why the student should do all his practice at once. Spaced-out practice is likely to be more helpful than one big blitz. Similarly, whether the student is practising a chain or exercising his grasp of a principle, it will usually be inappropriate to make him work continuously over the same ground. He needs to feel he is advancing, however slowly. The media should enable him to try out his skill or understanding in a variety of contexts and preferably allow for him to use it in reaching the next level of proficiency. If the capability acquired is not applicable at a higher level we must ask why it was taught in the first place. In fact there is a lot to be said for learning chains and associations – e.g., calculating statistics, naming flowers and rocks, defining technical terms – by their being continually encountered and coped with (practised) in a problem-solving context. This is more 'motivational' than trying to master them all first and only then looking round for a way to use them.

Fulfilling the Functions

I would not pretend that the above analysis of media functions is either complete or definitive. Indeed, how such functions interconnect, what their ramifications are and how they tie in with questions of strategy and sequence (let alone how they can best be fulfilled in specific instances) is all far from clear. We shall not have a definitive taxonomy of media function until we have a prescriptive and predictive theory of learning that will enable us to design infallibly effective learning experiences for every individual. Such a theory is not imminent.

Yet even this cursory examination of media functions reveals that most media are capable, to some extent, of tackling all six functions alone and unaided. If the teacher in the classroom can do it all, from motivation to encouraging practice, so too can books, tapes, films and the rest – to some extent. But, and here is the point, no single medium is superior on all functions and for all students. In any given situation some media will do a better job than others, so we still have to choose. Ideally, we will choose a combination of media according to which is best for each function and student. If we are forced to settle for just one medium we must decide which one has most benefits and least disadvantages overall.

Selecting Modes and Media
The Inadequacy of Research

The 'new' media especially have provided an enormously popular stamping ground for educational researchers (see Heidt 1980). And educational institutions have spent enormous sums of money installing audio-visual equipment and systems. But the decision to spend cannot have been justified by reference to the research findings. The fact is that very little of the vast published research on audio-visual media is of any help at all in deciding which media to use. Research into 'older' media, let alone combinations of old and new, is even less productive of insights. This overwhelming vacuity results variously from weak experimental design; insufficient detail in published reports; failure to ask research questions relating media effectiveness to characteristics of the learners, the situation and the objectives; and, above all, from the confusing interaction of the countless uncontrolled variables that are at work.

Peggie Campeau (1972), in her stringent critique of media research, identifies the kind of questions that researchers should be asking if they are to help us in media selection:

> What particular medium or combination of media will produce the most learning for Task A under Condition X, and why?
>
> What factors in Condition X maximise learning of Task A through a particular medium or combination of media and what factors interfere with such learning? Why?
>
> What learner variables should be taken into account in deciding which students will profit most from instruction by a particular medium (or media) for Task A under Condition X?

Of course, there is a daunting multitude of different 'tasks' and 'conditions' and of 'factors' and 'variables' (most of them uncontrollable by the teacher). In the words of Heidt (1980): 'the problem of relating *media* differences to *learner* differences cannot be solved by devising a comprehensive list of media characteristics and another list containing all relevant learner characteristics, the items of which would then only require mechanical matching.' Hence the difficulty of amassing valid and reliable evidence that might allow us to generalize from the situation in which it was collected to the teaching situations in which we find ourselves at various times. The best we can do for the time being is clarify a few rules of thumb.

Consider the Objectives

At least when the learning objectives are well defined, media selection may be fairly straightforward. If the most suitable medium for achieving a given objective is not immediately obvious, then it probably doesn't matter which of several media is used.

With certain objectives, we can make sure that the kind of stimulus mode presented by the medium is appropriate to the kind of capability the student is aiming to acquire. Thus, if the student is learning to 'distinguish between valid and invalid inferences that might be made from a particular historical source', the printed word may well be a suitable stimulus mode. But if he must 'state whether a musical passage played on the piano ends on the tonic or dominant', no amount of printed words or musical notation, or even human interaction, will help him unless he also has access to the stimulus of sound, either from recordings or a real piano. Again, the student who must 'identify which of a set of soil samples are sand, which clay and which loam' may get some help from words, printed or spoken, but he won't be able to make the discrimination until he gets his fingers on the realia – some soil specimens. Similarly, if the student is to be able to 'describe the motion of an amoeba' he must see one moving (or else he will be merely describing someone else's description); if microscopes and amoebae are not available, pictures will have to suffice – moving pictures on film, or video-tape 'flick-book'.

Bishop (1971) tells how one of his ceramics objectives ('the student will be able to describe the changes undergone by clay in the processes of drying and firing') suggests media and strategies, but also how these need to be related to the learning preferences of his students:

> The objectives themselves suggest teaching strategies. For example, the lessons on drying and firing might call for the student to construct several

samples for experimentation. Changes in weight and size could be recorded or even photographed as the samples dry to give the student his own evidence of the changes undergone by clay during the drying. One of the samples could then be bisque-fired and again the change noted. If the student places a bisqued sample and a bone-dry sample in water for a few minutes, he will gather more evidence about the metamorphosis of clay in ceramics. . . .

Some students are able to perceive the importance of these changes in clay on the basis of verbal information alone. Still others will be able to form the necessary concepts by observing teacher demonstrations, slides, or films on the subject. Yet others must work through problems which make it possible for them to see and to use the characteristics in the context of a real problem in order that their perceptions, and thus their concepts, become clear.

Knowledge? Skills? Attitudes?

Suppose we do not have very specific objectives? Our decisions about modes and media should still benefit from the recognition that different modes and media encourage *different kinds of learning*. Do we wish to develop a learning experience that affects chiefly knowledge, or skills, or attitudes? Thus, while knowledge of one kind or another may be conveyed by any mode or medium, we might expect attitudes to be affected more by media that involve human interaction than, say, by media that rely on written symbols. Some skills may best be developed through print, some may need moving pictures or realia, some (especially social skills) may call for human interaction media, and so on.

Even if we are concerned solely with knowledge, with subject matter content, we must recognize that different modes and media offer different kinds of knowledge. Knowledge of the 'same' topic or concept can be presented in alternative ways: verbally, pictorially, numerically, physically, socially and so on. Thus, the learner may experience, let's say, 'sex discrimination' by reading accounts of women's attempts to gain access to male-dominated careers; by viewing films or plays with such themes; by considering statistical evidence of women's representation in various careers over time; by herself being thwarted in the attempt to share in some activity normally reserved for males (e.g., football in schools); by discussing such experiences in company with other women and men; and so on.

All these ways of knowing 'sex discrimination' are different. We may feel the learner needs to experience all of them, and to make the connections between them, if his or her understanding is not to be partial or impoverished. The point is that *no one medium alone* can embody all kinds of knowledge, let alone foster all kinds of knowledge, skills and attitudes.

Students' Preferences

If more than one stimulus mode is appropriate to a given objective, we should aim to provide the student with the one that suits him best. Unfortunately, research allows few generalizations to help us here – apart from the rather obvious reminder that poor readers will learn better from spoken or recorded words than from printed material. Researchers have looked for differences in media-preference between young and old, bright and dim, anxious and non-anxious, introvert and extrovert, poorly and well-educated, male and female, dependent and independent, impulsive and reflective students without establishing any practical guidelines to help us suit the medium to an individual. Nevertheless, we know that some students will find human interaction motivating while others will not; some prefer to learn from print and some from sound recordings; some are not happy unless they see the real thing, and so on. As Bishop (1971) says:

> Some students need to work each area through in a physical way to form their concepts while others, because of differing background, experience and visual acuity, are able to form most of the necessary concepts from verbal information. It is as wrong to expect the student with little verbal skill to learn the concept when the only material presented is verbal as it is to force the student with strong verbal capabilities to work physically through each concept when he may be able to demonstrate quickly his understanding in another way.

If we are in doubt about our students' preferences we may need to go in for 'media overkill' – hitting an objective with several media in the reasonable expectation that between them they will satisfy all students. Since we have no exact science of who can best learn what from which, a certain amount of redundancy can be valuable. In the interests of individualization, we may need to give each student some opportunity to choose the medium that best suits his needs, abilities and interests. As Heidt (1980) remarks, the selection of media and methods is an activity in which we require the participation and cooperation of the learner.

There is also the probability that social interactions and personal relationships among students and between students and teacher will also affect the acceptability and effectiveness of any particular medium (see

Salomon 1978). That is, more than individual preferences may need to be taken into account.

Familiarity

As I suggested at the beginning of this chapter, our selection of media is also constrained by how wide a variety we are familiar with. The depth of familiarity is also important if we are to get the best out of a medium. Similarly, students too may be insufficiently familiar with a medium to learn as well as they might from it. Jean Ruddock (1980) describes the difficulties experienced by students who were expected to learn for the first time from free discussion in which the teacher acted as non-directive chairman (see also page 238).

Alternatively, students may be familiar with the medium, but in an inappropriate way. My colleague Duncan Brown (1980), in a study of the attitudes of new Open University students to radio as a medium, found that students came to their studies having listened to radio for news bulletins and music but, by and large, only students in the Arts Faculty and to some extent in the social sciences, regularly listened to talks, documentaries and dramas. In other words, students coming to mathematics, science and technology were familiar with the 'wrong' kind of broadcasting. This could be expected to cause them difficulties when they were exposed to university radio programmes that required them to concentrate and think – especially since the survey also revealed that about half of the students said they *never* listened to radio without doing other things at the same time! Maybe, as Jean Ruddock (1980) and my colleague Tony Bates (1982) suggest, we need to *teach* students how to learn from media to which they are not initially 'tuned in'.

Practicality and Cost

Student preferences and familiarity are not the only constraints upon our choice of media. We also have to consider practicality and cost. The best way to learn French may be to spend a year in rural Provence, yet we may have to settle for conversation classes in Brighton. The best way to teach an astronaut how to work in zero gravity might be to send him to the moon, but for reasons of economy and safety we start him off in a tank of water in Texas. Kefford (1970) illustrates how the 'obvious' medium, in this case a visit to a coal mine, needs to be closely scrutinized in terms of practicalities:

Clearly, a visit offers distinct advantages; these may include:

1 First-hand experience, including the sensations of sight, sound, touch and smell.
2 The opportunity for direct two-way communication including the facility of asking questions and getting answers 'on the spot'.
3 The opportunity to see the mine in the context of the community of which it forms a part.

But there are disadvantages also:

1 There are certain to be restrictions placed on the number of pupils who can visit the mine at one time.
2 Those who act as 'guides' may not necessarily be skilled in communicating ideas to children and this may result in confused ideas.
3 The timing of a visit may cause a disruption of the normal school timetable and the uneconomic deployment of staff.

As a result of weighing these advantages and disadvantages in the balance, the choice of the medium may not be quite so obvious. It is conceivable that a well-made film could be a better medium than an unsatisfactory visit and offer the advantage of large group participation without disruption of the normal timetable. The final decision must be taken on the basis of the objectives to be achieved. If, for example, the visit is seen as the means of providing stimuli for imaginative writing, the film may be an unacceptable substitute for direct experience. On the other hand, if the objective is a clear understanding of the processes by which coal is brought to the surface, the film will probably be the superior medium.

A case like this reminds us that, just as a given objective can often be attained through any of several media, so a given medium may help students attain more than one objective. For instance, a visit to a coal mine may help in learning to communicate with experts, as well as learning the processes of coal production. Such versatility may well be a reason for preferring one medium over another. Remember also that a medium may be influencing affective objectives even while you are aiming at cognitive ones. Thus, just as a doctor's prescribing tranquillisers will teach some people that medication is the way to improve personal relations, so a teacher's extensive use of the lecture method will teach students that the way to learn is to rely on the pronouncements of an authority.

Variety of Media

Of course, any medium, however appropriate to the objectives, will become tedious if used to the exclusion of all others. Variety is one good reason for combining media, even where one medium could (theoretically) perform all the functions. In combining media we must ensure that the student is not expected to respond to two incompatible stimuli at the same time, e.g., operating a piece of equipment at the same time as he reads a book on how to do it – here the instructions would be better given by tape-recorder. And in sequencing media we must ensure that the changeover from one medium to another is smooth, quick and not too frequent. Imagine the chaos if a class teacher tried to manipulate lecture, film, group-discussion, listening to records, writing, television programme, handling of specimens, practical work in groups, concluding discussion, all within the space of one hour! Sometimes we may have students continue to work with what for some of the objectives is a less than ideal medium – e.g., a series of still pictures within a text when a short film-clip would be really more appropriate – if we feel those objectives are not vital enough to warrant the cost and inconvenience of switching into a new medium.

Availability

Finally, we must take the availability of the media into account. Human interaction of several kinds is usually in abundant supply but may not always allow for individual tuition, simulation gaming, cooperative study, project teams and certain other special media. Printed symbols and still pictures are also readily available in the form of books, posters, charts, maps and so on, but there is a limit to quantity and variety. Realia may or may not be obtainable. For recorded sound we need to have not only the records and tape-players – enough perhaps to allow for individual and small group use – but also records and tapes appropriate to our students' learning objectives. So too with the need for suitable and sufficient films and film-projectors, video-tapes or cassettes and television replay facilities.

We may find it necessary to know what media our students have access to in their own homes. Clearly, television and radio and books are widespread, and the range of readily available media is expanding all the time. Far more students can now afford their own audio tape-players and pocket calculators than when the first edition of this book was published (1974). Now we see home video systems spreading fast and, who knows, maybe by the time of the next edition we'll be able to rely on most students having access to the household computer.

So our choice of media is sometimes limited because certain media are not available. Conversely, and paradoxically, our choice is sometimes limited because certain media are not only available but are virtually forced upon us. Thus, Open University course teams are under strong pressure (which thankfully they often resist) to use the television medium whether or not they foresee any particular educational function for it on the particular course they are planning. The argument is that students *expect* Open University courses to use television; hence, any that do not may be stigmatized as giving 'short weight'. School teachers will know of similar examples where individual scope for media selection (and even content selection) has been heavily constrained by a previous departmental decision to invest in a particular reading scheme, textbook or whatever.

Putting Media Together

The teacher designs the learning experiences out of what he and his students can do or make themselves, together with what he can buy or borrow from outside. They can plan and 'perform' their own interactions – lectures, conversations, discussions, excursions and so on. Especially if the teacher has the support and cooperation of colleagues, he can make and collect realia and pictures, and produce workcards, programmed booklets, tape-recordings, slides, short films or video-tapes and so on. Students, too, can produce learning resources from which their colleagues or successors can learn. For example, they may be tape-recording the reminiscences of the few remaining local veterans of the Great War, or photographing soon-to-be-demolished local landmarks. The teacher will also use media materials produced by outside publishers and curriculum developers – books, programmes, films, packages, multi-media kits. Before finding a place for them in his learning system he will need to be satisfied not only about their cost and likely effectiveness but also their relevance to his students' objectives. Data on these matters are not always too readily available.

Even with commercial materials the teacher is not limited to using them as they stand. He can produce 'learning packages' or assignment cards (as in the Dalton Plan of the 1920s), calling on students to do practical work; to read extracts from several books or programmes; to view extracts from various films; to collaborate with local people, other students and teachers; to organize their own fact-finding excursions into the environment; and so on. And he can link such assignments together by means of his own written or tape-recorded commentaries and suggestions, interspersing them perhaps with self-assessment exercises along the lines of 'adjunct programmes' (see Pressey 1964), and both scheduled and impromptu tutorials.

Using such a format of 'resource-based' learning (see Taylor 1971, Noble 1981, Clarke 1982) the teacher is free to select and combine media and strategies in the light of what he knows of his students' objectives and learning preferences and the cost-effectiveness and practicality of the many available options. But if the resulting resources and learning experiences are to exploit the individualization of learning that modern media make possible and if the teacher is to open up the curriculum, then students need a wide choice of resources. As David Hawkins (1965) puts it:

> . . .there must be at hand what I call 'multiply programmed' material; material that contains written and pictorial guidance of some sort for the student, but which is designed for the greatest possible variety of topics, ordering of topics, etc., so that for almost any given way into a subject that a child may evolve on his own, there is material available which he will recognize as helping him farther along that very way. Heroic teachers have sometimes done this on their own, but it is obviously one of the places where designers of curriculum materials can be of enormous help, designing those materials with a rich variety of choices for teacher and child, and freeing the teacher from the role of 'leader-drawer' along a single preconceived path, giving the teacher encouragement and real logistical help in diversifying the activities of a group.

Where the design of such multiplicity is beyond the time and resources of the individual teacher, he must look outside his classroom. He can join up with colleagues in his school to form curriculum development teams. He can exchange ideas and materials with teachers in other local schools through the operation of teachers' centres and other regional ventures. He has access to published material produced by teachers working in national curriculum development teams, to books and materials produced by publishers, to television and radio programmes and supporting materials produced by the broadcasting companies. He can call on people in his local community and send his students out to benefit from their special skills and experience. A wealth of learning resources can be made available if the teacher is ready to help his students use them.

Nevertheless, amid all this opportunity, teachers have only so much time and money available to them. 'Chalk-and-talk' or overhead projector-and-talk plus books will inevitably continue to be the most widely used media. There is no disgrace in this, provided those media are chosen and applied rationally; and provided they are supplemented by other media and methods where those can best embody the objectives or forms of knowledge required, or when special effects or variety are called for, or to cater for individual students' learning needs.

No doubt this chapter, and maybe others, will be found wanting by some readers because it does not extol the glorious possibilities opened up to us by micro-electronics. In fact, everything I have said is applicable, one way or another, to all the new media and systems that might spring from the 'chip'. For the moment, however, I prefer to give them a courteous but cautious welcome to the educational panoply. I wait to be convinced (as I have waited in vain on similar occasions in the past) that their technological splendour and ingenuity will not fast out-run our pedagogical ability to say anything worthwhile with them – or at least at a price we can justify compared with other media and methods. Until then, I feel some sympathy for the cynics, resistant to ed. tech. hype, who say, 'Computer-assisted learning is the medium of the future – and it always will be.'

All the same, our 'pedagogical ability' will not get its chance to rise to the occasion unless we make some effort now to evaluate the potential of the new technologies. For useful introductions, see O'Shea and Self 1982, Rushby 1979, and the series of information sheets published by the Council for Educational Technology, beginning with CET 1981.

Questions on Chapter 5

1 Would the distinction between 'stimulus modes' and 'media' give *you* any help in developing (or in describing) a course? If so, give some examples of how it would. If not, what do you find lacking in the distinction?

2 Which of the five stimulus modes are used in the course you have in mind? Are there any you think should be used but are not? If so, why are they not used?

3 Through which media are the various stimulus modes presented on your course? Are there any media that might be used in preference to some of them? If so, why are they not used instead? Are any of the media misused? If so, how?

4 Outline how one of the media used might be said to fulfil each of the

six functions mentioned on page 168. Which of the functions are most amply and least amply fulfilled? Why?

5   What might be the chief criteria (e.g., nature of objectives or types of learning, practicality, variety, etc.) that are used in determining the media of your course?

6   Are there any media you would like to have seen discussed at greater length in this chapter? If so, how might you find out what you feel you would want to know about them?

CHAPTER 6

EVALUATION AND IMPROVEMENT

The facts are always less than what really happens.
Nadine Gordimer

Thus far in our course planning, we have worked through the first two phases of the educational technology approach, dealing with objectives and the design of the learning. But, as we did so, the shadow of the two final phases – evaluation and improvement – has been rising to meet us. Not only may our decisions so far have been influenced by what we recall from the evaluation and improvement of similar learning experiences in the past, but we have also been well aware of the possible imperfections in what we are currently planning. We began thinking of criterion tests and evaluation while still ruminating on objectives.

What is Evaluation?

Having designed a learning experience and seen it in use by our students, we must ask: How is it working out? Is it doing any good? What effects is it having? Evaluation is the means whereby we systematically collect and analyse information about the results of students' encounters with a learning experience. We wish to understand what it is like to teach and learn within the system we have created; to recognize which objectives have been achieved and which not; and to ascertain what unforeseen results (beneficial or disastrous) have also materialized. In a sense, every course or learning experience (and certainly every interaction with an individual student) is a 'one-off' design, at least as far as the students are concerned. Yet, as teachers, we anticipate the need to create similar learning situations for other students in the future. Ideally, the insights gained from evaluation will help us develop and improve our teaching (or enhance the learning) not just for the present students but for future students also.

Micro- and Macro-evaluation

The spirit of evaluation should inform all our teaching decisions whether large or small. Of course, one kind of extempore, micro-evaluation enables us, for instance, to launch into a new line of argument when our student seems unconvinced or to seek out more congenial partners for a couple of students who appear unable to work together without constant bickering. This is the kind that goes on unceasingly as part of the teaching process. It has its parallel in the continuous self-assessment performed by the student himself as feedback shows him strengths and weaknesses in his learning. But, in addition, we need the planned-for *macro*-evaluation of learning experiences and systems *as a whole* – gauging the effects and effectiveness for different students of a set of work cards, a nature trail or a programmed tape-recording; assessing the contribution to students' learning made by the various elements in multimedia courses like those of the Open University, where correspondence texts, television and radio programmes, group tutorials, summer schools, self-help groups, assignments, experimental kits, gramophone records and the like all act together as part of the students' 'learning environment'. For this more systematic evaluation, we may need test exercises and examinations, attitude scales and 'opinionaires', as well as sensitive skills in interviewing, discussion and observation.

Although, in this chapter, we are more concerned with macro-evaluation than with micro-evaluation, the difference between them is perhaps relative rather than absolute. It depends on what we are regarding as the 'unit' of teaching. Consider a teacher, at the end of an afternoon's art session, reflecting on 'critical incidents' that arose during the course of it and inspecting the products of his students' work. Such evaluation may appear 'macro' compared with the myriad evaluative decisions through which he interacted with his students during the session itself; yet it appears 'micro' compared with the evaluation he will be able to make when his *series* of sessions is complete. Perhaps the most crucial distinction is that micro-evaluation, although it may well feed data into the macro-evaluation, has the primary purpose of sustaining and developing the teaching for the benefit of present students. Macro-evaluation, on the other hand, chiefly aims to benefit students in some future learning situation – either the present students on a subsequent course or, more usually, other students learning from an improved version of the present course.

Evaluation v. *Assessment*

We enter now another area of tortured educational semantics. Two words in particular cause confusion – 'evaluation' and 'assessment'. It is quite common in the UK to use these terms to refer to two rather different activities – assessment being just one aspect of evaluation. In North America, however, the one word 'evaluation' tends to do duty for both. Furthermore, even those who use the terms separately do not always clarify the connection between them, let alone show how they relate to other terms appearing in the same context, like 'testing', 'measurement', 'appraisal' and 'grading'. There is no space here for an extended analysis (see Rowntree 1977), but there are some distinctions and connections I must make clear.

Assessment we have already discussed in Chapter 4. What I am referring to is the assessment of a student's learning – finding out what the student's abilities and attitudes are and how they have changed since last assessed. This will not necessarily involve testing him or measuring his performance in any formal way. It may be enough to ask his opinions or unobtrusively observe him in action, and note that some personal trait or ability appears to be present in greater or lesser degree than hitherto.

One possible, but not essential, outcome of assessment is grading. Our assessment of the student's qualities and capabilities can be quantified with a score or percentage mark or letter grade. This allows for rough-and-ready comparisons with other students. It also enables outsiders, who do not know our student or perhaps the exact criteria by which we reached our judgement, to make decisions about him as if they did.

A more vital outcome of assessment, related to teaching our students rather than reporting on them to other people, is *diagnostic appraisal* — ascertaining the individual student's developing strengths and apparent weaknesses, and identifying his emerging needs. Given that the student has reached such-and-such a state, what can he or should he aim for next? What implications does this have for the ensuing teaching? Diagnostic appraisal does not involve grading, even though it may use test measurements or observations provided by assessment. Rather, it depends upon pedagogic judgements as to what learning sequences are possible and upon value judgements, both the teacher's and the student's, as to which are desirable.

It is also necessary, but not sufficient, to assess as part of a full *evaluation*. Evaluation is an attempt to identify and explain the effects and effectiveness of the teaching/learning system. Assessment reveals to us the most important class of 'effects' – the changes wrought by new learning in the knowledge, skills and attitudes of our students. In so far as effects on other people (e.g., teachers, parents, employers, etc.) are important, evaluation will also need data additional to that provided by student assessment. For instance, what are other teachers saying about our students? Are parents complaining about too much homework? How do people in the local shops and offices comment on the work our students are doing on their community project? Are students abiding by safety requirements? And so on.

Figure 6.1 shows how these concepts flow together in what I have called micro-evaluation – really the continuous use of feedback to adjust your teaching to minute-by-minute data about what is going on in the learning situation. By 'teaching' I mean not merely formal instruction but whatever the teacher does to promote the student's learning. Your assessment (A) of the student's learning, together with data about other events and developments in the teaching/learning system (N), enables you to evaluate (E) the effects and effectiveness of the teaching so far. The assessment also helps you to diagnose (D) the new needs of each student; and diagnosis and evaluation together go to determine the purpose and nature of the ensuing teaching (T) which continues until further assessment gives rise to more evaluation and diagnostic appraisal.

Figure 6.2 extends this pattern to encompass macro-evaluation – leading to insights into the *overall* effectiveness of a larger sequence of teaching and how it might be improved before being used with another set of students. This macro-evaluation (large E) would take note of all the individual evaluations of bits of the sequence but would, in addition, assess students on the sequence as a whole (large A) and take in non-assessment data about the effects of the sequence as a whole (large N).

Figure 6.3 shows the connection between assessment and grading. Students can be given a succession of grades (G) according to the assessments made at various stages. If these grades are to count towards some overall certificate of competency, the system may be called 'continuous assessment' – strictly speaking, 'continuous grading'. The student may finally be assessed (examined) on the abilities and attitudes he displays in relation to the unit as a whole (large A) and given a final, overall grade (large G) which may include a contribution from 'continuous assessment' as well as from examination.

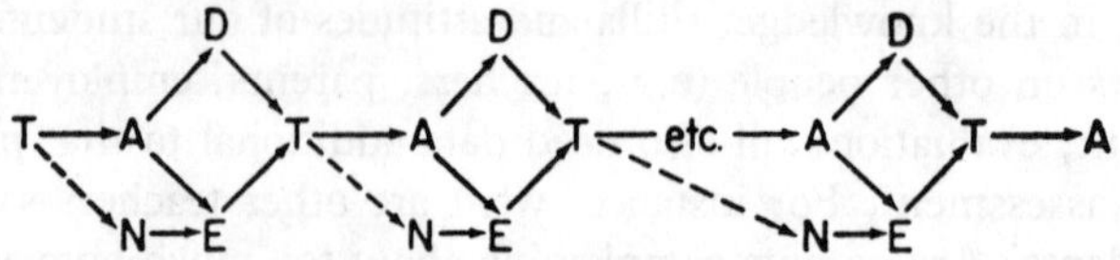

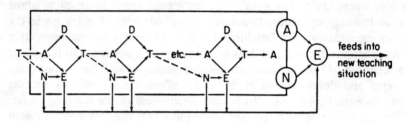

Figure 6.1 Assessment and micro-evaluation

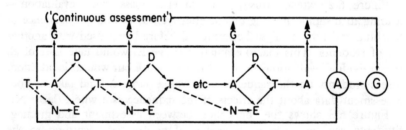

Figure 6.2 Assessment and macro-evaluation

Figure 6.3 Assessment and grading

A = Assessment of what student has learned
N = Data about other events in the teaching/learning system
E = Evaluation of teaching
D = Diagnostic appraisal of student's needs
T = Teaching
G = Grading

Who is Responsible for Learning?

A confusing ambivalence of purpose often sabotages our discussions of evaluation, assessment and grading. Who is on trial – the teacher or the student? If the student 'fails' his course, has he really failed it or has it failed him? How far is the student to be penalized because Bloom-type 'mastery learning' is not the norm? As Colin Kefford (1970) puts it, rather more polemically than some of us might care to hear:

> Perhaps the biggest single weakness of teachers is their reluctance to put their teaching methods on trial. For many teachers the whole process is an intuitive one and, as such, totally inadequate. If their pupils succeed in public examinations, teachers congratulate themselves on the efficacy of their teaching. If their pupils fail, excuses are sought out: the pupils are of poor quality this year; the facilities for homework are inadequate; the pupils did not work hard enough; the exam paper was badly devised. How seldom does one ever hear a teacher with the honesty to admit that his teaching methods may have been at fault.

Apportioning 'blame' for ineffective learning would be pointless were it not for the fact that assessment is often not so much for the student's benefit (in diagnosing his needs and helping him learn) as for the benefit of other people who will use a few crude soundings from it to determine what his life-prospects are to be. In the words of Donald McIntyre (1970):

> . . . although we spend an enormous amount of time and money on assessment, very little is obtained which helps teachers to teach. Instead, we give pupils marks or grades, that is, we concentrate on *judging* them, on saying how 'good' or 'bad' they are, on putting them in an 'order of merit'. Assessment of this . . . sort can make no contribution to effective teaching. Its function is rather to select pupils, gradually as they pass through our schools, for different positions in the socio-economic hierarchy of our society, positions for which we then proceed to train them.

Such political and economic interpretations can be attached to any grading decisions that arise out of assessment, but not to decisions of diagnosis and evaluation. Assessment itself can be a reasonably objective gathering of information. But the form it takes and the uses to which the information is put may vary with the assumptions that are being made about the division of responsibility in teaching and learning. 'Grading' seems to assume that the teaching is beyond reproach and that the student is to be rewarded according to how well he has discharged his responsibility to learn from it as revealed objectively by assessment.

'Diagnostic appraisal' makes no assumptions about the responsibility for effective teaching and learning; its value judgements about the student's apparent strengths, weaknesses and needs do not masquerade as objective truths about the student. 'Evaluation' may well make assumptions about responsibility, and assumptions that are diametrically opposed to those implied in 'grading'. That is, evaluation may assume that difficulties in the students' learning may conceivably be explained by shortcomings in the teaching — that is to say, in factors over which the teacher has some control, and that it is the *responsibility of the teaching to change* in such a way as to enable the student to learn.

In the 'real' world, of course, the assumptions and the practices are often as confused as the words. At different times a teacher may manage to operate from different assumptions. But problems can arise if he slips unwittingly from one set of assumptions to another or if he needs to cooperate with people whose assumptions he fails to recognize as being different from his.

Indeed any teacher who reckons to influence his students at all must accept the attendant responsibilities. Even if, paradoxically, he intends that his students should become increasingly responsible for planning their own learning, it is still his responsibility to ensure that the teaching/ learning environment is such as to support them, or at least not hinder them, in doing so. And if the planning is done chiefly by the teacher, based on objectives that are largely his, then his responsibility is so much greater.

Historically speaking, programmed learning made this particular moral breakthrough, by firmly accepting such responsibility for the student's attainment. If students did not learn from the programme, then the fault lay in the programme rather than in the students. In 'validating' a programme, the writers often adopted the so-called '90/90' criterion, modifying the programme until at least 90 percent of students were able to attain at least 90 percent of the objectives. Nowadays we might be more concerned to find *alternative* methods for the percentage of students who do not take to the basic 'programme' (whatever form it takes) rather than try to make it work for everyone. Thus, we would hope to achieve more than 90/90 with the system as a whole. Nevertheless, it was programmed learning that persuaded many teachers (and students) that, as far as humanly possible, the learning system should be adapted to the student rather than vice versa.

The Discomforts of Evaluation

Not surprising then, that evaluation is seen by some as a threatening activity. To carry it out at all implies that the teaching is no better than it ought to be. When the teaching we are evaluating is our own, considerable humility is needed to register its blemishes, especially if they call for more than superficial changes. And anyone involved in evaluating another's teaching, as educational technologists sometimes are, must bear in mind the uncheering warning of James Belasco and Harrison Trice (1969):

> . . . the evaluator is likely to be viewed with all the warmth and affection given to a motorcycle policeman hiding behind the last billboard you sped past. In short, although a conscience is necessary, no one wants one that plagues him too closely.

Added to which, evaluation can be costly and time-consuming. As an extreme example, the evaluation and improvement of the physics teaching materials produced in the USA by the Physical Sciences Study Committee is reported by Paul Marsh (1964) to have cost about three times as much as the original production. It is true that 'quick and dirty' partial evaluations may give people the impression they know what is going on in the learning system; but even if the impression happens to be accurate, such data can too easily be shot down in flames if it contradicts people's expectations. Yet how much time and money are people prepared to spend collecting information that may demand they spend *yet more* on major overhauls of the learning system? Especially when, as Patricia Kendall (1964) points out in her interesting account of the difficulties faced in evaluating an experimental medical course:

> . . . the creators of experimental programs. . .have little question about the efficacy of the changes they have introduced. They *know* that the courses they have developed are the best possible under existing conditions; and in the light of this assumed fact, systematic evaluation seems superfluous.

Evaluation can indeed be very difficult. How, for example, do you allow for the 'Hawthorne effect' – the artificial enhancement of student performance that may arise from any experimental newness of the system and the students' consequent response to what they perceive as 'special' treatment? How do you account for the umpteen 'contaminating' factors outside the learning system that may nevertheless influence performance? How do you prevent the easily tested objectives from weighing more heavily in the evaluation than objectives that are more important but less testable or less quantifiable? How do you adjudicate when the feelings of teachers and students towards a course are at odds with the cognitive results achieved? How much weight do you give to non-educational objectives (like goodwill in the outside community)? How do you collect all the necessary information, anyway, without, in so doing, exerting a contaminating influence on the results? If you are evaluating someone else's curriculum, how do you get their agreement as to what aspects are to be reported on and what action might be taken as a result?

How, in the final analysis, do you decide on the reliability of your interpretation of the data? Marten Shipman (1972a) shows, for example, how the diversity and uncontrollability of the variables involved in evaluations of such innovations as comprehensive schooling, de-streaming, the Initial Teaching Alphabet, smaller classes, etc., can result in the same data being interpreted to their advantage by both supporters and opponents of the schemes. The whole enterprise of evaluation bristles with problems, both conceptual and methodological. So effective evaluation can be unwelcome, costly, time-consuming and difficult. Why then do we persist in doing it?

Why Bother with Evaluation?

The chief function of evaluation is to understand what is happening in the teaching/learning system, with a view to sustaining, developing, and improving it. Can we pin down the cause-and-effect relationships between our teaching activities, students' learning activities, and the outcomes of those activities? If so we may be able to refine and elaborate our materials and methods until we can improve our teaching, and the students' learning, still more. At the very least we may be able to identify the students or circumstances for which they would *not* be appropriate.

Improvements

Why do we tolerate this trial-and-error approach? Why cannot we get the teaching 'right' first time? Because we do not have and probably never will have, a sufficiently water-tight science of learning. We are in much the same position as the motor-car manufacturer who puts his cars together on the best engineering principles, with advice from all kinds of experts, but who nevertheless finds it necessary to road-test each new model and carry out modifications before unleashing it on the waiting public. And, months after the launching, he may need to call back the car in large numbers to rectify a major but belatedly occurring fault.

Even the physician, with his rigorous, scientific heritage, is often forced to take this empirical approach with a patient.

Since we cannot guarantee the learning experiences we design, we must take steps to appraise their results. Random, informal observations will play their part in this, of course, but they are no substitute for systematic evaluation. This is dramatically illustrated in Figure 6.4 by Peter Warr et al. (1970) who report on an experiment in the training of airline managers where two series of information-giving courses were evaluated. In each series (A and B) the course was given five times to different groups and after each 'run' the attitudes and knowledge gained by the group were measured. But only for Series B were the teachers informed of the test results; so only in Series B were the teachers able to use systematic evaluation data in continuous improvement of their course. Figure 6.4 shows very clearly that the gain in knowledge by

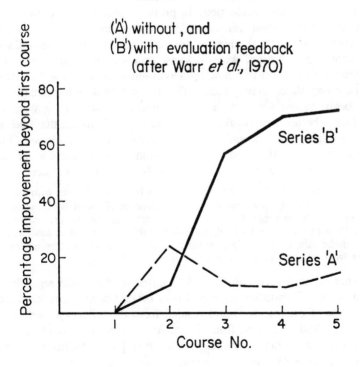

Figure 6.4   Improvement in course effectiveness

successive groups increased throughout Series B. By the end of Series B the average gain in knowledge as a result of a course was 70 percent above what it had been in the first run. But in Series A, where the teachers had not had feedback from systematic evaluation, the average gain in knowledge from the final course was only about 10 percent above that of the first run.

Information gained from evaluation may be used not only to benefit students on the present course but may also be generalized to improve subsequent teaching. If, for example, we find that students working in pairs on a particular programmed learning package learn just as much as students working alone and enjoy it more, we are likely to consider favourably the possibility of having students work in pairs on similar packages we devise in the future. See Nathenson and Henderson (1980, Chapter 7) for a discussion of the kinds of improvement in course effectiveness that can ensue from evaluation.

Furthermore, our evaluation, if properly recorded, can help *other* teachers improve their teaching. After more than a century of mass education and several decades of enthusiastic but uncoordinated educational researching, we still know excruciatingly little about how different people learn and how the environment of media and strategies can be manipulated to help them. With proper attention to evaluation we may begin to use some of the information at present being wasted to build up a better theoretical understanding of the learning that does and does not take place in and out of the classroom. John Dewey (1926) foresaw how little that understanding would advance unless we all have access to the recorded evaluations made by innovating teachers:

> . . . the successes of such individuals tend to be born and to die with them; beneficial consequences extend only to those pupils who have personal contact with such gifted teachers. . .the only way we can prevent such waste in the future is by methods which enable us to make an analysis of what the gifted teacher does intuitively, so that something accruing from his work can be communicated to others.

Whether or not we consider ourselves gifted teachers, and regardless of the amount of 'intuition' in our work, other teachers can learn from evaluation of our methods and results, from the failures as well as the successes. And so can we from theirs. As a teacher of doctors, much of the great Hippocrates' reputation was attributable to his courage in recording his work with the patients he *failed* to cure.

Of course, one often has the feeling, in wondering how to apply the results of research, that individual students and contexts are simply too different to justify generalizing the principles derived from research to teaching other students in other contexts. In the words of my colleague Gordon Burt (1976), 'the context overrides the general principle'. Admittedly, generalization from one context to another has its dangers, and we must keep alert for the differences (perhaps crucial) between the two contexts as well as the similarities. But without some attempt to adapt and apply earlier experience we learn nothing about teaching – hence the snide inquiry as to whether certain teachers have really had twenty years' experience, or merely the same year twenty times!

Proof and Persuasion

There is also a 'political' reason for evaluation. Sometimes it is necessary not only to improve the learning but also to *prove* it. Curriculum development is costly, in money, time and the cooperation of colleagues – especially if we make much use of the newer presentation media. (As in the Open University, for example, where one-fifth of the annual expenditure is devoted to television.) If we are to continue getting the funds and resources and manpower we need, we must prove that we can use them to good effect.

In the USA, because of anxiety about the billions of dollars spent on curriculum development without firm evidence of results, nationally funded projects must (since the 'Kennedy Amendment' of 1967) include plans for evaluation. Indicative of the same mood in the 1970s, commercial companies providing complete educational systems for certain school districts were signing 'performance contracts' (Davies 1971) whereby the fee paid to the company was to depend on the results achieved by students. (By and large, that particular innovation failed to prove its worth and has faded from the scene.) Similarly, since the mid-1970s, many US states have required the publishers of textbooks and other learning materials to provide evidence of their successful evaluation. (See the discussion of 'learner verification and revision' on page 216.)

Teachers in all countries are being made increasingly aware that they are competing with other sectors of the economy for scarce resources. A teaching institution has to justify the funds it requires from outside and it cannot do this unless the people within it can justify whatever proportion of the total each needs to spend. A fair claim on resources cannot be made without some commitment to open evaluation and building up a reliable 'track record'. The alternative to designing appropriate evaluation procedures of our own is often to be tacitly evaluated by other people's procedures, which may be neither systematic nor appropriate. Essentially, our efforts will be held in higher regard and given greater support if we convince others that we are achieving worthwhile results. 'Accountability' is a concept that UK schools and colleges are increasingly having to learn to live with (see Becher and Maclure 1978).

How Shall We Evaluate?

If it is to help us make decisions about teaching, an evaluation must enable us to understand what is happening in the learning situation and explain the relationship between causes and effects. In the words of Robert Stake (1967):

> A *full* evaluation results in a story, supported perhaps by statistics and profiles. It tells what happened. It reveals perceptions and judgements that different groups and individuals hold – obtained, I hope, by objective means. It tells of merit and shortcomings. As a bonus, it may offer generalizations ('The moral of the story is. . .') for the guidance of subsequent educational programmes. . .
>   . . .two main kinds of data are collected:
>   (1)   objective *descriptions* of goals, environments, personnel, method and content, and outcomes.
>   and
>   (2) personal *judgements* as to the quality and appropriateness of those goals, etc.

Both kinds of data may be collected by either of the two broad strategies of evaluation between which Malcolm Parlett and David Hamilton (1972) make so useful a distinction. The first is the traditional strategy that sets out single-mindedly to measure the extent to which a project has achieved certain specific, predetermined goals. This is related to the 'agricultural-botany' approach in which, for example, plants might be exposed to different experimental treatments and their different responses compared statistically.

The second strategy has more in common with the 'participant observation' approach of social anthropology. Here the evaluator enters into the project pragmatically, recognizing the problematical nature of dynamic, human situations, aware that objectives and priorities are constantly evolving, but seeking to understand the significant features of the process he is involved with and find illuminating interpretations of them. See Hamilton et al. (1977) for a wider discussion of this second approach which has become known as 'illuminative evaluation'.

The two strategies differ in their methodologies. The first is likely to base its findings on formal testing of students and the statistical analysis of achievement tests and attitude questionnaires. The second, on the other hand, is likely to emphasize sensitive observation, discussion and interviewing, and to communicate its findings through revealing analogies and anecdotes. The two strategies differ also in their focus. While the first asks, in essence, 'Have the *goals* been achieved?', the second asks, more openly, '*What* has been achieved?'

While both strategies can provide both objective descriptions and personal judgements, it seems to me that some emphasis on the second is needed if we are aiming to provide the kind of 'full' evaluation story implied by Robert Stake (above). I am sure it is needed if we are aiming to make realistic improvements in the teaching/learning system.

Questions of Procedure

Clearly, there is no one 'standard procedure' for evaluating a course or curriculum. An eclectic, 'applied common-sense' approach can combine elements of the 'agricultural-botany' and the 'illuminative'. The evaluator's 'tool-kit' may contain items borrowed from such diverse traditions as psychometrics, social anthropology, psychotherapy, social survey and market research, broadcasting audience research and programmed learning. We must select and use whatever tools seem appropriate to the peculiarities of the learning situation we are concerned with.

In developing an evaluation procedure we need to consider three main questions:

– What shall we identify and describe?
– By what means?
– Among which students and teachers and others?

I say 'in developing' rather than 'in setting up' because several possible answers to these questions cannot reveal themselves to us until *after* we have begun evaluating. The results we obtain from whatever procedures we develop must then be used to answer the overall, interpretative question: 'So what?'

Questions like the first three above have, as Stratton (1976) points out, an ethical or value component. That is, our answers to them determine the data that will be collected from our evaluation; and this data will be given status and authority that will perforce be denied to *other* data that might have been identified had we answered the questions differently. Hence, different evaluators might well paint different pictures of the 'same' curriculum, and arrive at different answers to the 'so what?' question. Particular care is needed here if we are evaluating *someone else's* curriculum. Otherwise, they will be able to ignore our data, saying 'He asked the wrong questions' or 'He came in too late' or 'He spoke to the wrong people', etc.

Inputs and Outputs as Data

The usefulness of our 'so what?' interpretations will depend to a large extent on how clearly we can identify the 'inputs' to the learning situation – purposes and approaches, materials and facilities, student:teacher relationships, styles of teaching and learning, staff and student capabilities and dispositions, external influences and so on. But if we are to find revealing explanations of what is going on, we must be able to link such 'inputs' (or contributory factors) with the system's 'outputs' – its results, outcomes and side-effects. We shall not be successful in making this connection unless we recognize that the inputs are themselves evolving – e.g., purposes being re-defined, teaching styles being modified, student attitudes changing, as they interact with one another. In effect, the inputs become outputs which, in turn, have the quality of new inputs, engendering a shimmering kaleidoscope of patterns, constantly developing new centres of interest and concern as the course proceeds.

Amid the flux, we are particularly concerned with how the 'inputs' affect the students' learning, and how they and their teachers feel about it. Hence our constant reference to observable behaviour – with what knowledge and skills and attitudes the students seem to be developing and displaying as they engage in the learning process, and with what they and their teachers tell us or show us about their trials and tribulations within the teaching/learning system.

Notice again that we should seek to identify *all* significant outcomes of the learning experience, not just those it was designed to produce. It is a naïve evaluator who asks only whether the project has achieved what it set out to achieve, and neglects to ask what else was achieved (for good or ill) *as well*. After all, students have been known, say, to learn how to solve algebraic equations faultlessly and yet end up hating mathematics, and their teachers, and themselves. More happily, a number of beneficial side-effects may accrue. Charles Silberman (1970), in discussing an evaluative comparison of achievements and attitudes in formal and informal British primary schools (Gardner 1966), notices that:

> Some of the most interesting differences among the two groups in the Gardner study showed up not in the test results themselves but in what the testers had to report about the way children went about taking the tests. A test measuring children's ability to concentrate on a task of their own choice, for example, showed no significant difference in results. But children in the informal schools picked a task 'much more quickly' than did youngsters in the formal schools. More of the 'informal' children chose tasks involving working together with others, and many would stop their own task to help other children, e.g., 'Kenneth stopped work to mix paint for Edward; on seeing the tester look at him he said, "I'm not changing you know — just doing this for him".' The children in the informal schools also volunteered with great frequency to help the tester arrange the materials and clean-up afterwards. And more than twice as many children in the informal schools picked reading as the task on which to be tested. These kinds of differences showed up in a great many tests; in general, children from informal schools were most relaxed, showed less anxiety and more initiative, independence, and self-confidence, and had an easier relationship with their peers and with the testers.

Any evaluation worthy of the name must be alert for unexpected learning outcomes, whether good or bad. They may well tell us more than the expected outcomes about how to modify and *improve* the course or learning experience. (Notice that the evaluation quoted above used observations and anecdotes about revealing incidents as well as the results of formal testing.)

Teachers also may develop unexpected attitudes. For instance, many of our part-time Open University tutors have urged us frequently to revise our courses (even if successful and still up-to-date) to save them the tedium of taking students through the same material year after year. Such evaluation data would be easier to respond to were it not for the fact that equal numbers of tutors ask us to keep the content constant so that, having once come to grips with it, they can concentrate on the students!

We may also need to evaluate the social and political outcomes *outside* the immediate learning situation. For example, is the course or learning experience having an effect on other teachers, other students, the psycho-social 'organizational climate' of the school, on parents, potential employers, politicians or the taxpayer at large? Again, to quote Open University experience, a few years ago we had to recognize, as part of our evaluation of one educational studies course, that strongly worded articles and letters were being written in the educational press, criticizing the allegedly Marxist bias of the course.

The Evaluators

By what means do we describe and measure the inputs and the outputs, the processes and the perceptions in teaching and learning? To begin with, who should do it? Is it fair to expect the designer of the learning experience to be judge and jury in his own case, or is it preferable to have the evaluation carried out by a collegue who is not otherwise involved in the project? One would certainly have qualms, for example, about allowing a 'performance contractor' to do his own evaluation. Perhaps the answer is that the 'insider' and the 'outsider' have complementary roles to play in evaluation. Michael Scriven (1967) points out that:

> . . .evaluation proper must include as an equal partner with the measuring of performance *against* goals, procedures for the evaluation *of* the goals. [My italics]

And here the curriculum developer is well advised to get an opinion from 'uninvolved' colleagues as to the relevance and value of his aims and objectives – and perhaps of the likely appropriateness of his proposed content, strategies and media too. Such a colleague (a 'critical friend') might be asked to comment along the lines of a *checklist* like the following (see Rowntree 1981, for more examples):

- Are the aims and objectives sufficiently explicit?
- Do the aims seem relevant to the needs of the students?
- Do the objectives support the aims?
- Is there scope for students to develop additional aims and objectives?
- Is the content up to date?
- Is it accurate?
- Are there any important omissions?
- Do there seem to be any faults of emphasis?

To compensate for our common human tendency to see what we expect to see and ignore the unexpected, it may be wise when evaluating outcomes also to enlist the participation of an 'univolved' evaluator who can afford to be more sceptical than those who have invested a great deal of emotional capital in the venture. All depends, of course, on the relationships that can be achieved within the teaching team. Teachers in Britain, from primary school to university, are not yet used to exposing their work to the eyes of colleagues, and we must wait to see whether 'team-teaching' and the 'open classroom' help us throw off the mantle of privacy.

Nor should we neglect to enlist the students as evaluators. What have been the best and worst features of the teaching as they have perceived it? What does each individual feel he has got out of it? Of course, we should not go looking for consensus. As Norman MacKenzie et al. (1970) point out:

> There are those who want to be entertained, there are those who want an easy pass, there are those who want to cover as much vocationally relevant material as possible, there are those who want to think deeply, and there are those who want to browse and explore.

J.P. Powell (1981) records the contradictory comments made by students about a teacher-training course, e.g.:

> 'To those who feel free to use their personalities and the personalities of their students as best meets the learning situation, such a course is highly congenial and highly informative. I enjoyed the class and believe I learned a lot from it, including from the other members.'

> 'I entered this course with expectations of coming out with information. . . . Somehow I felt I was being forced to do something I was not prepared for.'

> 'Overall the course was an exciting event for me . . . if it was starting again next Tuesday, or if we were carrying on from where we left off, I would certainly sign up to do it again.'

> 'The methods used for conducting the course were too difficult for me to understand. . . . There was something wrong when a group of students rejected the approach of the teacher while the other group preferred to continue the same approach. The teacher failed to compromise the needs of the two groups.'

Clearly, the 'same' learning experience will mean different things to different students. We become better teachers if we know how those differences arise and how they operate. Richard Miller (1972) and Colin Flood-Page (1974) have produced useful reviews of the extensive literature on using students' contributions to evaluation in higher education. But students of all ages should be encouraged to reflect upon what is happening to them educationally; and the children quoted by Edward Blishen (1969) in *The School That I'd Like* indicates the powerful insights that might be forthcoming.

Student views may be solicited in questionnaires or in discussion (or both). Either of these may be based on an agenda of issues such as that suggested by Will Bridge (1978) in Figure 6.5. Nehari and Bender (1978) describe an inventory which the student can use to indicate 'the extent to which he perceives the course as having had some impact, i.e., to have made a difference and to have produced change and growth'.

Choice of Methods

As for the variety of methods with which to collect information about the outcomes, we discussed several at the end of Chapter 3. We considered paper-and-pencil tests and situational tests, obtrusive and unobtrusive methods, short- and long-term measures, subjective and objective data. We noted that any system of assessment and evaluation is likely to need a mixture of techniques to cover all important possible outcomes – written tests of cognitive objectives; situational observations of psycho-social skills and attitudes; administrative statistics like rate of drop-out or number of students signing up for subsequent runs of the course; questionnaires measuring individual personality development or the psycho-social climate (healthy or otherwise) of an institution. This latter may be revealed by such measures as the high school or college characteristics index (Stern 1970) designed to find out how students really perceive the environment in which they spend so much of their time. Paul Ramsden (1979) reports his use of a questionnaire that shows up how students' feelings about their departments are likely to affect their attitudes to their course work. (See also Parlett 1977.)

Figure 6.5 illustrates the kind of information looked for, and the variety of means used to gather it in the evaluation of the Schools Council's *Science 5–13* project, which produced a number of 'units' of materials (and methods) for primary school science teaching (see Harlen 1975). It is interesting to note that, in order to cancel out the effects of differences in reading ability, the children's tests, including both cognitive and affective items, were based on 8mm film loops rather than on print. First-hand classroom observation by members of the project team played a large part in evaluation, as did reports and questionnaires from the participating teachers. Indeed, from the point of view of suggesting revision to the units, teachers' reports and classroom observations were

Theoretical instruction
Relevance of content to course objectives, and whether the latter were clear.
Adequacy of time allowed, including time for personal study.
Suitability of teaching methods.
Availability of personal guidance.

Clinical experience
Coverage of all necessary skills.
Relation of theory to practice.
Adequacy of preparation for clinical practice.
Opportunity to practise skills thoroughly under supervision.

Assessments
Amount of preparation and information given on the assessment programme.
Conduct of the various assessments.
Availability of counselling and help where assessments show up difficulties.

General evaluation of course (so far)
The course member's judgement of his or her achievement of course objectives.
Suggestions for improvement from course members.

Figure 6.5   An agenda for evaluation discussion (from Bridge 1978)

considered far more helpful than formal test results. This is not necessarily bad news for the proponents of objectives; maybe just a reminder that many of the most important objectives are to be observed informally in classroom activity rather than in paper-and-pencil tests.

Stages of Evaluation

In our discussion of assessment, we noted that, when assessing students, you can concentrate on their performance during the course (continuous

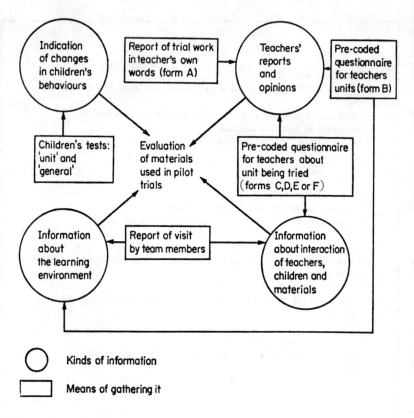

Figure 6.6   Evaluation procedures in *Science 5–13* (after Nisbet 1972)

assessment) or on their performance at the end of it (examination). A similar distinction has been made by Scriven (1967) between evaluation in the process of developing and improving a course or unit of teaching (*formative* evaluation) and evaluation after the course or unit is finished and in regular use, to sum up the results of applying it (*summative* evaluation). (Here, 'formative' approximates to micro-evaluation, and 'summative' to macro-evaluation.) Just as one might wish to regard an examination simply as the final item in a student's continuous assessment, so one might prefer to regard a summative evaluation as a final contribution to formative evaluation.

Scriven admits that it can be difficult in practice to distinguish between formative and summative evaluation; and it would be a rare teacher who felt able to disregard the implications of an authoritative summative evaluation when thinking about improvements to his course. In fact, summative evaluation is often done mainly to help some 'outside' agency make a 'go/no go' decision about the continued funding of a project (see Hawkridge 1970). But it can also be valuable, for example, in helping another teacher or institution decide whether to adopt, or how to adapt, your innovation.

Surely we must assume that *all* evaluation is potentially formative. Then we can perhaps more usefully distinguish between the evaluation of learning experiences, strategies or packages *prior* to incorporating them into a new learning system and the *continuous monitoring* of the system as a whole which cannot begin until the system is put into serious operation. Both types of evaluation are built into the Open University's approach to course design (see Rowntree 1971 and 1976).

The first kind of evaluation can take place in two stages – what I have called *preliminary evaluation* followed by *developmental testing* (see Rowntree 1981).

Preliminary Evaluation

Interestingly enough, evaluation can begin before students ever come into contact with a course; even before the course exists in any coherent sense. I have recently been involved in producing an updating course on drug therapy for family doctors. Before a word of that course appeared on paper, I spent time touring medical in-service training centres with a colleague to discuss with potential students and tutors the kinds of ideas and approaches we had in mind to develop in the course. I was in no doubt that this was a form of evaluation, and certainly the resulting course turned out very differently from the way it might had we not arranged those preliminary consultations.

Various factors may be considered in preliminary evaluation, and a few that interest me are listed below. (Those we covered in the drug therapy discussions are second, third and fifth in the list.) We may wish to evaluate:

- Our curriculum development processes.
- The proposed aims, objectives and content of the course.
- The proposed teaching methods.

- The materials and facilities that might be used by students.
- The institutional setting within which students will be studying our course.

I have already mentioned the possibility of obtaining evaluative comments from 'critical friends'. Such people, persons whose views the course developer(s) can respect, may be subject experts, other teachers, experienced students or educational technologists. To begin with, they may be able to comment usefully on the ways we set about developing our curriculum (the first factor listed above). This can be very necessary if we are working in a team situation (see Crick 1980) where we can get into interpersonal conflicts that may more easily be dissolved with the help of insights from a fairly dispassionate observer.

If we are selecting or preparing learning materials for our course, they can be subjected to some form of *content analysis* (see Burt 1976 and Rowntree 1981) to determine their academic acceptability, e.g., are they true to the nature of the subject and do they avoid undue bias? This can be an important step if we are to avoid wasting time and money testing with students the effectiveness of material that is intellectually dubious. Checklists may be helpful, see page 208.

Critical friends can also be asked to consider the proposed methods, materials and facilities (factors three and four in the list above) and speculate about their *likely* effectiveness. Again, we may wish to provide them with checklists showing the kinds of questions to which we would like them to address themselves (see Rowntree 1981). Undoubtedly, changes will be made as a result of such informed opinion, but it is no substitute for developmental testing.

Before we go on to discuss developmental testing, notice the final item in the list of factors for preliminary evaluation. That is, our course planning will need to take into account the settings in which our students will be working. This takes in more than just the physical aspects of the setting – e.g., are the students studying at home or on campus, or both? it includes also the kinds of social relationships existing among them and between them and teachers, and the 'organizational climate' of their school, college or department. For example, the kind of course that would be 'at home' in a comprehensive school whose climate is akin, say, to that of a small progressive school might not be so in one whose climate more resembled that of an old-fashioned grammar school (see Parlett 1977).

Developmental Testing

However we develop our teaching, we cannot be sure how it will really work with our students until they have begun upon our course or curriculum. In the meantime, we can approach that kind of knowledge by trying out aspects of the teaching on *other* students in developmental testing.

Developmental testing is derived from the 'validation' procedures of programmed learning. It can be applied, however, to many learning experiences other than programmes. In a typical validation, the writer of the programme may begin by sitting with perhaps half a dozen students, one at a time, while they work through an early draft of his programme. He will note whether or not the student is responding appropriately to the questions and exercises within the programme but will interrupt only if the student seems to be having difficulty. He will make a note of any extra oral help he needs to give the student, together with any comments the student may offer as to the difficulty, relevance, interest or effectiveness of various parts of the programme. Having tested the student beforehand to check whether he has already achieved any of the objectives, the writer tests him again afterwards to discover how much has been learned. From observing, interviewing and testing a student, the writer will gain valuable insights into possible improvements to his programme. He may then revise it before trying it out on another student, or he may wait until he has accumulated results from several individuals and then revise the programme before submitting it to a full-scale 'field trial'.

In such a field trial, a sizeable group of students, say twenty or more, will work through the programme under the same kind of conditions in which it is likely to be used in practice. Again, students will be given the criterion test before and after the programme to ascertain what has been learned, and they may well be given attitude questionnaires also. In addition, since the programmer will not this time be sitting with each student, they will be asked to record their responses to the various exercises in the programme and to make a note of any passages they find dull, obscure, difficult, condescending, infuriating or whatever. Having collected and sifted the evidence arising from such a trial, the programmer may dig deeper by interviewing some of the students and teachers who took part, before he revises his programme yet again. Since the purpose of the trial was to determine whether the programme will effectively enable students to reach the objectives under 'normal' conditions, the writer should now know whether he can safely publish the programme or whether it needs a further trial first.

Such evaluation, though often rough-and-ready, is a good deal more relevant than that enjoyed by most teaching materials. Most textbooks, for example, are accepted for publication because they look good to a teacher acting as 'reader' rather than because they have been shown to work well with students. (But then, of course, the decision to buy will usually be taken by teachers rather than students so this procedure makes commercial, if not educational, sense.) Again, few educational films or television programmes are ever tried out on students before being 'published'. All this is a great pity because teaching materials and techniques can usually be improved dramatically by quite simple developmental testing of the kind that originated in programmed learning.

In the USA, much pressure has been exerted on the developers of learning materials to provide evidence of their effectiveness. One form has been applied under the slogan 'LVR' (Learner verification and revision). Since the mid-1970s, many states have laid down criteria by which they expect materials to have been tested before being offered for adoption in the school systems. See Engler (1976) and Thiagarajan (1976) for comments on the pros and cons of this requirement.

It is important to note that Kenneth Komoski (1974), who coined the term LVR, saw it not as a form of developmental testing only, but as a commitment to 'continuing the gathering of data from learners on both effective and affective results of a product's use both *before* and *after* publication, for as long as the product under consideration has "market life"'. In other words, LVR implies also what I call continuous monitoring.

Continuous Monitoring

Developmental testing is not a complete evaluation. Not every element in a learning system can be realistically tested in isolation from the rest of the system. Even with those that can, there may be a limit to how far we can generalize from the results of limited testing. Once the elements are being used 'for real', in an integrated system, in natural conditions and spread over a considerable period of time, by students who are not consciously performing as 'testers', then the results may be quite different from those in the 'clean' developmental testing situation, no matter how closely we tried to simulate 'realistic' conditions. Indeed, it may be difficult even to sustain an adequate level of effort from students who are not taking the course 'for real'. (See Henderson et al. 1980.) The system as a whole is far more complex than the sum of its parts, for the parts interact in unexpected ways. For this reason we need 'continuous monitoring' of cause and effect while the course is in progress, and perhaps follow-up of long-term effects afterwards. (Even with such monitoring, however, it can be difficult to sort out the individual effects of the various components in a multi-media system. See Bates 1972 for an analysis of evaluation problems in the Open University.)

Continuous monitoring should systematically collect and interpret feedback from a wide variety of sources, inside and outside the immediate teaching/learning situation. What, for example, can we learn from the in-jokes, local jargon, and running catch-phrases that course-members develop by way of asserting their 'we-ness' over the weeks? What do we learn from the remarks of teachers in other subjects or departments about the way they view our students (and our teaching)? The monitoring should persist throughout the 'life' of a course or curriculum, continuously providing information whereby it may be improved, diversified, enriched and, in the fullness of time perhaps, declared redundant.

In continuous monitoring, I distinguish between *casual evaluation* (simply noticing things of interest relating to the course) and *deliberate evaluation* (arranging for data to be collected at intervals through questionnaires, formal assessment, interviewing, discussions, etc.). Both approaches yield worthwhile insights and complement one another in building up a picture of how the course is progressing. In Rowntree (1981) I recommend the keeping of a course *log book*, which sits happily with the idea of the course as a voyage (of discovery, naturally) whose story is worth recording. In this log book you might reckon to write down, at no more than weekly intervals, the emerging strengths, weaknesses and unexpected features of the course or curriculum, and what you are doing about them.

Some Problems and Pitfalls

As may already have become apparent, the enterprise of evaluation is not without its difficulties, both conceptual and practical. Two areas, in particular, in which these arise concern where to look for data and how to interpret it once it has been collected. The first of these we may look on as question of appropriate sampling.

Problems of Sampling

Of course, in deciding what to look for in an evaluation, and how to look for it, we must also decide *where* to look for it – among which students, teachers and others? Choosing a suitable sample is often a problem when evaluating. No matter which students you expose to the learning experience they will be merely a sample of all the students who could or will be exposed to it. How far can the responses of such a sample help us judge the appropriateness of the 'experience' for other students (different in many ways) who will follow? How *representative* is our sample? A crucial question this, for if different teachers give different answers they are liable to attach different interpretations to any evaluation data that come from the sample.

In choosing a sample to help in developmental testing, we need students who are at the same stage of learning as the 'target population' – the students for whom the experience is eventually intended. Perhaps we need to find students who have attained all the prerequisites but none of the intended objectives. However, if the target population is likely to be of mixed attainment, then the *mixture* may need to be replicated in the sample. Clearly, we must know a great deal about the students we are working with – not just their attainments but also their personalities, learning styles, socio-economic backgrounds, motivations and so on – for all these should, ideally, be similar in both sample and target population. In the early days of programmed learning, often only the brighter, faster students were offered as 'guinea pigs', on the grounds that they would come to least harm! Naturally, if our sample is super-normally qualified they are likely to give an over-optimistic prediction of our teaching effectiveness – because they will have been able to surmount the obstacles we unwittingly put in their way.

When monitoring a course in progress, we may be able to collect information from *all* the students involved. But if the numbers are large, or if we wish to pursue an in-depth investigation of some particular problem, we may again be faced with choosing a sample representative of the students as a whole. And if the investigation lasts some time, we may have the further problem of maintaining the representativeness of the sample, for students may be continually dropping out of it, and some types of student more frequently than others.

This problem intensifies if we wish to follow up the sample some time after our students have left us. Belasco and Trice (1969) describe how even an elaborate 'detective network' failed to get full information on more than 55 percent of former patients two years after undergoing therapy for alcoholism. They therefore had to cope with urgent questions as to whether the 'traceability' of a patient was a function of his sobriety and stability and whether behaviours observed in the now reduced sample might not be untypical of the group as a whole. Generally speaking, however, educational researchers and evaluators have not paid much attention to discovering just what students retain from education once their schooling is over (see Henrysson and Franke-Wikberg 1979).

Even when the sample contains all our students, we are still considering but a sample of all their potential responses. No matter how many tests and questionnaires we apply, no matter how frequent our observing and interviewing, we cannot pretend to be aware of the full potentiality of response in each student. How much do we know of how such students might respond at other times or in other circumstances? Let alone of how other students, even if broadly similar, might respond?

We need to be always sceptical about the typicality of our sample and the confidence with which we can generalize from it. This applies equally whether we are sampling among students, teachers, parents, employers or whoever. Without such scepticism, we can be led astray by vociferous but unrepresentative feedback.

We may also need to consider a sample from *outside* our learning system. For instance, evaluation may well indicate that students exposed to our learning experience do, indeed, learn. But can we be sure that they have learned *from* the experience? Perhaps they have learned from some outside experience or have simply 'matured'? And even if we are sure they have learned from the experience we designed, is it not possible that they might have learned even more from some *alternative* experience?

Comparison with alternatives is implicit in any evaluation, and often needs to be made explicit. If we are fully to judge the relative effectiveness of our curriculum, we might need to identify a 'control' group following some other curriculum (or none at all) whose development you could compare with that of your 'experimental' group. An ethical problem can arise here if the only way of getting a comparable control group is to split the available students into two groups and deprive one of what we believe to be a valuable educational experience. Of course if this control group can be exposed to the experience later on, then the problem is eased; otherwise, we may prefer to make do with an outside control group, who would not have been exposed to the learning experience anyway, even if they are less comparable. Usually our 'control group' data will be what we happen to remember of past students whom we have taught in some other way.

Statistics, Averages and Individuals

In analysing evaluation data, how much quantification and statistical work is called for? The 'number-crunching' approach may go all the way from simple counting (e.g., how many students attained each objective) to complex statisticulation like factor analysis (e.g., to pin down the underlying factors responsible for intricate relationships assumed to exist among inputs and outputs in the learning system). Undoubtedly, many educators feel that measurement and statistics are already over-emphasized in evaluation. Some would suggest that if a relationship is not obvious without high-level statistical computation it is probably not worth bothering about. Such sceptics are scornful, for instance, of the statisticians who pronounce the gain in learning of a group of students to be 'statistically significant' (because it is too big to have occurred by chance) when it is clearly insignificant educationally (because it is too meagre to be worth the time and trouble spent acquiring it).

The role of quantification and statistics is now far from certain, even in such apparently simple matters as comparing the gains in learning made by different groups of students. The present state of the once-proud psychometric art was heralded in the title of a paper by Martyn Roebuck (1971): *Floundering Among Measurements in Educational Technology*. Certainly, the qualitative and the quantitative approaches to evaluation tend to attract different clienteles. David Hawkridge (1970) writes of a running battle between the 'intuitive' and the 'analytic' evaluators which is at its fiercest around the choice of analysis techniques. The most we can say at present is that we had better encourage the retention, and hopefully the complementary interaction, of both approaches until we all know considerably more about what we are doing in education.

One special warning. In evaluating the effects of a learning experience on a large number of students, we must not lose sight of the diversity of effect among *individuals*. Of course we will wish to cumulate results to get a general picture. How many students felt this way and how many that? What percentage attained each of the objectives? What was the average amount of learning? Has this group gained more or that? Which of these two treatments did students prefer? But we also want to know which individuals got what out of the experience and why. Thus, it might appear, from a comparison of the 'average' amount learned, that a class taught by 'discovery' methods gained no more from the experience than a similar class taught by straight exposition. On comparison of individual students, however, it could turn out, for example, that 'confident' children had done far better in the 'discovery' group than in the 'exposition' group, but 'anxious' children had done far better in the 'exposition' group. Thus, while group averages might suggest that there was nothing to choose between the two methods, a closer look at individuals suggests that the two methods each have advantages for different kinds of children.

A classic illustration of the dangers that lie in wait for the unwary consumer of group statistics is given by George Miller (1972) in his report of a US Army project of 1945 designed to persuade soldiers that the war with Japan would be long and difficult. Since there was some dispute as to whether people are more convinced by hearing both sides of an argument or one side only, two parallel radio programmes were made – one presented only the reasons for expecting a long war while the other presented arguments on the opposite side as well. A number of soldiers were asked several questions about the war, including: 'What is your guess as to how long it will take us to beat Japan after Germany's defeat?' They were then split into three groups, one acting as the 'control' group while each of the other two groups listened to one or other of the two radio programmes.

Afterwards, they were all questioned again. Although the soldiers in the control group showed no appreciable shift in their opinions as to how long the war would last, both groups who had listened to the radio programmes showed a significant shift in opinion – but both in the same direction and to the same degree. In both groups, whether they had heard the one-sided programme or the two-sided one, the percentage of soldiers believing the war would last more than eighteen months increased from 37 to 59 percent. Does this mean that individuals are equally persuaded whether they hear a fair presentation or a biased one? Not quite. The experimenters probed beneath the surface and compared the educational levels attained by the soldiers in the groups. At once it became clear that the persuasiveness of the two-sided programme was due to a big shift in the opinions of students who had graduated from high school and a relatively small shift among non-graduates; conversely, the equal overall persuasiveness of the one-sided programme was due to a big shift among non-graduates and a relatively small one among graduates. In short, the better-educated soldier tended to be more impressed by a fair-minded argument and his less educated colleague by a biased argument. As happens so often, 'on the average' comparisons between mixed groups had been masking real differences between individuals.

This masking effect of averages possibly accounts for the findings of writers like Stephens (1967) who reviewed many evaluations of educational variables – e.g., school attendance, independent study and correspondence courses, educational television, team-teaching, ability grouping, discussion *v*. lecture, programmed instruction, amount of time spent in study, progressivism *v*. traditionalism and so on – and suggested that none of them seemed to make consistent and significant differences to the effectiveness of learning. Of course, this conclusion is highly debatable. Neal Gross et al. (1971), for instance, argue that many promising innovations are reported as ineffective when it would be fairer to say that they had never been properly implemented. (See also my comments on Dubin and Taveggia (1968), on page 151 for the additional possibility that methods have not been properly *evaluated*.) Stephens explains his findings by invoking the theory of 'spontaneous schooling' – briefly that perhaps 95 percent of a student's potential growth is determined by long standing and powerful psycho-social factors in the backgrounds of both student and teacher, leaving educational innovations no room to produce any but minor changes. But the theory ignores the possibility that a new method may appear no better *overall* than other methods for the reason that it has been far better for some students and far worse for others. It also ignores the fact that a method may achieve similar 'equal effectiveness' overall by being better on some objectives and worse on others.

What we need to ask in evaluation is not only, how much have students learned from such and such an experience?, but also, how do the processes and results of learning vary from student to student? The ideal of evaluation is not the best method for all but the best method for each.

How far you push your evaluation analysis will largely depend on your need, ability and willingness to utilize the results. If your course or learning experience turns out to be, let's say, only '50 percent effective' (by whatever quantitative or qualitative criteria you are using), then, clearly, much analysis and improvement is needed. And even if the course or experience is '100 percent effective'(!), you may still be able to increase its efficiency by modifying it so that it requires less time and resources to achieve the same objectives. And what if the course or experience were, say, 90 percent effective? To raise its effectiveness to 100 or even 95 percent might well take more effort and resources than would be required to turn the 50 percent course into a 90 percent course. Beyond a certain point of perfection, the further efforts even of educational technology may face diminishing marginal returns – or even *reduce* the overall effectiveness due to some unforeseen link-up in the system. So should you spend your time seeking greater perfection, or would it be better spent producing another 90 percent effective course? Clearly there is no ready answer to this. The relative cost-benefits of the two lines of action can be determined only in the light of local priorities. How much is the learning worth?

From Evaluation to Improvement

Now for the 'so what?' of evaluation. Evaluation helps us to understand and make sense of what is going on in the teaching/learning system. As a result we should be better able to sustain and develop the students' learning and improve our teaching. Evaluation tells us what has worked and what has not. It tells us how students are, in their different ways, coping or failing to cope. It may even suggest why. Although we have no better theory for re-designing courses than we have for designing them in the first place, at least we do now have this improved empirical picture of what actually happens once students have begun to grapple with the learning experience.

Undeniably, there is a large subjective element in evaluation, from deciding on appropriate criteria to weighing up the relative importance of conflicting pieces of feedback. Nevertheless, many teachers have found that evaluation provides a 'distancing' stimulus whereby they can re-examine their teaching as if through someone else's eyes, and thereby see the solecisms and violations of pedagogy that had somehow escaped all their preliminary scrutinies.

What Kinds of Improvement?

Many different kinds of improvement may be made at different stages of evaluation. Some may take place before the teaching strategy is finalized, as a result of preliminary evaluation. Some may take place during developmental testing. Some may take place once the course is under way, as a result of continuous monitoring. Yet others, the product of summative evaluation, may not be possible until students have worked right through the course or a particular module of it. Thus, *some* improvements will benefit future students only, or perhaps the present students on a later section of the course, rather than the present students on the section of the course that has just been evaluated.

The possible improvements are as varied and as difficult to categorize as the materials, strategies and courses being evaluated. Quite simple evaluation exercises may suggest, for example, that some objectives have to be modified or abandoned because the related parts of the course are taking up a disproportionate amount of the students' time. Perhaps some sections of the teaching material are weak in argument or insufficiently supported by evidence. Perhaps students turn out to be weaker in some prerequisite skills than was expected, and 'remedial' or 'preparatory' experiences need to be designed. Perhaps some objectives are not being attained because a vital step has been omitted from the learning sequence or because the sequence contradicts some underlying hierarchy. Perhaps the teaching strategy needs to be revised so as to tie in better with the objectives (especially in the affective domain). Perhaps the media chosen were sometimes inappropriate or mishandled. Perhaps more illustrative examples, or practice opportunities, or revision, or knowledge of results was needed. Perhaps the system did not take enough account of students' individual differences. Perhaps the system in some ways demanded too much of the administrators and over-loaded the organization. Perhaps students are developing strong antipathies to certain parts of the course, or to the teacher, or to one another, and these are showing up as 'discipline problems'. Perhaps some of the local community have been offended by aspects of the teaching and will impede further developments unless we find a way of influencing or mobilizing public opinion. In the fourth phase of the educational technology approach, the designer of learning experiences must retrace the kind of thinking he did in the first and second phases – armed this time with his own knowledge of results (see Figure 1.1, page 19).

Consider an actual example of the kind of improvement that can result from thorough evaluation. Tyler (1971) describes how the evaluation of a course based on contemporary social problems revealed, by the end of the first year:

> . . . that the students had acquired a great deal more information about these contemporary problems, that they had shifted their attitudes slightly in the direction of greater social and less selfish attitudes, but that their attitudes were much more confused and inconsistent than before, that they

had not gained any skill in analysing social problems, and that their ability to interpret social data was worse because the students were drawing more unwarranted conclusions than before.

Having analysed all available data, the teachers decided that the balance of the course was wrong, too much ground having been covered with too little time devoted to critical analysis, interpretation and application. The course was then revised in time for its second 'run'. The number of social problems dealt with was reduced from twenty-one to seven, and the reading required was cut by more than half. This left more time free for thinking and arguing about the material presented. Then, at the end of the second year, it was found that:

> . . . although the students had not gained quite so much in the range of information acquired, they had gained greater consistency in social attitudes, had gained greater skill in analysing social problems, and had become able to draw better generalizations from the data presented to them.

More examples of how evaluation through student feedback has led to changes in course materials and teaching methods are discussed at length in Nathenson and Henderson (1980). By and large, we may say that the more students, and the more typical the students, who have been through our course the more confident we can be about making major changes to it. Minor changes, e.g., those that are reversible while the course is in progress, can be made almost on a hunch with little risk. Major changes, however, unless they are based on wide and representative evaluation may turn out to be premature and counter-productive. Such big 'improvements' as changing the basis of the assessment system or replacing the subject-matter content, may best be implemented gradually over a number of cycles of the course.

Evaluating Other People's Innovations

So far we have assumed that you are evaluating your own or a colleague's teaching/learning system. But few individual teachers or even institutions are rich enough in time, talent and resources to develop all the learning materials their students need. Perhaps we should all be taking more seriously the possibility of our drawing upon strategies, materials and systems developed by other teachers elsewhere. Until recently, no doubt, most of us have exhibited the 'not-invented-here syndrome' – unless we designed the teaching ourselves, it cannot possibly be appropriate to *our* students. However, the recent and continuing cuts in educational spending may make this academic isolationism a luxury we can no longer afford. As James (1979) says, in considering the likely impact of micro-electronics on education:

> The continuously increasing people-costs involved in the production of good teaching material will far outweigh the savings due to the employment of micro-electronics unless there can be very extensive communal use of material. The problem is political and personal rather than technical.

So how can we find out about and appraise potentially useable strategies, materials and systems developed by other people elsewhere? The search for new possibilities in teaching should be continuous. We will pursue it through professional meetings and the literature, through research reports, publishers' and manufacturers' catalogues, museum and library lists and through the grapevine of informal personal contact which often anticipates all other sources. On hearing of a promising innovation we will ask after its objectives, its methods and its outcomes. Sometimes (especially if a summative evaluation has already been carried out) we will receive adequate information on all three aspects, sometimes not. Before deciding whether to adopt (or adapt) the innovation, we may wish to visit some institutions using it and carry out our own interviews and observations. Henry Brickell (1969) offers a useful approach to appraising other people's innovations, and from it we can derive twelve key questions to be asked about any new materials, approach or curriculum which we are thinking of adopting or adapting to our needs:

– *How suitable?*	Are its objectives, methods and outcomes appropriate to our students?
– *How effective?*	Does it achieve satisfactory results?
– *How big?*	How much time, staff and resources does it need? How many subjects? What range of students?
– *How complete?*	Does it need extra supporting material?
– *How complex?*	Is it difficult for teachers and students to work with?
– *How flexible?*	Is there room for innovation and adaptation by teachers and students?
– *How different?*	Is it sufficiently distinct from other approaches in outcome, method, cost, or whatever?

– *How repeatable?*	Are there any special factors (e.g., unusual teachers or local resources) to hinder repetition elsewhere?
– *How compatible?*	Would it interfere or fit in with the rest of the existing system?
– *How ready?*	Can it be started this week/term/year, etc.?
– *How 'samplable'?*	Could we give it a trial run and abandon it if unsuccessful? Or would the decision commit us for some considerable time ahead (e.g., a computer system)?
– *How expensive?*	What are the initial installation and running costs?

Brickell's questions might help us decide whether, or to what extent, we might take up someone else's teaching innovation. The more suitable, effective, complete, flexible, different, repeatable, compatible, ready and 'samplable' it is (and the less big, complex and expensive), the easier it will be for us to adopt or adapt. Jean Ruddock (1980) offers a set of questions that has some overlap with Brickell's, but puts more emphasis on the demands that will be made on teachers and students in coming to terms with the innovation once the decision to use it has been made:

- How would one know if one had grasped the essence of the new ideas? (That is, how would one know if one were 'doing' the innovation properly?)
- What skills, attitudes or patterns of behaviour do teachers *and* pupils need to develop in order to proceed with the new approach?
- How have other teachers and pupils acquired these new skills, attitudes or patterns of behaviour?
- Were there any special resources or organizational arrangements that were essential to the introduction of the new approach?
- What problems did the teachers encounter?
- What were the apparent pay-offs for teachers, pupils and others?
- What were the apparent costs (in human terms as well as in terms of resources) of introducing the new approach?
- What issues or questions emerge that might merit further research?

So, questions such as we have looked at in this section can help us evaluate an innovation and decide whether to take it up and, if so, how.

Once taken up and implemented, of course, it will need to be subjected to the same kind of evaluation procedures we considered earlier in the chapter. All in all, the evaluative approach I have suggested is in line with the suggestion of Stenhouse (1975) that the teacher might think of himself as a *researcher* in his own classroom.

The Critical Ingredient in Educational Technology

There has not been space in this book to do more than hint at the many contentions and unsolved problems that surround evaluation. What seems certain is that evaluation will grow in importance in the years ahead and that its problems will intensify – especially since we now increasingly question the *aims* and *ideologies* as well as the effectiveness of educational systems. We no longer succumb quite so amenably to the technological fallacy: assuming that because something is technically feasible, or even effective in practice, it must also be desirable. More and more we are likely to need the kind of *supra*-evaluation applied, after the event, to the Apollo space programme. Granted that a system has been splendidly effective, and even efficient in terms of its use of resources, was it worth doing at all and would the resources have been employed better elsewhere? As Fred Wilhelms (1967) points out:

> It is one thing for a history teacher to organize a continuing feedback to guide him in teaching his class. It may take quite a different order of evaluation to tell whether his history teaching would be more effective if he injected more economic and anthropological content into it. It may require still something more to guide a school's relative investment in the social studies as against the sciences and the humanities. . . . The most important educational choices often involve whole blocks of curriculum, or programs differing in *kind* rather than in detail; if evaluation is to live up to its responsibilities, it must provide data for this order of choices too.

The evaluation of aims and ideologies must be a task for philosophers and social critics as much as for teachers and educational technologists. It is one that will be happily shared, vigorously if sporadically, by parents, employers, politicians, women's rights groups, ethnic minorities, the mass media. . . and just about anyone who believes education to be capable of achieving something worthwhile that is not being achieved at present. The continuing interest in what I called 'educational pathology' (see page 4), and the 'alternative' perspectives offered by such periodicals as *Libertarian Education, Radical Education* and *Hard Cheese*, are indications that supra-evaluation has taken its place alongside micro-evaluation and macro-evaluation.

In fact, the three levels of evaluation must be carried out in parallel in any evolving educational system. Each is weaker if unaccompanied by the others. Unless aims and objectives, inputs and outputs and the relationships between them all are constantly under critical review, even the most high-minded systems can break down and fail to deliver, while even the most smoothly running can become irrelevant and dangerous.

I have come to see evaluation as the critical ingredient (no pun intended!) in educational technology. That is, I believe it to be the unifying concept, the essential pursuit that will remain, like the smile of the vanished Cheshire Cat, when so many of our other less unique concerns have faded into relative insignificance.

Many people still assume that *prescription* is the heart of the matter in educational technology – deciding how to design an episode of learning, starting from an analysis of aims and objectives and going on to apply the appropriate principles of learning. While such activity is still to be engaged in by educational technologists, we may do well to query the uniqueness of our contribution thereto. After all, what is the source of our insights, our flashes of illumination, our bright ideas for new ways to reach the students? Perhaps they come not from that part of oneself that one calls the educational technologist but rather from some other, older part over which one has less conscious control – from what Albert Einstein, seeking to identify the source of scientific knowledge, recognized as 'intuition, resting on sympathetic understanding of experience'. Robert Pirsig (1975) follows Einstein in pointing out that there is nothing in scientific method to account for the genesis of scientific hypothesis. The contribution of scientific method is to *evaluate* the hypotheses which have arisen outside of it.

So it may be with educational technology. It contains nothing that would enable us all to generate identical good ideas about how and what to teach in a specific situation. But once we have thought of a few possibilities, through 'intuition, resting on sympathetic understanding of experience' (including our individual experiences of educational technology), it does enable us to describe and explain and, above all, to evaluate their potentialities and effects. In the words of Karl Popper (1972), talking of scientific knowledge: 'Our starting-point is common sense, and our great instrument for progress is criticism.'

Let me illustrate by describing a piece of teaching I saw at an Open University summer school. Imagine a tutor meeting his class of twenty students for the first time. His initial objective is that they will have 'broken the ice' and be all on first-name terms by the end of the hour. *How* is he to relax them? *How* is he to teach each student twenty other names? (No, not transcendental meditation followed by programmed learning!) What he does is to say his own name and then get the student on his right – they are all sitting in a rough circle – to say first the tutor's name and then the student's own name. The next student round to his right is now asked to name the tutor, then the student on his left, then himself. The next student names the tutor, each of the students on his left, in order, then himself. And so the naming goes around the circle, eased on its way by considerable jollity and growing mutual supportiveness among the students, until the twentieth student is (yes, *is*) able to name all the others – and so is everyone else in the circle. A brilliant piece of instructional design, but one owing absolutely nothing to educational technology. Of course, we can explain it – multiple-discrimination, backward chaining, the encouragement of a group-identity by means of a shared initiation ceremony, and so on; and we can evaluate it – establishing whether or not students really are attaching names to people and not just to positions in a room, whether it lasts beyond the coffee-break, whether students have been turned on or off by the experience; but we cannot invent it. Not *as* educational technologists, anyway.

So what? you may say. Only that, when it comes to educational design, we may be no more productive of insights than any other good teacher. We have our general principles, of course, derived from research. But we also know how often the context over-rides the general principle. Advance organizers may sometimes work and sometimes not, but how do we decide whether to use what kind here and now? Small steps in learning may be a good thing and give the pupil confidence to move forward – but not if they bore him and fail to offer a satisfactory challenge. Immediate knowledge of results has a lot to recommend it – but so does a delay long enough to let the student develop a new perspective on his response (an essay, for instance). General principles may be useful in describing teaching in general but become problematical when designing teaching in particular. There we are thrown back, to a large extent, on our native wit or on our experience (if sufficiently evaluative) of how various teaching purposes and ploys have worked out in comparable situations in the past.

Hence the inevitability of evaluation as the basic, unifying activity in which all those calling themselves educational technologists can join together. Not only is it essential to the enterprise, but there are styles to suit all proclivities. The armchair speculator can evaluate the aims and ideologies underlying the curriculum in question. The anthropologically minded can analyse his participant observations of human interactions in course teams and feed back his interpretations so that all are aware of the forces pulling and pushing at their decisions. The empathetic 'student's friend' can vet the course materials in advance and anticipate snags the students are likely to encounter when working with them. Others can set about finding out what seems to happen when the teaching actually takes place: the positivist empiricist relying on his questionnaires and test-results and other archival data; the subjectivistic phenomenologist getting out among students and tutors to establish what it is like to be learning and teaching in the system we have created. All parties contribute their descriptions and interpretations, identifying the good, the bad and the peculiar. We can see where the teaching needs to be improved and, on the basis of the *specific* experience, not just general principles, we may see ways of improving it that would not otherwise have occurred to us. It is the fundamental, prior commitment to such evaluation and improvement that distinguishes the educational technologist (whether he accepts that appellation or not) from other participants in the processes of teaching and learning.

Questions on Chapter 6

1 If a colleague said to you: 'How else can you evaluate your teaching except by checking how much your students have learned?', what would you say to him?

2 What considerations would lead you to evaluate your own teaching? For whose benefit might you do so? What would you hope might result from such evaluation?

3 Which aspects of your own teaching do you think might benefit from evaluation by a sympathetic but critical colleague? What problems would you see in carrying out such evaluation?

4 Think of a particular course and describe how it might be evaluated. What methods would be used? What kinds of questions would be asked? Of whom? What forms of data might be collected? How might it be analysed? What problems would you foresee?

5 How might 'preliminary evaluation' have been used on the course

you have in mind (or how might it yet be used if the course is still in the planning stage)? If you see no use for it, why not?

6   What kinds of improvement might you expect to see made to your course as a result of evaluation? If you already have experience of evaluating a course, recall some of the improvements that were made (if any) as a result. Did any of these 'improvements' turn out to be unproductive or even counter-productive? Why?

7   Which set of questions, Bricknell's or Ruddock's (pages 226–227) would *you* find most useful in evaluating other people's innovations? Why? What questions of your own would you like to add to your chosen list?

8   To what extent do you agree with the author that evaluation (rather than, say, objectives) is the essence of educational technology? If you disagree, what would you suggest is the critical ingredient? How would you justify this?

9   What do you see as the significance for evaluation of the quotation from Nadine Gordimer at the beginning of the chapter?

CHAPTER 7

PUTTING EDUCATIONAL TECHNOLOGY
TO WORK

Our little systems have their day;
They have their day and cease to be.
                              Alfred Lord Tennyson

In this final chapter, we must consider how educational technology can
be put into operation and spread more widely. Here, perhaps, we should
distinguish between the *processes* of educational technology (the four
phases) and the *products* (curriculum innovations). It is probably fair to
say that we shall not achieve widespread and effective adoption of the
products of educational technology unless we aim, at the same time, to
gain widespread adoption of the processes by which they were produced.
In short, if teachers are to avoid becoming mere technicians applying
other people's curriculum innovations, they will need sufficient
educational technology skills to play an active and *critical* role in
curriculum innovation.

Implementing Innovation in Education

With most innovations it is necessary to win the goodwill and active
involvement of other people. As an individual teacher, you may be able
to introduce, say, programmed learning materials, simulation games or
discovery methods, without interfering too much with colleagues' work.
But if you want to adopt, say, team-teaching or a new set of curriculum
objectives, you will need the cooperation of at least some of your
colleagues. If you want to bring in the initial teaching alphabet or to
de-stream, then the whole school has to agree. An innovation like comprehensivization must be planned by the local education authority; while
the decision to lengthen or shorten the period of compulsory schooling
can only be taken at national level.

In fact, there are few significant innovations, however seemingly self-
contained, that do not have knock-on effects somewhere else in the

system – even if it is only the teacher in the next room banging on the dividing wall because he thinks your class is getting too excited. At whatever level the innovation is introduced – class, department, school, LEA, nation – it may be necessary to gain the approval of people at a 'higher' level just as it is necessary to win the support of those at 'lower' levels. Indeed, it often seems reasonable to regard the school or college, rather than the individual teacher, as the tactical unit for innovation. The headteacher or principal then assumes a key role as the facilitator of change (see Hoyle 1972, Macdonald and Ruddock 1972). 'Community educators' like Eric Midwinter (1972) might focus on the local community rather than on the school, but would still see the headteacher as a cardinal facilitator of change in the locality. Then again, the need to coordinate action and support at several levels may sometimes best be met by a 'change agent' from right outside the local system. Hence, the development in the 1960s and 70s of agencies like the Schools Council, the Nuffield Foundation and the Council for Educational Technology, all working for deliberate and continuous change in curriculum.

Barriers to Innovation

Getting an educational innovation accepted is not easy, especially if you are in a hurry. The much-admired child-centred practices of British primary education, for example, have evolved over the last forty years (though the ideas on which they are based are at least a century old) and are still not totally diffused throughout all primary schools (see Kogan 1971 and Galton et al. 1980). Likewise, in the USA, John Goodlad (1977) embarked upon a study of 158 classrooms in 67 elementary (primary) schools in order to check out 'the prevailing assumptions that sweeping curricular, organizational, and instructional changes had occurred during the preceding decade'. However, he reports:

> This was not what we found: the much-touted reforms appear to have been non-events, at least in our sample. Textbooks predominated as the medium of instruction; telling and questioning, usually in total class groups, constituted the prevailing teaching method; the inquiry or discovery approach to learning was seldom evident; there was little individualization of instruction; and an astonishing amount of time was taken up in control, classroom routines, and what appeared to be scarcely more than busy-work.

Paul Mort (1964), writing of the diffusion of innovation in US education, suggested that half a century had tended to elapse between the identification of an educational need and the development of an acceptable way of meeting that need. Diffusion of the innovation among 3 percent of schools then took fifteen more years, followed by twenty years of rapid diffusion reaching most but not all of the remaining schools. Mort's wise words carry a warning for us all:

> . . . knowledge of the slowness of spread of an innovation – among the teachers in a school, among the schools in a school system and from school system to school system – is essential. Lack of such knowledge has resulted in the abandonment of many good innovations before they had a chance to put down roots.

Our schools, colleges and universities are constitutionally resistant to change. 'Yes, but . . .' is the automatic response to would-be innovators. In view of the hordes of unvalidated fads and fancies with which education is constantly assailed, this stance has some survival value. It only becomes deplorable when the instinct for self-preservation swamps the need for self-renewal. Different participants, e.g., the 'old guard' *v.* the 'young turks', will, of course, differ in their views as to whether or not this is happening in their particular institution.

Clearly, as I suggested at the end of Chapter 6, some innovations 'take' more easily than others. In general, the less disruptive it is to ongoing practices and teacher attitudes, the more chance an innovation has of being adopted. Thus, new teaching aids are more readily adopted than new learning materials which in turn are more acceptable than new curriculum purposes. All of these are more easily adopted than new organizational structures, and perhaps new roles and personal relationships (involving attitude shifts on the part of teachers) are most difficult of all to implement. In the short term, for instance, it is easier to mechanize a classroom than to democratize it.

Admittedly, the time may not appear ripe at present for widespread innovation in education. Teachers are still reeling, in the UK at least, from the combined effects of falling numbers of pupils in school (due to the passing of the 1960s' 'bulge' in the birth-rate) and the stringent cut-backs in educational expenditure. With budgets being pruned, with some educational services being cut out altogether (e.g., peripatetic music teaching), and with the ever-present possibility of being made redundant, the morale of the teaching profession is at a low ebb. Why should individuals put their careers (or more basically their job-security) at risk by forsaking traditional practices in order to pursue a new ideal to which their colleagues and the institutional hierarchy may, at least initially, be none too sympathetic?

Yet, paradoxically, many such beleaguered teachers see their best chance, both of surviving personally and of regalvanizing their institution, as lying in their capacity for identifying new educational purposes and of inventing or adopting new ways of accomplishing them. A case in point here might be the recognition by many UK further education colleges that student numbers can be increased by catering for people who have not traditionally enrolled as students; hence the spreading adoption of 'open learning' systems (Coffey 1978, Noble 1980) and the support for an 'Open Tech' system (MSC 1981) to encourage colleges in Open University-style 'distance teaching'.

However, getting itself invented or adopted is but the first hazardous stage in the life of an innovation. The innovation will be a failure unless it then becomes institutionalized. Kurt Lewin (1958) makes the point quite vividly when he identifies three periods in the implementation of an innovation: unfreezing, changing and refreezing. During the 'unfreezing' period, previous practices are being softened up and people are getting prepared for a change. During the 'changing' period, they have set aside the old ways and are trying out the new. During 'refreezing', the new ways harden into a new, enduring system. It is during this latter period that the innovation will be most at risk. If enthusiasms fade and people slip back into the comfortable old ways, then refreezing may take place *without* incorporating the innovation.

Too often, innovations have started well, like the Dalton Plan of the 1920s (see Parkhurst 1922), and yet have failed to get institutionalized. Ron Wastnedge (1972), in answering the plaintive question: 'Whatever happened to Nuffield Junior Science?', reveals how an apparently effective project – aimed at introducing a Froebelian approach to science learning in primary school – just fizzled out because the project's funding ended and teachers were left without the support they still needed. This has not been the only project where the innovator, whether an individual teacher or some local or national team, has failed to ensure sufficient resources, motivational or material, to see things through to institutionalization.

But, of course, some innovations are doomed long before refreezing sets in. Neal, Gross, *et al* (1971), in their well-documented analysis of an unsuccessful attempt to introduce 'Leicestershire' methods into a US primary school, identify five barriers to implementation:

- The teachers' lack of clarity about the innovation.
- Their lack of the kinds of skills and knowledge needed to conform to the new role model.
- The unavailability of required instructional materials.
- The incompatibility of organizational arrangements with the innovation.
- Loss of staff motivation.

They lay most of the blame for this on the implementation strategy used by the director of the project. Apparently, he failed to anticipate teachers' difficulties or to recognize and cope with them as they arose during the period of attempted change. Such factors are undoubtedly responsible for many of the early deaths recorded in the literature of would-be innovation. Interestingly, the authors make no comment on the fact that evaluation of the success of the innovation came a mere six months after the participants were first persuaded to undertake it. Perhaps Paul Mort's comment applies here?

Planning for Change

Successful implementation of innovations seems to depend on what has been called *planned organizational change* (see Bennis, *et al.* 1968, Havelock 1970, Hoyle 1970). Various different strategies have been suggested to accomplish such change. Clearly, some kind of 'systems approach' is essential, since any failure to comprehend in its fullness the social system inside which the potential innovators presently play out their roles and relationships is likely to result in what Eric Hoyle likens to 'tissue rejection'. According to Champness and Young (1980), would-be innovators in educational technology are often insufficiently attentive to the social interactions and personal relationships that will determine whether a new medium or system succeeds or fails. In fact, since innovation essentially calls for *changes in behaviour* among the participants, it represents a learning problem in its own right. Perhaps, therefore, we can usefully apply something of the approach we have been developing in this book. Can we teach people to innovate?

To begin with, what objectives – in terms of new knowledge, skills and attitudes – are required of the potential innovators? (See page 227 for the list of questions suggested by Jean Ruddock 1980.) How might they be thinking and acting once they have got the innovation successfully institutionalized? Will they be demonstrating new roles and relationships, manifesting new attitudes, organizing things in new ways? And who is the 'target population'? Teachers certainly and pupils, classroom 'helpers', headteachers and principals, parents and others? And, to discriminate further, will all teachers be expected to operate in similar ways or will role-differentiation and specialization be required? What are the 'entry behaviours' of these people? How amenable and prepared are they to begin with? Just how far are we expecting them to change their ways? Have the expected changes been identified, or will they at least be admitted as desirable, by the people themselves? 'Self-initiated and self-applied innovation will have the strongest user commitment and the best chances for long-term survival,' says Havelock (1971).

And how is the necessary 'learning experience' to be designed? What 'enabling objectives' need to be attained by participants? As Neal Gross and his colleagues point out, participants need to gain not only knowledge *about* the proposed innovation but also the *know-how* to modify their own thinking and actions accordingly. What are the appropriate media through which to reach these preliminary objectives? Just as it is fatal for the innovator to forget that his potential colleagues know less than he does about the nature of the innovation, it is equally fatal, as both the Wastnedge and the Gross et al. case studies indicate, to rely overmuch on printed communications as a means of putting them in the picture. Courses, conversations, seminars and workshops seem to make a far more effective introduction. These will, where appropriate, be supported by observation of the innovation (or one that is similar) at work in a *similar* school setting elsewhere and discussions with the people who have already implemented it.

Teachers, like students, naturally need to be shown, rather than merely told. And, by the way, there is much to be said for inviting at least some of the intended beneficiaries, i.e., the students, to take part in the preliminary planning for innovation. Jean Ruddock (1980), argues the need for teachers and pupils to be regarded as *partners* in learning how to live with a curriculum innovation. She tells how students of the Humanities Curriculum Project were unable to take on the new roles required of them by its emphasis on open discussion with teacher as a non-directive chairman until they had seen *videotape of other students* learning that way.

Of course, the potential adopters of the innovation will continue to learn during the 'changing' period as well as during the 'unfreezing'.

Much of the training must be aimed at the working *group* rather than at the individual teacher. Belasco and Trice (1969), while somewhat sceptical about the amount of cognitive growth accruing from training, are very confident about the affective or 'ceremonial' aspects. They identify three phases of group training – separation, transition and incorporation – which sound remarkably like Lewin's phases of innovation. They see such training as a ceremony whereby members of the group are led to recognize the distinctiveness of their group and to identify with it, building cohesive bonds among themselves and reducing internal aggressions. Training thereby softens the stresses of organizational change for the individual who is passing from a known role into a new one. They warn that: 'Role passage without structured ceremony to symbolize the change may well produce inappropriate performance in the new role.' In other words, without the morale-building that can result from successful training, there may be no 'incorporation' (institutionalization).

Even while aiming at the working group, the training will still have to be individualized, for some participants will need to learn more or differently than others. How can the individual evaluate his own success while learning new ways? How can individual difficulties and anxieties be picked up in good time? How can the individual be helped to cope with them? How can he be rewarded for the extra time and effort demanded of him? The innovator needs to establish sensitive feedback mechanisms for the early identification both of teething troubles and of portents of disaster. Also needed is a regular forum in which the participants can discuss their joys and sorrows in a supportive atmosphere, getting their personal experience into social perspective and, hopefully, recharging their psychic batteries. Evaluation and improvement will thus continue throughout the 'changing' and 'refreezing' periods.

During these phases of implementation, 'systems thinking' may reveal that the school *organization* needs to change in order to accommodate the innovation. For example, teachers may simply be unable to plan and coordinate their new activities unless they get more free time than has hitherto been allowed. Again, certain existing features of timetabling, space utilization, subject specialization, streaming, discipline, student assessment, distribution of decision-making power between headteacher and staff may, if unchanged, undermine the objectives of the innovation (see Gross et al.).

'Systems thinking' will also emphasize that training and reorganization prove of little avail unless teachers and students are provided with all necessary *equipment and learning materials*. Many projects, hoping to strike while some political iron was hot, have got started before they were fully 'tooled up'. Some survive a premature birth and some do not. John Downing and Barbara Jones (1966) tell how, in the first experiment comparing the initial teaching alphabet (i.t.a.) with the traditional alphabet in the teaching of reading: 'Children in the i.t.a. classes were at a disadvantage in respect of the shortage of supply of i.t.a. materials and there were delays in supplying the schools with properly produced i.t.a. books for the library corner.' Neal Gross and his colleagues report that eight out of ten teachers in the project we considered earlier: '. . . complained bitterly that the amount of curricular materials placed at their disposal . . . was inadequate', and conclude that one of the major barriers to successful implementation was that: '. . . the administration, in effect, was requiring teachers to carry out an innovation that required unique types of instructional material that were not available.' This will sound only too familiar to the many teachers who became permanently disenchanted with programmed learning after being persuaded into experiments with teaching machines that soon ground embarrassingly to a halt for lack of the promised programmes. Such early starvation of essential materials can be survived only by the most powerful of innovations and the most dedicated of innovators.

The fact that successful institutionalization may take months (or years) raises severe problems for the maintenance of staff motivation. Participants may find the task of starting a project more exciting, and better supported, than that of keeping it going. Unless the feedback mechanisms continue to operate effectively, frustrations and disillusion can suddenly appear and build up rapidly to a destructive overload. Besides which, as Marten Shipman (1972b) points out in describing the trials of the Nuffield Integrated Studies Project:

> The pressures on teachers to go back to traditional methods are strong. They spring not only from the strain and effort of innovation, but also from the security of established work. While schools are concentrated on classroom teaching, it is difficult for a minority of teachers to use another system because they may be judged inefficient on the criteria established for the traditional way. The classroom teacher is trained for this job, he fulfils the expectations of pupils and other staff. He receives the support of the school organization. He utilizes buildings designed for this method. The innovator sacrifices these supports. . . . He is suspect, feels hostility and lacks supports. He can be seen as a lackey of alien powers. He can be

accused of monopolizing resources. He is a marginal man, on the fringe of the group to which he really belongs. Yet he has to bear this while making extra effort.

Not surprising, then, that innovation in education proceeds at a snail's pace. Nor can we be optimistic that the snail will move in the 'right' direction. Teachers are often accused of misdirecting and of emasculating innovations by adopting only those features that sit comfortably in the existing system. Innovations are 'blunted on the classroom door' according to Goodland and Klein (1970) who found (in the USA) '. . . a considerable discrepancy between teachers' perceptions of their own innovative behaviour and the perceptions of observers'. Many teachers may secretly espouse the cynicism of Taylor (1969) in a 'bluffer's guide' for teachers that is too true to be funny (even if it's really meant to be) and has been disturbingly popular:

> New and revolutionary teaching methods are constantly being thrown-up. Not often by teachers, who are far too busy in the classroom, but by others who see their ratings in the educational charts slipping and who need to claim the public eye. These methods normally have but a brief life and are seldom adopted in depth, so don't bother with lengthy courses of instruction. However, it is as well to know what they are all about – the elements are quickly assimilated along with the relevant vocabulary. Used while the method is enjoying its brief vogue, it gives a pleasing up-to-date impression.

Although, at first glance, *Bluff Your Way in Teaching* might appear to be simply the staffroom's answer to *The Little Red Schoolbook* (Hansen and Jensen 1971), it soon emerges that while the latter urges sympathy for teachers and insists that teachers and pupils are essentially on the same side, the former characterizes pupils as the opposition.

Barry Macdonald and Jean Ruddock (1972) identify the phenomenon of 'innovation without change'. An innovation like Nuffield French can be taught extremely badly by teachers who acquire the materials without the necessary training and who either slavishly adhere to them or else wantonly mix them up with other conflicting methods. Even the 'grand' innovations like comprehensivization and de-streaming are easily subverted by people or systems lacking in the necessary goodwill or professional responsiveness. Stephen Ball (1980) reports how a secondary school introduced mixed-ability teaching but without obtaining the social mixing between working-class and middle-class children that the headteacher had hoped would result; teachers' attitudes and expectations encouraged the 'streaming' mentality to continue within mixed-ability classes. As T.S. Eliot pointed out: 'Between the idea/And the reality/ Between the motion/And the act/Falls the shadow'.

The Innovatory Climate

Certainly adaptation is more usual than adoption. Even the most receptive schools rarely swallow innovations whole, and may make numerous modifications. This can be healthy. It may indicate that a school or college is rejecting changes 'imposed' from without and is thoughtfully developing its own innovations suited to local conditions. Jean Ruddock (1980) discusses the kind of information teachers may need in order to make such rational modifications to an 'imported' innovation (see also page 227). In cases like this, what may get institutionalized is not the originally intended innovation, or even just a local variation on it but, more productively, the habit or *climate* of innovation. Watson and Glaser (1965) describe it well:

> Following any important change comes a period during which the new equilibrium is being stabilized. Yet that condition, too, is only temporary. The organization that has accepted an innovation may need a breathing spell in which to consolidate what it has learned. But if the organization is geared to continued growth, its members will value forward-moving change as a recurrent and desirable phenomenon. From the plateau on which equilibrium is regained, the cycle of change can be launched again.

The virtue of developing an innovatory climate is that it is then less likely to allow any one innovation to become over-institutionalized to the extent that it can *never* be unfrozen again. When Tennyson wrote: 'Our little systems have their day; they have their day, and cease to be,' he was not to know the tenacity of modern education. Too many of our 'little systems' keep rolling on, long after 'their day' is past. Every strategy for implementing an innovation needs to include a self-destruct mechanism. That is, the innovators must keep a weather eye on the future to ensure that, with changing trends in society, the innovation is constantly reviewed and renovated – or replaced. Ideally, we should stop regarding 'innovation' as a 'thing' (e.g., a new course), or even as the processes whereby a particular new 'thing' is institutionalized (e.g., 'We innovated last year!'), and begin to embrace it as a continuing commitment to development and growth in education. Many people, not least its own staff, are watching to see whether the Open University (itself perhaps the major innovation in higher education this century) will, after a dozen or so years of establishing its traditions, be any more encouraging of *new* approaches to *new* problems than are most institutions in higher education. Let us not be complacent because we innovated in 1970!

But this innovatory climate is rarely to be found in our educational institutions. It seems an essential prerequisite for successfully introducing an 'innovation' and yet, paradoxically, is unlikely to arise except out of a school's previous experience of successful innovation. The individual teacher cannot introduce too much change unless the institution also changes and the institution cannot change unless society changes. Our present well-meaning tinkering may even be hindering true reform, as John Bremer (1971) implies:

> No changes in an educational system will be of any significance unless the social organization of education is totally changed, that is, unless the system itself is changed. Nothing less will do, for it is the whole system that defines the nature and function of the parts. As a consequence, imaginative and fruitful ways of helping students to learn become, ultimately, only new ways of subordinating the student to the present system, only another way of keeping the student under control. New methods, new materials and new machinery are used as new means of continuing the old pattern of fitting students into a pre-ordained social structure.

This problem underlies the distinction between *liberal* and *libertarian* approaches to education as outlined, for example, by Nagara (1981). It is also, as I implied in Chapter 1, a problem that all educational technologists should keep somewhere in sight, however pragmatic may be their efforts after 'improvement' in their particular corners of the system.

The Role of Educational Technology

In recent years, the UK school curriculum has become a battleground of debate. Perhaps until the student revolts of the late 1960s it was more or less taken for granted – the teachers' 'secret garden' as it was dubbed by one government minister. Then came the Black Papers, stridently criticizing various aspects of teaching method and pupil attainment in primary and secondary schools and, soon after, the 'accountability' crusade was under way (Becher and Maclure 1978) with its rallying cry perhaps being sounded by the then Prime Minister, Mr James Callaghan, in the speech that launched the 'Great Debate':

> To the teachers I would say that you must satisfy parents and industry that

what you are doing meets their requirements and the needs of their*
children. If the public is not convinced then the profession will be laying
up trouble for itself in the future. . . . It will be an advantage to the teaching
profession to have a wide public understanding and support for what they
are doing. (TES 1976)
(*Notice that the children are seen to 'belong' to industry as well as to the
parents.)

In 1976 the government also established the Assessment of Performance
Unit to monitor national standards of pupil-attainment in what the
Department of Education and Science will inevitably thereby be identifying as the 'key' areas of the curriculum. Furthermore, the idea of a
nationally agreed 'common core' curriculum has increasingly come under
serious consideration. Certainly a series of 'consultative documents' and
other official publications (e.g., DES 1977, 1979, 1980, 1981) has made
plain the government's intention to intervene in curriculum to an extent
unknown, perhaps, since the Second World War, and the 1980
Education Act has done much to require that schools become more open
to scrutiny and evaluation from outside.

Consequently, schools have already begun to re-define their
curriculum activities with a view to making them more clearly justifiable,
locally and nationally. Different but equally powerful pressures are being
felt by teachers in further and higher education. At all levels we are
being asked what we are doing, and why, and what we might be doing
instead. Teachers are being forced to clarify and articulate their
educational purposes and procedures, and to develop imaginative new
strategies to deal with newly emerging problems, as they may never have
been before. Not only their job-satisfaction but maybe even their jobs
may depend on it.

Given the anxieties, ambiguities and realpolitik that permeate so much
of the present-day curriculum ferment in schools and colleges, teachers
probably have more need than ever for some kind of *rational* framework
for their debates and decision-making. Such a framework I believe we can
draw from the problem-solving approach of educational technology.
Whether the educational technology thinking is fed in by specialists
working with teaching teams or by the teachers developing 'ed. tech.
attitudes' of their own is immaterial. They are not alternatives and both
may occur within the same institution, as we have observed in the Open
University.

These exponents of educational technology will find themselves faced with problems of varying degress of complexity. My colleague Clive Lawless (1980) puts his finger on four issues to which they must actively address themselves if they are to claim anything like a responsible role in curriculum development:

- By what criteria are the content, skills and outcomes for instruction chosen?
- What values lie behind the content and practices of the educational system?
- With what model of the student and how he learns does the system operate?
- How is the system to promote variety of approach, especially in the individualization of instruction and in evaluation?

Educational technology will certainly persist in alerting us to problems in education. It does not, as the cynic would suggest, invent the problems. They have always been with us. But it does drag them out from where they have been allowed to hide under the cosy structures of tradition. And each one we drag out brings a dozen others slithering after it. Consequently, this book is full of unanswered questions, both expressed and implied. Here, as the warning tip of the iceberg, are just a random few of them:

- Why is deliberate education necessary?
- What is to count as worthwhile knowledge?
- Who should decide subject-matter and objectives?
- Can we avoid emphasizing trivial but easily measurable learning?
- Where in the world (literally) shall we find appropriate learning resources?
- Do learners need teachers?
- Can learning be both personal and pre-packaged?
- Can we use research findings to improve learning?
- Should the student be expected to adjust to his course, or vice versa?
- How can assessment be used to aid learning rather than to inhibit it?
- How dare we allow students to fail?
- Is it fair to label students with public grades and marks?
- How can we find out whether our teaching has achieved anything of lasting value?

- How much education is each student entitled to?
- How can education be continuously renovated?
- Should the system we are improving be replaced?
- How should decisions be made about questions like those above?

Of course, there can be no easy, universal or enduring answers. Systems being what they are, no such question can even be debated without taking into account several of the others also. And whatever answers we tentatively come up with can never be valid for all situations, let alone all times. So the debate must continue indefinitely, itself an integral component in the system and vital to its self-renewal.

Whether the educators involved in such debates regard themselves as educational technologists or not is of no importance. What matters is that the awkward questions should continue to be raised, that the systems relations *between* them should be recognized, and that they should be tackled with assessable, though not necessarily measurable, outcomes in view, and with the expectation of such evaluation as will lead to development and growth rather than to complacency and decay.

Evaluating and Improving Educational Technology

So there is a continuing role for educational technology – *provided* educational technology is willing to learn from its experience and improve itself. Since the first edition of this book (1974) I have become aware of weaknesses that are ripe for correction. These have been touched upon here and there in earlier chapters. Now let us draw them together and consider what we must do to transcend them.

I described in Chapter 1 how the early tools technology gave way to a more sophisticated 'systems technology'. Now this concept of educational technology has also revealed its inherent tensions and contradictions. Until well into the 1970s the concept suffered no serious set-backs. Perhaps its proponents gravitated unconsciously towards milieux in which it would be reasonably acceptable and avoided those likely to offer any fundamental challenge. However their expansion into new subject areas or levels of education, together with a growing criticism (among teachers as well as students) of the manipulative, authoritarian and non-interactive nature of much of education, has eventually led to demands that educational technologists re-think some of their hitherto taken-for-granted tenets. In a sense, they are being asked to apply the systems approach *to themselves* – to regard their approach as a means to an end which has been evaluated and is now in need of improvement.

So where are the weak spots in the systems technology? To begin with it is evasive on the subject of ends. For all its stress on objectives it does not deal very convincingly with the questions 'Which objectives are most worthwhile?' or 'Where should objectives come from?' Individual educational technologists may, as people, have their opinions; but there is nothing in the systems approach to put educational technology's blessing on their preferences. Critics have insisted on drawing educational technologists' attention to the realization that the choice of objectives (of ends) has ethical and political dimensions. What we choose to aim at depends on the values we subscribe to, even if unconsciously. Likewise, what we help students achieve carries implications as to what we see, or at least accept, as their future roles in the socio-economic structure of society. These are still uncomfortable notions for the kind of educational technologist who is content to accept that others should decide what is to be learned, leaving him to concentrate on how it should be taught.

Even the 'magical' question 'What *exactly* do you want your students to *do*?' is not always greeted too sympathetically. Many teachers, especially in post-secondary education and in the more humanistic disciplines, do not accept that desirable outcomes can always be so predicted in advance – or at least not with the kind of exactness that would seem to be necessary if means are to be tailored to fit the ends. They may persist in requiring that students should display creativity, or originality of interpretation, or willingness to explore new dimensions of understanding. Much to the resentment of some educational tech-nologists, such aims are not easily translatable into behavioural objectives, let alone into test questions with right and wrong answers.

Moreover, even when an obliging teacher has expressed a set of teaching aims that the educational technologist *can* turn into behavioural objectives, all is not necessarily well. The educational technologist may prescribe the means to attain those objectives – e.g., suggest a certain combination of media, a certain sequence of concepts, a certain teaching strategy – only to be faced with the devastating question: 'How do you know?' Until recently, teachers have usually been too polite, or too mystified by the 'expert' status accorded the technologist, to ask him to *justify* his recommendations. Now that they are being asked, many educational technologists find that they do not know the basis of their supposed expertise. Or at least the basis they propose may look no sounder than alternative bases that would have supported quite different recommendations. The so-called 'findings' of research into learning are notoriously partial or contradictory.

So the grand outcome of the educational technologist's much vaunted 'systematic approach' has often appeared to be little more than a hunch; an educated guess; an intuition. Now this is not to decry the importance of intuition in educational design. Quite the contrary: wisdom, good judgement, creative intuition may well be the most important ingredients. But, and this is the point, they are not to be exercised exclusively by the educational technologist.

So we have seen weaknesses in educational technology's consideration of ends. We have seen more weaknesses when it comes to recommending means of attaining those ends. Can there be still more? Unfortunately, yes. Once the learning experience has been designed it is then, according to the educational technology approach, tried out, evaluated and improved. The weakness lies in the meaning to be put on 'improved'. How radical a change does the approach allow? Educational technologists have been criticized for taking too narrow a view of the evaluation process. They often ask the question 'Have the objectives been achieved?' when they should perhaps be asking '*What* has been achieved?'. The latter question recognizes an unpalatable fact, long given due weight in the trials of new drugs – that is, new treatments may produce unplanned, even unwanted, *side*-effects. Sometimes, in medicine or in education, these side-effects may be benign and important; they may even be more worthy than the original objectives of special encouragement in future 'trials'. But the systems approach, looking for attainment of pre-determined goals, would be unable to respond to the implication that the goals might be changed. While small adjustments could be made to the aims and objectives, major changes would imply that educational technology had 'made a mistake' earlier on.

Various other embarrassing considerations arise in the context of assessment and evaluation. It is worth pondering the influence of the fact that low-level cognitive objectives are usually easier to test for than are higher level abilities, especially in the affective area. This gave the educational technologist an interest in sponsoring some kinds of educational ends rather than others – because not all ends allowed him so visibly to perform his special rites. And how is the educational technologist to react when evaluation reveals that students appear to be pursuing objectives of their own as well as (if not instead of) those of his 'client', the teacher? Does he instantly recognize that they too are his clients? Does he feel bound to help them reach their objectives also? Or would he regard that as subversive of their 'true' interests, which are only properly defined by him and the teacher? Enough to say that the systems approach was not designed to deal with such problems. Nor was it designed to account for *external* factors having more effect on the outcomes than do the closed little worlds of learning created by educational technology. Educational technologists are only just beginning to recognize that their best-laid plans may be sabotaged by the mass-media or by the social norms and expectations prevailing among his student's family and friends.

There is more that could be said. But the malaise of educational technology should already be apparent. In essence, it seemed not to know what it was doing, or why it was doing it, or on what grounds it might have considered doing something else instead. This is not to imply that educational technologists are stubborn or stupid. But we have been extremely busy – often too busy to reflect on what we were doing. Family doctors, nowadays, can sometimes be heard voicing a similar regret about quite similar shortcomings. Because of time pressures and the demands of institutional politics we have often been persuaded into acting fast and decisively – even though we may have doubted the ethics of a particular project or felt our knowledge-base was inadequate to generate high-quality advice. But the awkwardness of the real world has been breaking in upon our cosy systems approach. Hence our recognition that if educational technology is not to become increasingly irrelevant, if it is not to lose what credibility it retains in educational circles, it must subject itself to re-appraisal. But will anything of value remain? I do believe so, or I would not have produced this book.

Towards a Responsible Educational Technology

I find myself, in this chapter, talking not just of educational technologists but also of 'educational technology'. I hope it will be understood that I am not thereby trying to 'reify' educational technology (as the Continental philosophers say). That is, I am not trying to pretend it is a thing with a coherent, timeless existence of its own, independent of the people who practise in a *variety* of ways but *choose* to use the common umbrella term for their activities. Indeed, I have already implied (page 10) that 'educational technology *is* what educational technologists *do.*'

Consequently, when I suggest that 'educational technology' needs to become 'responsible', it is not because I am under the impression that all educational technolog*ists* are irresponsible at present. On the contrary, my desire is to highlight and accelerate certain evolutionary tendencies which I believe are *already* in motion among some of the practitioners of educational technology.

The last major evolutionary step took our technology from tools into systems. Although some 'tools technologists' are still to be found co-existing with the 'systems technologists', by and large most people who started with a tools-orientation have long ago adopted at least some semblance of a systems approach. The next evolutionary step, I believe, is to be discerned among certain of the systems technologists who are beginning to stand back from what they are doing, and observing themselves doing it; criticizing their own beliefs and actions; and attempting to explain them, justify them, or at least relate them to the beliefs and actions of other people with whom they might be collaborating. It is this reflective spirit that we must nurture in order to achieve a responsible educational technology.

So I move from describing what *is* to recommending what *ought* to be the nature of educational technology. But the 'ought' (or 'must') is not a moral imperative. It is more of a political imperative. That is, I believe that, unless educational technology develops somewhat along the lines I suggest, it will soon be regarded as having nothing distinctive to say and will very properly be allowed to die.

So how shall I describe this responsible educational technology whose emergence we must accelerate and nurture? I may already have conveyed a rough picture – by sketching out some of the weaknesses it must overcome. But let me be more specific.

The Role of Knowledge

To begin with, educational technology – unlike, say, 'educational studies' or 'educational science' – is meant to have influence on the real world. To paraphrase Karl Marx's dictum: 'The task is not simply to understand an educational situation but to *change* it.'

So knowledge is chiefly the means rather than the end. Although action towards a desired end, whether successful or not, will doubtless produce, as a subsidiary end, some *new* knowledge that may be used to help inform future action. Effective use of knowledge would thus appear to be the key. But what kind of knowledge?

Self-Knowledge To begin with, educational technology needs knowledge about itself. That is to say, it needs to be conscious of its role and status and responsibilities. In different institutions or at different times, educational technologists may play many roles; they may initiate new teaching on their own; they may advise other teachers, perhaps as members of teams; they may produce teaching material based on the suggestions of colleagues; they may evaluate and improve materials produced by others; they may act as the institution's pedagogic conscience; they may be the visiting consultant or the general practitioner. All such roles will have their time and place – but they need to be very carefully chosen in relation to the needs of the educational technologist's colleagues as *they* perceive them. Educational technology cannot be, and should not be, responsible to itself alone.

By analogy with 'community medicine', it is not too fanciful to propose the need for 'community educational technology'. By this I mean, quite simply, that the most acceptable and effective educational technologists are those who take a full part in the activities of their school or college. That is, they will involve themselves, for example, in societies and committee work neither just because they enjoy it nor because 'We've all got to do our bit', but also because they believe it enhances their professional credibility and because their peculiar problem-solving approach may actually turn out to be of help in quite unexpected situations. They may even prevent some problems from arising.

Clearly, by wider community involvement, the educational technologist gains political and institutional knowledge. He learns about the prevailing bonds and allegiances and antipathies among departments and faculties and individuals; he comes to understand the local traditions, the norms, the priorities, the pressure-points, the no-go areas, the 'ideas in currency'; and he gets to know who are the obstructionists and who the opinion-leaders.

Educational technologists need to know where they stand in relation to the various interest groups in their project or institution – and perhaps in relation to others in the wider society with which it interacts. This implies social and historical knowledge of how various others came to be what they are, and how they feel about it. Educational technologists must reflect on how they relate to this larger world. Whose criteria (e.g., of 'successful action') do they have to satisfy besides their own? To whom are they responsible? What are the limits to their power? They may not be satisfied with the answers to such questions, but, unless they are openly discussed and answered realistically, they may find themselves generating much disappointment among colleagues and frustration for themselves. (The relationships between educational technologists and 'clients' or colleagues are discussed in Davies 1975, Eraut et al 1975, Farrar 1978, Hedberg 1980, Lewis 1980 and Macdonald-Ross 1976.)

Knowledge of values   Secondly, educational technology (and thereby the people who profess it) needs to know what ends it values and what ends other people might value. That is, it needs an ethical awareness of alternative consequences of its actions. Without this, it cannot claim to be acting responsibly. The educational technologist must become capable of justifying his actions and his immediate objectives in terms of higher-order aims that reveal his ideal of the 'educated person' – the qualities he values for their own sake not, like objectives, as contributory to some higher purpose. He must be prepared to debate this value-base with his collaborators, who may well have different value-bases. He must have reflected on what he considers worthwhile in people and in society so that he can help evaluate the proposed goals of educational projects as well as (or sometimes instead of) students' attainment of them. Without a well-reflected ideal of what is worthwhile, the educational technologist may be dismissed as an amoral pragmatist from whom, perhaps, education can expect technical competence but not moral responsibility. Naturally, educational technologists will not all have the same value-base. We can expect to see Marxist educational technologists, liberal educational technologists, libertarian educational technologists, and so on; hence all the more need to make their value-allegiances clear to colleagues.

Pedagogical knowledge   By this I mean cause-and-effect knowledge about teaching and learning. Largely it will be probabilistic in nature — e.g., 'Students are likely to learn in this way or that if we expose them to this or that kind of teaching.' In other words, it is the knowledge that enables the technologist to recommend a suitable treatment, from a number of alternatives, because he *predicts* that it is the one most likely to succeed.

What sort of knowledge is this? Its basis must lie in observation, description and analysis. That is, the educational technologist cannot begin to suggest, say, simulation games or distance learning as possible solutions to certain educational problems unless he has actually learned of their existence and made an effort to understand their special qualities. He also needs to know how differently students orient themselves towards learning; how they perceive the functions of different components in the teaching situation as they relate to the students' own priorities; how they work out the meaning of new ideas and fit them to existing experience; and the different ways they may use the ideas once they have incorporated them. Such knowledge is attainable only by listening carefully to students.

The educational technologist also needs reliable knowledge relating differences among media or strategies to differences among students in situations similar to those in which he is working. This might be called 'scientific knowledge'. It can, in principle, be gained from reading the reports of other people working in similar areas.

But, as William James pointed out at the beginning of the century, talking particularly of psychology, 'Teaching is an art, and science never creates art forms directly.' Scientific knowledge has to be transmuted by a sceptical and creative mind. While the educational technologist should always be looking out for principles drawn from scientific inquiry, he should be prepared to see his particular context *over-ride* the principle. That is, the situation he faces may contain new elements (both positive and negative) making it so different from that of the researcher that the principle cannot be adopted, or not without serious modifications. To make such a decision, the educational technologist needs another kind of knowledge – call it proto-scientific, intuitive, experimental. This is practical knowledge based on his reflections about his (and perhaps his colleagues') previous experience. The acquisition of such practical knowledge will be difficult unless the technologist can accept *ambiguity*: he must not feel threatened by having to work in an experimental frame of mind rather than with a fixed and secure set of recipes and rules.

Subject-matter knowledge The educational technologist also needs knowledge of whatever subject or discipline he is helping to teach – calculus, health and environment, economics or whatever. On the one hand, lack of such knowledge has often led to the educational technologist being relegated to technician status. On the other hand, it has often blinded him to the fact that even the so-called experts may not know the subject as well as they might – or at least not in ways akin to those through which his students need to come to apprehend it. So, the educational technologist is doubly discouraged from engaging with the perhaps fundamental problem of what knowledge-structure underlies the teachers' teaching and the students' learning, and how coherent it is, and how far commonly perceived by all participants.

The need for such an engagement with *what* is taught, as well as with the why and the how, becomes even more urgent with the increasing popularity of interdisciplinary or issue-based courses, e.g., science and society, pollution studies, contemporary issues in education. For in such courses the subject-matter has to be negotiated and *decided* rather than simply being accepted out of the traditions of some established discipline.

How Will the Knowledge be Applied?

The 'educational technologist' is to be seen as one of several participants in any educational situation. He may or may not adopt the title of educational technologist. Applying the responsible educational technology approach may be just one aspect, though an important one, of his work as a teacher or a curriculum developer.

On the basis of his well-reflected sense of values, he should therefore be involved in early debates about the purpose of the enterprise he is working within. As well as clarifying his own values as they relate to possible purposes, he should consciously act to help other participants, including students, to articulate their values and purposes. As a consequence, he should be able to help make clear the implications of adopting one set of ends rather than the others. He can also impress on colleagues the mutability of ends and show how intentions change and initial goals get re-defined as students progress through the learning experience.

He should also be able to help colleagues remain aware that the distinction between means and ends is always a tenuous one. Any given end, e.g., mastering statistical inference, can become a means to attain some further end, e.g., thinking critically. Similarly, what was chosen as a means, e.g., Skinnerian reinforcement, can impose itself as an end, e.g., students may become dependent on rewards that are extrinsic to what they are supposedly learning.

His recommendations for a particular design for the learning experience, e.g., choice of media, teaching strategy, conceptual structure and sequence, will be grounded in both scientific and practical knowledge – his own and that of his colleagues. He will also accept that even the students may have some valuable ideas as to how best they might be taught – though they may not be able to express these in usable form until they have been through the learning experience. The educational technologist will be properly encouraging of intuition in the design of learning. Always, however, he will look for justification of proposed methods in some wider theory of the conditions that bring about learning.

The responsible educational technology will have an open attitude to evaluating the effects of teaching. It will ask not simply 'Has the learner learned what we (or even he) wanted him to learn?' but 'What has he learned? How has he changed? Can this be explained in terms of the teaching as he experienced it?' Thus, the technologist will be open to changing not just the teaching (the means) but also the ends – relegating any objectives that no longer seem so important and recognizing objectives that have since come to assume special significance (for good or ill). He will be open also to the idea that the understanding gained in evaluating a project will be liable to change not just the way he improves that project but also the way he tackles future projects. Because of this continual accretion of practical knowledge, he will recognize that he would be unlikely to tackle the same project in the same way if he were faced with it again. He sees teaching as a learning experience for *all* participants.

In summary, a responsible educational technology, or rather the people practising it, would be seeking clarity about educational ends; relating means to ends on the basis of scientific and practical pedagogical knowledge; and constantly improving both individual projects and the knowledge-base — through evaluation in which the emphasis is on what happens and why rather than on the attainment of pre-specified goals. The educational technologists would be those who remembered, though all around might have forgotten, the need for constant creative evaluation of the communal experience.

★   ★   ★

My only remaining question is whether it isn't time for us to finally stop using the label 'educational technology'. Educational technology is one possible means to an end. But perhaps we would circumvent much understandable suspicion among potential colleagues, and gain ourselves a more open hearing, if we were to emphasize that end rather than the means – and re-name our profession *educational development*.

Questions on Chapter 7

1   Recall a curriculum innovation that you have been concerned with or affected by. Whose agreement had to be obtained before it could be introduced? How was that agreement obtained? How would you assess the innovation's success?

2   What would you say were the most significant innovations you have seen introduced in institutions you have been concerned with (either as teacher or student)? Why were they introduced? What problems were encountered? If none were introduced, why do you suppose this was?

3   What innovation would you most like to see introduced into your present institution? What would you expect as the major difficulties in introducing it? What might be done to overcome them?

4   Do you see your own role in curriculum development in your institution increasing or decreasing over the next few years? Why? Whoever will be involved in the discussion and decision-making about curriculum in your institution, do you believe they might usefully use educational technology ideas? If so, which ones? If not, why not?

5   What questions would you like to add to those listed on pages 245–6? Which of the questions on the present list do you regard as most vital?

6   How would you reply to a colleague who said: 'It's none of the educational technologist's business to be questioning the purposes and ideologies of education – he should concentrate on finding more effective ways of teaching?

7   In the second half of this chapter, do you feel the author strengthens the case he has been making for educational technology in the rest of the book, or does he undermine it? What do you regard as the most important points made in this section? How might they affect your activities as an educational technologist?

8   What's in a name? Could the label under which educational technologists operate really make any difference, e.g., to their reception by colleagues, to their sense of professional identity, or to their effectiveness? If so, what label would you advise them to use? Or do you believe it is too late to change?

EPILOGUE: CONVERSATION WITH AN EDUCATIONAL TECHNOLOGIST

'What is the use of a book,' thought Alice, 'without pictures or conversation.'

Lewis Carroll

As a relief from the monologue of the previous couple of hundred pages, you may like to consider the following discussion – a conversation between a teacher (T) and an educational technologist (E) which takes place in the common room of a large college to which one of them (never mind which) has recently been appointed. After a brief introductory exchange, E broaches the topic that leads into the following dialogue which touches on several of the issues we have considered in this book (though not always as aptly or convincingly as we would have done!):

T: I don't believe I know what your field is. . . exactly?

E: Educational technology. I'm an educational technologist.

T: Are you indeed? And what might that be? Something to do with computers? Computer-assisted instruction, is it – and that sort of thing?

E: Well, I'm interested in computer-assisted instruction, but I don't have anything to do with it, not personally. Nothing as complex as all that. Actually, I'm more concerned. . .

T: No, hang on; let me think. You don't sound at all like the kind of person we have round when the televisions and tape-recorders and overhead projectors go on the blink. But maybe you do something in that general line – trying to persuade us teachers to use more audio-visual aids. . . giving advice on how to use them better. That kind of thing?

E: I certainly *could* do that. In fact it *is* something I do every now and again – advising on this or that audio-visual medium. But I don't really see myself as a hardware man in the sense you're thinking of, I'm not that sort of educational technologist.

T: Aha! I think I've got you now. It's not so much what you call the hardware, perhaps, as what goes into it. You must be a maker of educational films, or tape-recordings, or television programmes. Is that what you mean by educational technology?

E: I know I'm repeating myself but, again, it's sort of yes *and* no. I have done that sort of thing. I've produced television programmes and made sound-recordings, for instance. But I could get along quite well as an educational technologist if I never did it again!

T: Perhaps you'd be advising other people on how to do it, though?

E: No, even if I never again did that either, I could still be practising educational technology. Perhaps I'd better tell you what I do, and put you out of your misery – before I forget what it is myself!

T: No, don't do that. I like a puzzle, and this is beginning to intrigue me.

E: Well, I don't mind if you don't. Next question?

T: OK, I'm trying to think of a different line. What I can't fathom is why you brush off every suggestion that involves machines. Ah, how about *teaching* machines? (Sees E's eyebrows beginning to rise in a now-familiar way.) All right, don't say it. . . . You're interested. You've done some. But it's not really 'where you're at' (as they say). Am I right?

E: Absolutely.

T: Thank heavens: at last I'm right about something! But, as I say, I still can't see why I'm getting nowhere with the machines idea. Surely educational *technology* must have something to do with machines – tools, equipment, complex apparatus?

E: Well, I've got to admit that many people do take that line. They think of educational technology as being the tools – the equipment, the machines – *used* in education.

T: But isn't that what *any* kind of technology is about?

E: Ah well, it may be *about* machines etc. in the sense that they're usually *involved* in it. In fact, technology of the kind I'm talking about often *results* in machines being invented and used.

T: You mean your kind of technology can *give rise* to the use of machines, equipment, tools and so on?

E: Exactly. The tools etc. may be a product of the technology, but they're not the technology itself. Technology existed before the machines and could go on existing even if they all disappeared. It's more a state of mind than a set of objects.

T: Now you really are getting mysterious. Do you mean . . . (What is it the philosphers would say?) . . . that machines are 'sufficient but not necessary' for there to be a technology?

E: (Pausing.) Now your making *me* think. I'm not too sure about the 'sufficient' bit. Certainly they're not *necessary* (as I see it) to have a technology. For one thing – something we've not really mentioned yet – the technology might consist of a set of *techniques* rather than a set of tools. Or both tools and techniques together, of course.

T: But you doubt whether tools, or machines, would be sufficient on their own – to make your kind of technology?

E: Yes, I'm pretty sure you could have a set of tools (techniques as well, maybe) without having a technology. I think it would depend on how they were used, on what went on in the minds of the users. Were they being used in a technological way or in . . . I don't know . . . let's say in a religious way.

T: Oh yes, I can see how machines might be used as objects of veneration – little tins gods, literally. I'm old enough to remember teaching machines – and all the people who went around the country preaching their virtues – even though there were hardly any programmes to use in them.

E: That's just what I mean. And when the stuff *is* used, it's often used in a fairly unthinking way.

T: You mean without thinking whether the tool is really suited to the job in hand, and whether it's being used in the best way . . . that sort of thing?

E: Yes, and certainly without thinking whether any of the tools need to be modified – or even be pensioned off and replaced with *new* ones – in response to changing circumstances and new needs.

T: The same must be true of techniques.

E: I think so. You can certainly apply a teaching technique – lecturing, practical work, field-trips, homework, exams, etc. – without giving much thought to it. (To the technique that is, as opposed to the content.)

T: And even if you're thinking about the content, it may never occur to you to question whether the content is actually *worth* teaching.

E: True enough.

T: Yes, many teachers just keep on using the same old techniques automatically – I suppose we all do to some extent – without ever considering the whys and wherefors.

E: Often they were taught like that themselves. Then they tried it out as teachers, found it worked well enough, and just kept on doing it.

T: Hence the old crack about the kind of teacher who has had not twenty years' experience but the same year twenty times!

E: That hits the nail right on the head. Such a person could not be a technologist to my way of thinking, no matter how many tools or fancy techniques he'd been using.

T: So, let's make sure I've got this clear – your kind of technology. It's not enough to have machines, and it may not even be necessary – but even a set of techniques will not be enough unless you've got the right attitudes to go with them – unless you use them, and think about them, in the right kind of way?

E: That's about it. The way I see it, you could be using all kinds of tools and techniques but still not have a technology, still not be any kind of technologist. You might be a technician, perhaps, or even a craftsman, or you might just be some trendy who thinks that promoting the latest methods and media might give him the edge over his rivals. But you wouldn't be a technologist. Not my kind anyway.

T: So, even though I was using what other people might describe as a technology – of tools and techniques, you wouldn't call me a technologist unless I was *thinking technologically*.

E: You've got it. If you were thinking technologically about the tools and techniques you were using in education, then I'd say you were an educational technologist. But, of course, that leaves us with one big unanswered question.

T: Quite. What do you mean by 'technologically'? I think I know now what you *don't* mean by it! But how would you know I was thinking *technologically*? I suppose you'd expect to see me re-inventing the blackboard!

E: Well, you may laugh, but that's already been done. Somebody found that it could be visually more effective to paint chalkboards *green*! But no, although you might end up re-designing something, or using old things in new ways, I'd be happy to call you an educational technologist (my kind that is) so long as you were choosing and using your tools and techniques *rationally*.

T: Rationally? You'd want me to be able to say why I was using the ones I'd chosen? To explain my choice? To give you reasons?

E: Ideally, yes. At the very least, you would need to recognize that explaining was a relevant thing to be doing – that you *should* be able to give reasons. Though you might sometimes feel you couldn't *yet* give an adequate justification of a particular technique (or tool) you were using.

T: So that's it then? Your technology is a matter of using tools and techniques (or maybe techniques on their own?) in such a way that you can justify your use? Or at least feel guilty when your justification seems less convincing than you'd wish!

E: Well, that's the bare bones of it. Though I expect you'll be pressing me, in a moment, to say *what sort* of justification I'd be looking for! But, before you do, there is one other vital aspect that we've managed to gloss over so far.

T: Just one, eh! What is it?

E: Simply that the techniques must actually *work*. They must be effective in achieving some *purpose* or desired result. If they're not effective, you won't even bother trying to justify them.

T: Yes, we have rather taken that for granted. Actually, all this reminds me of how . . . was it Plato . . .? defined knowledge – as 'justified true belief'. It seems to me like you're defining technology as 'justified true technique' – if we take 'true' here to mean 'effective'.

E: Mnh. I think I like that. It should do us quite nicely to be going on with – if we also let 'technique' include all the associated tools, machines, hardware, software, etc. So, all right. For the moment, let's say educational technology is the application of justified true techniques in education – or in teaching and learning if you want to be a bit more down to earth. But . . .?

T: Yes, it's a big BUT! The question you knew I'd be asking – what do you mean by *justification*?

E: Well, I don't want to seem sneaky, but I really would be interested to hear what *you* think I mean by it. You seem pretty good at mind-reading!

T: And pretty susceptible to flattery! But I suppose I am beginning to get some idea of how your mind works. All the same, I think I'll find it easier to say what you *wouldn't* accept as justification.

E: Go ahead, then. Give me an example.

T: All right, suppose I'm teaching in a certain way – teaching kids to read using the initial teaching alphabet, let's say. And you ask me why.

E: I'm asking you to justify your technique, yes.

T: Right. Well, for a start, it wouldn't be enough for me to say: 'It's working. The kids are learning to read.'

E: No, it wouldn't be enough. As we said in our definition, the justification is needed *in addition* to the truth (or effectiveness) of the technique.

T: Quite. Then again, it wouldn't satisfy you if I said I've taught kids this way before – several times perhaps – and it's always worked.

E: It would be better – assuming you were telling the truth – but not good enough. Not good enough to convince me you were teaching like an educational technologist.

T: Right. And how about if I told you I'd tried other methods of teaching reading as well, and this one had always been the most effective?

E: Again, that *could* help justify your choice; but it wouldn't convince me.

T: No, I thought not. We want something more than claims of effectiveness. But I'll come back to that in a moment. Now then: let's say I told you that I'd met the originator of the technique and been very impressed by him, or that some of my best friends had recommended it, or that I personally feel good when teaching that way?

E: No, No and No!

T: As I thought! I was just getting those out of the way. But I do believe I have an inkling of what you're after. What you require, as an educational technologist, is some kind of *theory* justifying the techniques we use.

E: You're getting warm.

T: You'd want me to justify the technique (say, the initial teaching alphabet) in terms of theories about how children learn to read, about how what is known of such learning relates to the specific characteristics of, in this case, the initial teaching alphabet. . . .

E: Yes, go on.

T: And I suppose you'd like to see objective evidence from controlled experiments – scientific evidence I suppose you'd call it – into how the technique had worked . . . what results it had achieved, with what kinds of learners . . . how it compared with other techniques, and so on.

E: Yes, I think technology is a matter of applying scientific findings . . . to a large extent.

T: You wouldn't be satisfied with one single teacher's experience of the method. It wouldn't be sufficiently objective for you.

E: No, I'd certainly be wary about generalizing from it – to recommend it to other teachers, or even to apply it myself with any confidence.

T: So you'd want some scientific experiment and comparison – done by some disinterested researcher, or researchers?

E: As an educational technologist, yes. I'd be looking for educational techniques that could be justified in terms of scientific evidence and underlying theories that would explain the results. To take your example, not just knowing in what circumstances kids learn better with the initial teaching alphabet (if they do) but *why* they do.

T: So, for you, techniques are justified if their results can be explained in terms of scientific evidence and underlying theories?

E: That's it.

T: Well, it does occur to me that there's another kind of justification which you are ignoring altogether. To my mind, a technique could be fully justified in the sense we've just discussed, and yet be definitely *not* justified in another, maybe more important sense.

E: Can you give me an example?

T: Easily – I'll make it fairly extreme: Suppose I were using a 'justified true technique' – one that you'd have to approve – in order to teach kids how to pick pockets or how to kill one another with a single blow.

E: Ah, I see what you mean. You have me in a corner.

T: How do you feel about the technique now? Does it still seem justified?

E: I take your point. No need to twist the knife! You're wanting me to comment not just on whether the means is justified (the technique) – but also on whether the end, the *purpose*, is justified?

T: I'm certainly curious to know whether *you* think it is relevant to inquire about the purpose? Or do you always take the worthwhileness of the end for granted?

E: That's quite a difficult one. I certainly don't think the means justifies the end – even in less extreme circumstances. Personally, I would expect the teacher to be able to justify what he was doing in terms of its worthwhileness. Why does he value the kind of learning that he is trying to bring about?

T: But you didn't mention this kind of justification earlier. Maybe you don't regard it as part of technological thinking?

E: I'm not sure. Maybe I just take it for granted. After all, I did talk about using techniques *rationally*. It surely would not be rational to use them in teaching something one found abhorrent or even something that seemed less valuable than some alternative that one might just as easily be teaching.

T: So, anyway, we've got round to the idea that educational technology involves being rational about both ends and means. Both have to be justified.

E: Yes, I'm sure that's right – though I'm not sure that all educational technologists would agree that justifying ends is part of the technology.

T: Well, it would be a pretty dangerous kind of technology that had no moral awareness about the purposes it was applied to.

E: I agree. You don't have to convince me. After all, educational technologists should be expected to work with both kinds of educational theory. . . .

T: There are only *two* kinds!

E: Well, what I was going to say is they should be able to work both with *empirical* theory – the kind that deals with effects of teaching – and also with *evaluative* theories – the kind that discusses what is *worth* teaching.

T: In the light of some beliefs or ideals about the nature of humanity, society, knowledge, culture and so on?

E: Exactly. And both need to be referred to in educational technology – or so I believe, anyway.

T: So educational technology is in the business of understanding the purposes and processes of teaching and learning.

E: Certainly. But not, I would say, for their own sake. As a technologist, I want to apply that understanding to *practical activities* – to the practical activities of education, since I am an *educational* technologist.

T: But is that any different from other people working in the area of educational studies? philosophers of education? psychologists? sociologists? historians of education? And so on?

E: Oh, I think so, don't you? For one thing, an educational technologist would glean understandings from all those disciplines. And from others: like media research, communications theory, anthropology and so on. He wouldn't recognize the boundaries at all.

T: And for another thing . . .?

E: Yes, perhaps the main difference is that those disciplines put the emphasis on description and interpretation – on *understanding* the educational world. But, as Karl Marx said: 'The important thing is not merely to understand the world but to *change* it.' And that's what makes educational technology different. It's trying to change the world – the world of teaching and learning, anyway. For the better, of course!

T: Well, I'll try to resist the idea of educational technology being a secret Marxist conspiracy! I'm sure I see what you mean about your commitment to change – to improvement. And God knows there's plenty of room for improvement in education. But you plan to do this *how* exactly? Just remind me.

E: Given that we've decided what is most worth teaching?

T: Well, it's a big 'given'. But, all right, if it helps you.

E: OK, we improve things by designing teaching materials and learning experiences rationally – using the most reliable knowledge available. And I'd look for the chosen methods to be justified, made reliable if you like, by some kind of theory demonstrated in scientific evidence.

T: That all sounds very grand. Quite praiseworthy. But isn't it a bit more difficult than it sounds?

E: I never said I had an easy job!

T: No, I don't mean difficult in execution. I mean difficult in principle. It seems to me you're wanting to lean very heavily indeed on science.

E: What else is there?

T: I'll think of something in a minute! But first I've really got to register my doubts about how much you can really learn from scientific research findings. How much of value in practical teaching, that is.

E: What sort of doubts do you have?

T: Where shall I start? To begin with, there's the matter of whether scientists are asking the right questions in educational situations. For one thing, a lot of footling inquiries are carried out in highly artificial circumstances, or over too short a time period to yield any believable results. Often researchers just can't get the time or funds to carry out the inquiries they'd really like to tackle; but they've still got to produce some publications.

E: I think you're being unduly cynical there.

T: Yes, I know it's not all like that. More seriously, though, I've a feeling that much educational research may be too firmly rooted in the status quo. Researchers may show us, for example, that intelligence test scores give reliable predictions of future academic success. But this may be an artefact of the system in which they did the experiments. Change the system, employing teachers with different skills and different expectations about children's capacity to learn, and the association between intelligence test score and later success might disappear – making it useless as far as your educational technology is concerned.

E: No, on the contrary, educational technologists would want to *use* the knowledge that there was no necessary association – provided it could be demonstrated scientifically and accounted for in terms of what kind of teacher-skills, pupil-motivations, etc. made the difference.

T: But my point is that such knowledge would never become available if scientific knowledge is too bound to the status quo – if it's unable to conceive of, or get facilities to experiment with, quite different assumptions about education.

E: Yes, I accept that science does have that limitation. But I think you're making altogether too much of it. A lot of research is pedestrian, I admit, and unlikely to transform the way we look at things. But it's not true of all science. There are always *some* educational theorists and researchers coming up with significantly new perspectives on education – and looking for ways of testing out their ideas. You've really got to assume that we educational technologists can pick out the *best* of the knowledge crop!

T: Point taken. I certainly don't want to discount *all* research because some is unusable. So I won't pursue another quibble I had in mind – that so many theories and so many research findings are ambiguous or even contradict one another.

E: Yes, we'd just have to be wary about the ambiguities and contradictions – to use that knowledge more tentatively.

T: All the same, there's a more fundamental problem about how much use you can get out of even the best scientific knowledge – once you're dealing with practical learning situations.

E: And what's that?

T: Well, it's to do with the matter of generalizing and particularizing. As I understand it, science works best with large numbers of events.

You said yourself that you wouldn't put much faith in a single teacher's account of his experience.

E: Not in recommending his techniques unreservedly to others, no.

T: And in order to understand the technique and use your knowledge of it you'd need more evidence. You'd need the scientific observation of more teachers, more pupils, more situations. All of this would go to produce more robust evidence and a more articulated theory of what was going on with the technique being examined. Would this really help you?

E: Surely it would. I'd be able to generalize from the evidence and use the underlying theory to see how that educational technique might apply in another situation.

T: Ah, but could you? I can see how you might generalize. It's the particularizing that worries me. Science seems to be very good on producing general laws – that's its job. But it's not so hot when it comes to predictions in particular cases.

E: I'm not sure I follow you.

T: All right, take the scientist who could tell you with practically 100 percent certainty how a billion or so gas molecules would behave if you heated their container. He wouldn't have a clue if you picked out a single one of the molecules and asked him to predict its behaviour.

E: Sorry, I still don't see what point you're trying to make.

T: Well, bring it a bit closer to home. Your educational scientists may well prove that children who score highly on intelligence tests do better academically, *in general*, than those who don't, or that children learning to read with the initial teaching alphabet learn faster, *on average*, than those using other methods. But so what? You see, as a teacher I'm not dealing with children 'in general'.

E: Of course not. You're dealing with particular individuals.

T: Absolutely. So how do I know whether to treat them like those the researchers found to be limited by intelligence or like those who could succeed nevertheless? Or, with the initial teaching alphabet, how do I know whether I'm in the 'average' situation where the method appeared to work best or whether I'm in one of the other situations where a different method might work best – at least with some of my pupils?

E: But that's why we look to science – to give us more and more detailed evidence. To explain finer and finer variations – so we can adapt the principles to more and more specific circumstances.

T: Well, I just don't believe it. I can't see how we'll ever conceivably have a science that will tell *me* (not the teacher in the next room) how best to deal with a learning problem that *this* child (not the one next to him) is facing right *now* (not on some other occasion when the circumstances may be slightly but crucially different). When science does come up with learning principles, they're easily over-ridden by a change of context. Doesn't the new context – Form 4e on a wet Friday afternoon, say – so often unleash factors that the researcher couldn't have controlled (and might not even have anticipated) in his experiments?

E: Often enough, I suppose.

T: And doesn't that make all the difference when his ideas are tried out in a new situation? Even the fact that a particular teacher has got enthusiastic about a particular technique – irrationally maybe – might enable *him* to teach better with that technique than with any number of alternatives that objective evidence tells us *ought* to be more effective but which just don't turn him on. Contexts are no respecters of scientific principles of learning.

E: Have you finished! Now you've paused to get your breath back, I'd just like to say that I don't entirely disagree with you. I hope that not many educational technologists are bone-headed enough to think that principles can be just picked up 'off the shelf' and plugged into their colleagues' teaching.

T: They'd get short shrift if they did!

E: All the same, some principles are more easily, or more widely, applicable than others. . . . No, don't ask me to list them! But the important thing is that most theories and principles are at least illuminative or *suggestive*. By which I mean it's worth keeping alive to the new ideas coming out of educational research and other people's practical experience. Because we can always consider how they might work in our situation and, if we like the sound of them, we can try them out – tentatively at first, perhaps, see where the snags are, and either modify them or replace them with more promising methods.

T: Fair enough: but who needs educational technology come from the realms of science to tell us this? Isn't it what all teachers do – or *should* do anyway – if they're being professional?

E: Quite probably, yes. But, as you said earlier, many teachers find they can 'get by' without developing their methods. What I'm suggesting, really, is that the educational technology approach involves not just using scientific *knowledge*. . . .

T: Which may be pretty thin on the ground?

E: All right. . . but also using scientific *method*. By that I mean a hypothesis-testing method.

T: Now how would you explain that?

E: Well, educational technology would want the teacher – the 'professional' teacher, as you called him – to think of himself as a tester of hypotheses about teaching and learning. That is, he'd start with hypotheses, insights, about what purposes might be worthwhile, or about possible ways of achieving the purposes. . .

T: From science?

E: Maybe from science, maybe from philosophy, maybe from his experience or from that of his colleagues, very often from the suggestions of his students. But quite often his hypotheses would seem to come right out of the blue. After all, there's nothing in science itself to generate new hypotheses. Even Einstein once said they came from 'intuition, resting on sympathetic experience'.

T: So you do allow for inspiration.

E: But of course. Inspiration, intuition, wisdom, good judgement. These underlie all innovation and growth in education. Science itself doesn't produce the new ideas.

T: Anyway, once you've got them . . .?

E: Yes, though scientific method doesn't produce the hypotheses, it does enable you to evaluate them and elaborate on them once you've got them.

T: I'm not sure I know what you mean by scientific method here.

E: Simply that you regard your hypotheses experimentally. You try them out with learners, expecting to find that they work with some and not with others, and to different degrees. You'll be trying to account for these differences, using whatever scientific or practical knowledge seems relevant. And you'll expect to modify your original hypothesis (as a scientist would) in the light of your experience – perhaps working out variations on the basic idea to suit different circumstances, perhaps combining it with elements from other approaches and so on.

T: Well . . . I don't know. I suppose you're entitled to call that educational technology, if you like. But to me it just sounds like *applied common sense*.

E: Sensible I'm sure it is. But I can assure you it's not very commonly applied. If it were, teachers would be seeing themselves as experimenters, constantly developing and refining their tools and techniques, and adapting them continuously to changes in their pupils and the world about them.

T: Well, I glimpsed the Marxist slant on educational technology a few minutes ago, but now you're beginning to sound like a Trotskyist! What you're after in education is *continuous revolution*!

E: As long as you say 'trotskyist' with a small 't'! But seriously, if teachers were to take this kind of educational technology approach to their work, they would be constantly learning about teaching – and probably never teaching in quite the same way a second time.

T: However, as you say, applied common sense (as I called it) is not applied very commonly. Exciting though it may be, I can quite see why not.

E: Oh certainly. Most teachers feel under far too much day-to-day pressure to think about the 'continuous revolution' in techniques. Most ask only for a few hints and tips that will make their job a bit easier. And who can blame them?

T: Is that why people like you are needed – to act as the conscience of us all and keep prodding us to learn from experience – as all good teachers should be doing?

E: I suppose so. But, fortunately, there are always a few teachers who *are* educational technologists, often without knowing it. And they're often very influential with their colleagues. Don't get me wrong. I'm not saying the educational technologist is in any way better than the intuitive teacher.

T: I should think the better educational technologists are the ones who are most intuitive, anyway.

E: Other things being equal, yes, I'd agree. And the intuitive approach in the hands of a brilliant improvisor could be expected to be more effective than the educational technology approach employed by someone without much flair. But the educational technologist would be trying to do something different. He'd certainly welcome any effective intuitions, but he'd be looking for ways of externalizing them, making them public, discussing them in such a way that other teachers could get some benefit from them – perhaps by using them to spark off new intuitions (hypotheses) of their own.

T: So, educational technology isn't going to make brilliant teachers of us all?

E: No, that's too much to hope for. I'd be happy if it merely helped us all become as good as we've got it in us to be.

T: Well, I'll drink to that!

E: Good, I'm glad you mentioned that. I see the bar is just about to open.

T: Right. Let's go to it.
  (They went.)

Questions about the Conversation

Were there points within the conversation when you felt the teacher might have asked other important questions or pursued an issue further? Alternatively, were you ever disappointed with the educational technologist's answers? What would *you* have wanted to say, either as T or as E, at those points in the conversation?

QUESTIONS ABOUT THE BOOK AS A WHOLE

1   At the end of his first chapter, the author mentions the tension in educational technology between what he calls manipulation and facilitation. Do you think he has got his own position sorted out? If so, what is it? Or do you think he still has a foot towards both ends of the spectrum? If so, does it matter? And where do you stand?

2   Are there any issues discussed in the book that you think are not properly the province of educational technology? Conversely, are there any areas of concern to the educational technologist that you think have been unfairly neglected?

3   What would you say to someone who suggested that educational technology is just another name for curriculum development?

4   Suppose your institution has been granted funds to appoint an educational technologist. Write a job-description for the benefit of applicants for the new post.

5   For each chapter of the book, draft some questions of your own that you would like to discuss with other people who have read the book.

6   Can you think of colleagues in your institution who might benefit from reading and thinking about any of the material in this book? If so, make up an 'anthology' amounting to no more than ten or twenty pages and add your own brief introduction and any necessary linking comments. How might you get your colleagues to consider the material?

7   Have your ideas and/or attitudes regarding education, teaching, learning, etc. changed in any way as a result of reading this book? If so, in what ways? If not, what *did* you get out of it that kept you reading this far!

REFERENCES

Books and Articles

Where a book or aticle is particularly useful as background reading to one of my seven chapters, I have indicated the chapter number in the margin alongside it; an asterisk (*) in the margin denotes an item of relevance to educational technology as a whole.

Abercrombie, M.L.J. (1969) *The Anatomy of Judgment* Hutchinson, London (first published 1960)

Abercrombie, M.L.J. (1970) *Aims and Techniques of Group Teaching* Society for Research in Higher Education, London

Allen, P.S. (1978) 'Developing a remedial Keller Plan course' in *Studies in Higher Education* 3, No. 2

Apple, M.W. (1979) *Ideology and Curriculum* Routledge & Kegan Paul, London

Archambault, R.D. (1967) Introduction to *Tolstoy on Education* translated by Leo Wiener, University of Chicago Press

Asbel, B. (1972) 'The case of the wandering IQs' in Gnagey, W.J. et al. (1972) (see below)

Austwick, K. and Harris, N.D.C. (1972) *Aspects of Educational Technology* Vol VI Pitman, London

Ausubel, D.P. (1959) 'Viewpoints from related disciplines, human growth and development' in *Teachers' College Record* 60, pp 245–254.

(4) Ausubel, D.P. and Robinson, F.G. (1969) *School Learning* Holt, Rinehart and Winston, New York

Baggaley, J., Jaimeson, C.H. and Marchant, H. (eds) (1975) *Aspects of Educational Technology* Vol VIII Pitman, London

Bajpai, A.C. and Leedham, J.F. (1970) *Aspects of Educational Technology* Vol IV Pitman, London

Ball, C. and M. (1973) *Education for a Change: Community Action and the School* Penguin, London

Ball, S. (1980) *Beachside Comprehensive* Cambridge University Press, Cambridge

(1) Banathy, B. (1968) *Instructional Systems* Fearon, Palo Alto, California

Bandura, A. (1970) *Principles of Behaviour Modification* Holt, Rinehart and Winston, London

Banks, B. (1969) 'Report on an auto-instructional course in mathematics' in *Programmed Learning and Educational Technology* 6, 1 Jan. 1969, pp 31–39

Barber, T. et al. (1971) *Biofeedback and Self-Control* Aldine, Chicago

Barnes, D. (1971) 'Language and learning in the classroom' in *Journal of Curriculum Studies* 3, No. 1, pp 36–37

Bates, A.W. (1972) 'The evaluation of broadcasting at the Open University' in Austwick, K. and Harris, N.D.C. (1972) (see above)

(5)   Bates, A.W. (1982) 'Learning from audio-visual media: the Open University experience' in *Teaching at a Distance: Research Supplement No. 1* Open University, Milton Keynes

Beard, R.M. and Senior, I.J. (1980) *Motivating Students* Routledge & Kegan Paul, London

Becher, T. and Maclure, S. (1978) *Accountability in Education* NFER Publishing Company, Slough

Becker, H.S., Geer, B. and Hughes, E.C. (1968) *Making the Grade: The Academic Side of College Life* Wiley, New York

(6)   Belasco, J.A. and Trice, H.M. (1969) *The Assessment of Change in Training and Therapy* McGraw-Hill, New York

Bell, P.B. and Staines, P.J. (1981) *Reasoning and Argument in Psychology* Routledge & Kegan Paul, London

Bennett, S.N. (1976) *Teaching Styles and Pupil Progress* Open Books, London

(7)   Bennis, W.G., Benne, K. and Chin, R. (eds) (1968) *The Planning of Change* Holt, Rinehart and Winston, New York

Bernstein, B. (1971) 'Open schools, open society' in Cosin, B.R. et al. (eds) *School and Society: A Sociological Reader* Routledge & Kegan Paul, London

Bishop, A. (1971) 'Mathematics' in R. Whitfield (1971) (see below)

Bishop, L.K. (1971) *Individualizing Educational Systems* Harper & Row, New York

(4)   Bligh, D., Ebrahim, G.J., Jaques, D., and Warren Piper, D. (1975) *Teaching Students* Exeter University Teaching Services, Exeter

Blishen, E. (ed) (1969) *The School That I'd Like* Penguin, London

Block, J.H. (1971) *Mastery Learning: Theory and Practice* Holt, Rinehart and Winston, New York

(2)   Bloom, B.S. (ed) (1956) *Taxonomy of Educational Objectives: Cognitive Domain* David McKay, New York

Bloom, B.S. (1971) *Individual Differences in School Achievement: A Vanishing Point?* Phi Delta Kappa International, Bloomington, Indiana

(3)   Bloom, B.S., Hastings, J.T. and Madaus, J.F. (1971) *Handbook on Formative and Summative Evaluation of Student Learning* McGraw-Hill, New York

Bobbit, F. (1924) *How to Make a Curriculum* Houghton Mifflin, Boston

Bono, E. de (1973) *CoRT Thinking: Teachers' Notes* Direct Education Services, London

Boocock, S.S. and Schild, E.O. (eds) (1968) *Simulation Games in Learning* Sage, Beverly Hills, California

Bremer, J. and Von Moschzisker, M. (1971) *The School Without Walls* Holt, Rinehart and Winston, New York

Brickell, H.M. (1969) 'Appraising the effects of innovations in local schools' in Tyler, R.W. *Educational Evaluation: New Roles, New Means* (the 68th Yearbook of the National Society for the Study of Education) University of Chicago Press

Bridge, W. (1978) *Course Evaluation Package* Joint Board of Clinical Nursing Studies, London

Bridge, W. and Elton, L. (eds) (1977) *Individual Study in Undergraduate Science* Heinemann, London

(4) Briggs, L.J. (1968) *Sequencing of Instruction in Relation to Hierarchies of Competence* American Institutes for Research, Pittsburgh, Pennsylvania

(*) Briggs, L.J. (1970) *Handbook of Procedures for the Design of Instruction* American Institutes for Research, Pittsburgh, Pennsylvania

(4) Brophy, J.E. and Good, T.L. (1974) *Teacher-Student Relationships* Holt, Rinehart and Winston, New York

Brown, D. (1980) 'New students and radio at the open university', *Educational Broadcasting International*, vol 13, No 1

Brown, G.I. (1971) *Human Teaching for Human Learning: An Introduction to Confluent Education* Viking, New York

(4) Bruner, J.S. (1960) *The Process of Education* Harvard University Press, Cambridge, Massachusetts

Bruner, J.S. (1964) 'Some theorems on instruction, illustrated with reference to mathematics' in Hilgard, R. *Theories of Learning and Instruction* (The 63rd Yearbook of the National Society for the Study of Education), University of Chicago Press

Burt, G. (1976) 'Detailed evaluation and content analysis' pp 43–53 in Rowntree (1976) (see below)

Buswell, C. (1981) 'Packages in the classroom' in *New Society* 16 April 1981, pp 98–99

Butler, F. and Cavanagh, P. (1969) 'The role of the teacher in theory and practice in classroom programmed instruction' in Dunn, W.R. and Holroyd, C. (1969) (see below)

Buzan, T. (1973) *Use Your Head* BBC Publications, London

Calder, J.R. (1980) 'In defense of the systematic approach to instruction and behavioural objectives' in *Educational Technology* May 1980, pp 21–25

(1) Callahan, R.E. (1962) *Education and the Cult of Efficiency* University of Chicago Press

Campeau, P.L. (1972) *Selective Review of the Results of Research on the Use of Audiovisual Media to Teach Adults* Council of Europe, Strasbourg

Cantor, N. (1972) *Dynamics of Learning* Agathon, New York (first published 1946)

Caton, B.J. (1972) 'Transcript' (pp 43–44) and 'A Practical Attempt at Collaborative Learning' (pp 49–58) in Esland, G. et al. (1972) *The Social Organisation of Teaching and Learning Units* 5–8 in Course E282 Open University Press, Bletchley

CET (1981) *Thinking About Microcomputers: First Steps* Information Sheet No. 1 Council for Educational Technology, London

(*) Chadwick, C.B. (1979) 'Why educational technology is failing (and what should be done to create success)' in *Educational Technology* XIX, No. 1, January 1979, pp 7–19

(*) Champness, B. and Young, I. (1980) 'Social limits on educational technology' in *European Journal of Education* 15, No. 3, pp 229–239

Chazan, M., Laing, A. and Jackson, S. (1971) *Just Before School* Blackwell, Oxford

Claridge, G. (1970) *Drugs and Human Behaviour* Penguin, London

Clarke, J. (1969) 'The use of programmed systems in the development of the integrated day in the primary school' in Dunn, W.R and Holroyd, C. (1969) (see below)

Clarke, J. (1982) *Resource-based Learning for Higher and Continuing Education* Croom Helm, London

(*) Clarke, J.L. (1981) *Educational Development: A Select Bibliography* Kogan Page, London

Clarke, J. and Leedham, J. (eds) (1976) *Aspects of Educational Technology X* Kogan Page, London

Coffey, J. (1978) *Development of an Open Learning System in Further Education* Working Paper 15 Council for Educational Technology, London

Coladarci, J.J. (1956) 'The relevancy of educational psychology' in *Educational Leadership*, 18 (1956), pp 489–492

Cole, H.P. (1972) *Process Education* Educational Technology Publications, Engle-wood Cliffs, New Jersey.

Coulson, E. (1971) 'Chemistry' in Whitfield, R. (1971) (see below)

Covington, M., Crutchfield, R. and Davies, L.B. (1966) *The Productive Thinking Program* Educational Innovation, Chicago

Cowan, J. (1975) 'The ability to appraise one's own work' in *Higher Education Bulletin* 3, No. 2, Spring 1975, pp 127–128

Cowan, J. (1980) 'Is systematic curriculum design always feasible?' in *Programmed Learning and Educational Technology* 17, No. 2, May 1980, pp 115–117

Crick, M. (1980) 'Course teams: myth and actuality' in *Distance Education* 1, No. 2, pp 127–141

Davie, R., Butler, N.R. and Goldstein, H. (1972) *From Birth to Seven: The Second Report of the National Child Development Survey* Longman, London

Davies, I.K. (1971) 'Developing accountability in instructional systems technology' in Packham, D. et al. (1971) (see below)

(*) Davies, I.K. and Hartley, J. (eds) (1972) *Contributions to an Educational Technology* Butterworth, London

Davies, I.K. (1975) 'Some aspects of a theory of advice' in *Instructional Science* 3, pp 351–373

Dean, J. (1972) *Recording Children's Progress* Macmillan, London

(4) De Cecco, J.P. (1968) *The Psychology of Learning and Instruction* Prentice-Hall, Englewood Cliffs, New Jersey

De Cecco, J.P. (ed) (1972) *The Regeneration of the School* Holt, Rinehart and Winston, New York

DES (1977) *Curriculum 11-16* HMSO, London

DES (1979) *Aspects of Secondary Education in England; A Survey by HM Inspectors of Schools* HMSO, London

DES (1980) *A Framework for the School Curriculum* Department of Education and Science, London

DES (1981) *The School Curriculum* HMSO, London

Dewey, J. (1926) *The Sources of a Science of Education* Liveright, New York

Dixon, J. (1972) *Growth Through English* Oxford University Press, London

Dore, R. (1976) *The Diploma Disease* Unwin, London

Downing, J.A. and Jones, B. (1966) 'Some problems in evaluating i.t.a.: a second experiment' in *Educational Research* 8, pp 100–114, and reprinted in Entwhistle, N.J. and Nisbet, J.D. (1972) (see below)

Dressel, P.L. (1971) *College and University Curriculum* McCutchan, Berkeley, California

Dubin, R. and Taveggia, T.C. (1968) *The Teaching-Learning Paradox: A Comparative Analysis of College Teaching Methods* University of Oregon, Portland, Oregon

Dunn, W.R. and Holroyd, C. (eds) (1969) *Aspects of Educational Technology* Vol II Methuen, London

Edgeworth, F.Y. (1890) 'The element of chance in competitive examinations' in *Journal of the Royal Statistical Society* LIII, September/December 1890 pp 400–475 and 644–663

Edwards, D. (1979) 'A study of the reliability of tutor-marked assignments in the Open University' in *Assessment in Higher Education* 5, No. 1, December 1979, pp 16–44

Eggleston, J. (1971) 'Biology' in Whitfield, R. (1971) (see below)

Eisner, E.W. (1967) 'Educational objectives: help or hindrance?' in *School Review* 75, Autumn 1967, pp 250–260

Elkan, W. (1974) 'Bringing economics back to earth' in *The Times Higher Educational Supplement* 13 December 1974, p 13

Elton, L. (1977) 'Educational technology – today and tomorrow' in Hills, P.J. and Gilbert, J. (eds) (1975) *Aspects of Educational Technology XI* Kogan Page, London, pp 236–241

Engler, D. (1976) 'Learner verification: a fine grain analysis of go-go empricism' in *AV Communication Review* 24, No. 1, pp 5–20

(*) Entwhistle, N.J. and Nisbet, J.D. (1972) *Educational Research in Action* University of London Press, London

(*) Eraut, M., MacKenzie, N. and Papps, I. (1975) 'The mythology of educational development; reflections on a three year study of economics teaching' in *British Journal of Educational Technology* 6, No. 3, October 1975, pp 20–34

(*) Eraut, M. and Squires, G. (1973) *An Annotated Select Bibliography of Educational Technology*, 2nd ed, Council for Educational Technology, London

(5) Erickson, C.W.H. (1972) *Fundamentals of Teaching with Audio-Visual Technology* Collier-Macmillan, New York

Esland, G. et al. (1972) *The Social Organization of Teaching and Learning* Units 5–8 in Course E282 Open University Press, Milton Keynes

Evans, H. (1978) *Pictures on a Page* Heinemann, London

Farnes, N.C. (1973) *Reading Purposes, Comprehension and the Use of Context* Units 3–4 in Course PE261, Open University Press, Bletchley

Fairbrother, R. (1975) 'The reliability of teachers' judgements of the abilities being tested by multiple-choice items' in *Educational Research* 17, No. 3, pp 202–210

Farrar, E.H. (1978) 'Evaluation of the role of the educational technology adviser' pp 39–54 in Coffey, J. (1978) (see above)

Flanders, N.A. (1970) *Analysing Teacher Behaviour* Addison-Wesley, London

Flood-Page, C. (1974) *Student Evaluation of Teaching: The American Experience* Society for Research into Higher Education, London

Fogelman, K. (1976) *Britain's Sixteen Year Olds* National Children's Bureau, London

French, W. et al. (1967) *Behavioral Goals of General Education in High School* Russell Sage Foundation, New York

Fritts, H.C. (1966) 'Growth-rings of trees: their correlation with climate', *Science*, 25 November 1966, 154, pp 973–979

Furbank, N. (1973) Personal note to the author

(*)   Gage, N.L. (1963) *Handbook of Research on Teaching* Rand McNally, Chicago

(**4,5**) Gagné, R.M. (1965) *The Conditions of Learning* Holt, Rinehart and Winston, New York (2nd edition, 1970)

Galton, M., Simon, B. and Croll, P. (1980) *Inside the Primary Classroom* Routledge & Kegan Paul, London

Gardner, D.E.M. (1966) *Experiment and Tradition in Primary Schools* Methuen, London

(*)   Gerlach, V.S. and Ely, D.P. (1971) *Teaching and Media: A Systematic Approach* Prentice-Hall, Englewood Cliffs, New Jersey

Gibbs, G. (1981) *Teaching Students to Learn* Open University Press, Milton Keynes

Gilbert, T.F. (1962) 'Mathematics: The Technology of Education', *Journal of Mathematics*, 1962, I, reprinted as supplement to *Recall*, Longman, London (1970)

Glasser, W. (1968) *Schools Without Failure* Harper & Row, New York

Glenn, J.A. (1977) *Teaching Primary Mathematics: Strategy and Evaluation* Harper & Row, London

(*)   Glock, M.D. (ed) (1971) *Guiding Learning* Wiley, New York

Glynn, E., Pearce, J.P. and Willott, A.S. (1970) 'A simple mobile feedback classroom' in Bajpai, A.C. and Leedham, J.F. (1970) (see above)

Gnagey, W.J., Chesebro, P.A. and Johnson, J.A. (1972) *Learning Environments* Holt, Rinehart and Winston, New York

Goldschmid, B. and Goldschmid, M.L. (1976) 'Peer teaching in higher education: a review' in *Higher Education* 5, pp 9–33

Gombrich, P. (1962) *Art and Illusion: A Study in the Psychology of Pictorial Representation* Phaidon, London

Goodlad, J.I. (1977) 'What goes on in our schools?' in *Educational Researcher* 6, No. 3, pp 3–6

Goodlad, J. (1977) 'What goes on in our schools?' in *Educational Researcher* 6, No. 3, pp 3–6

Goodlad, J.I. and Klein, M.F. (1970) *Behind the Classroom Door* Charles A. Jones, Worthington, Ohio

Goodman, P. (1971) *Compulsory Miseducation* Penguin, London (first published 1962)

Gray, K. and Sare, G.T. (1970) 'Programmed Learning in Surrey schools' *in Visual Education*, March 1970, pp 7–14

(**3**)   Gronlund, N.E. (1971) *Measurement and Evaluation in Teaching* Macmillan, New York

(**7**)   Gross, N., Giacquinta, J.B. and Bernstein, M. (1971) *Implementing Organizational Innovations* Harper & Row, New York

Hack, W.G. et al. (1971) *Educational Futurism*, 1985 McCutchan, Berkeley, California

Haddon, F.A. and Lytton, H. (1968) 'Teaching approach and the development of divergent thinking abilities in primary schools' in *British Journal of Educational Psychology* 38 (2), pp 171–179

Hajnal, J. (1972) *The Student Trap: A Critique of University and Sixth-form Curricula* Penguin, London

(**6**)   Hamilton, D. et al. (1977) *Beyond the Numbers Game: A Reader in Educational Evaluation* Macmillan, London

Hansen, S. and Jensen, J. (1971) *The Little Red School Book* Stage 1, London

Hargie, O.D.W. (1978) 'The importance of teacher questions in the classroom' in *Educational Research* 20, No. 2, pp 99–102

(6) Harlen, W. (1975) "Science 5/13 Project' in *Evaluation in Curriculum Development: Twelve Case Studies* Macmillan, London

Harrison, R. and Hopkins, R. (1969) 'The design of cross-cultural training: an alternative to the university model' *Journal of Applied Behavioral Sciences* 3, No. 4, pp 431–440 and reprinted in Bennis, W.G. et al. (eds) (1968) (see above)

(2) Harrow, A.J. (1972) *A Taxonomy of the Motor Domain* McKay, New York

Hartog, P. and Rhodes, E.C. (1935) *An Examination of Examinations* Macmillan, London

(7) Havelock, R.G. (1970) *A Guide to Innovation in Education* University of Michigan

Havelock, R.G. (1971) The utilisation of educational research and development' in *British Journal of Educational Technology* 2, No. 2, May 1971, pp 84–98

Hawkins, D. (1965) 'Messing about in Science' in *Science and Children* February 1965, quoted in Holt, J. (1970), p 145 (see below)

Hawkridge, D.G. (1970) 'Design for evaluation studies' in *Evaluation Research: Strategies and Methods* American Institutes for Research, Palo Alto, California

(*) Hawkridge, D.G. (1981) 'The telesis of educational technology' in *British Journal of Educational Technology* 12, No. 1, January 1981, pp 4–18

(4) HE (1979) Special issue of *Higher Education*, Vol 8, devoted to papers on 'Student learning in its natural setting'

(7) Hedberg, J.G. (1980) 'Client relationships in instructional design' in *Programmed Learning and Educational Technology* 17, No. 2, pp 102–110, plus a response 'Client relationships and consulting realities' by G. Isaacs, pp 111–114 in the same issue

(5) Heidt, E.U. (1980) 'Differences between media and differences between learners: can we relate them?' in *Instructional Science* 9, pp 365–391

(6) Henderson, E. et al. (1980) *Development Testing for Credit: An Account of Open University Experience 1976–79* IET, Open University, Milton Keynes

Henry, J. (1971) *Essays on Education* Penguin, London

Henrysson, S. and Franke-Wikberg, S. (1979) 'Long term effects of higher education' in *SRHE International Newsletter* (12) Society for Research into Higher Education, London University, pp 7–9

Hill, W.F. (1969) *Learning Thru Discussion* Sage, Beverly Hills, California

Hills, P.J. (1976) *The Self-teaching Process in Higher Education* Croom-Helm, London

Hirst, P.H. (1968) 'The contribution of philosophy to the study of the curriculum' in Kerr, J.F. *Changing the Curriculum* London University Press, London

Hirst, P.H. and Peters, R.S. (1970) *The Logic of Education* Routledge & Kegan Paul, London

Hoetker, J. (1970) 'Limitations and advantages of behavioral objectives in the arts and humanities' in Maxwell, J. and Tovatt, A. (1970) (see below)

Hoffman, B. (1967) *The Tyranny of Testing* Collier, New York

Holderness, G. (1973) 'Those anecdotes can be relevant' Letter in Open University newspaper *Sesame* 2, No. 4, May 1973

Holling, K. (1969) 'The feedback classroom' in Unwin, D. (ed) (1969), *Media and Methods: Instructional Technology in Higher Education* McGraw-Hill Book Company, Maidenhead

Holt, J. (1969) *How Children Fail* Penguin, London (first published 1964)

Holt, J. (1970) *How Children Learn* Penguin, London (first published 1967)

(*) Hooper, R.S. (ed) (1971) *The Curriculum: Context, Design and Development* Oliver and Boyd, Edinburgh

Hoyle, E. (1970) 'Planned organisational change in education' in *Research in Education* 3, May 1970, pp 1–22

(7) Hoyle, E. and Bell, R. (1972) *Problems of Curriculum Innovation* I Units 13–15 in Course E283, Open University Press, Bletchley

(7) Hoyle, E. (1972) *Problems of Curriculum Innovation* II Unit 17 in Course E283, Open University Press, Bletchley

Hoyt, D.P. (1965) *The Relationship Between College Grades and Adult Achievement* American College Testing Program, Iowa City

(3) Hudson, B. (1973) *Assessment Techniques* Methuen, London

Hudson, L. (1966) 'Selection and the problem of conformity' in Meade, J.E. and Parkes, A.S. (1966) *Genetic and Environmental Factors in Human Ability* Oliver and Boyd, Edinburgh

(7) Humble, S. and Simons, H. (1978) *From Council to Classroom: an Evaluation of the Diffusion of the Humanities Curriculum Project* Macmillan, London

Illich, I.D. (1971) *Deschooling Society* Harper & Row, New York

Illiffe, A.H. (1966) 'Objective tests' in Heywood, J. and Iliffe, A.H. *Some Problems of Testing Academic Performance* Department of Higher Education, University of Lancaster

Insel, P.M. and Jacobson, L.F. (1975) *What Do You Expect? An Enquiry into Self-fulfilling Prophecies* Cummings, Menlo Park, California

Irvine, D.J. (1979) 'Factors associated with school effectiveness' in *Educational Technology* May 1979

Jackson, B. (1964) *Streaming: An Education System in Miniature* Routledge & Kegan Paul, London

Jackson, P.W. (1968) *Life in Classrooms* Holt, Rinehart and Winston, New York

James, C. (1972) 'Flexible grouping and the secondary school curriculum' in Rubinstein, D. and Stoneman, C. (1972) (see below)

James, E. (1979) Review of 'Micro-electronics: their implications for education and training' in *Programmed Learning and Educational Technology* 16, No. 2, pp 183–184

Jones, R.M. (1972) *Fantasy and Feeling in Education* Penguin, London (first published 1968)

(2,3) Kapfer, M.B. (ed) (1971) *Behavioral Objectives in Curriculum Development* Educational Technology, Publications, Englewood Cliffs, New Jersey

Kaufman, B. (1964) *Up the Down Staircase* Prentice-Hall Englewood Cliffs, New Jersey

Kearney, N.C. (1953) *Elementary School Objectives* Russell Sage Foundation, New York

Keddie, N. (1971) 'Classroom knowledge' in Young (1971) (see below)

Kefford, C. (1970) *A Programmed Approach to Environmental Studies* Blandford, London

Kendall, P. (1964) 'Evaluating an experimental programme in medical education' in Miles, M.B. (1964) (see below)

Klug, B. (1974) *Pro Profiles* NUS Publications, London

Kogan, M. (1971) 'English primary schools: a model for institutional innovation?' in Green, T. *Educational Planning in Perspective* Futures/IPC Science and Technology Press, Guildford

Kogan, M. (1976) *The Next Ten Years: A Speculative Essay on Educational Futures* National Development Programme in Computer Assisted Learning, London

Kohl, H. (1972) *36 Children* Penguin, London

Komoski, P.K. (1974) 'Learner verification: touchstone for instructional materials?' in *Educational Leadership*, February 1974, pp 397–399

(2) Krathwohl, D.R., Bloom, B.S. and Masia, B. (1964) *Taxonomy of Educational Objectives II: Affective Domain* David McKay, New York

Krech, D. (1967) 'The chemistry of learning' reprinted in Gnagey, W.J. et al. (1972) (see above)

Kuhn, T.S. (1970) *The Structure of Scientific Revolutions* Chicago University Press, Chicago

Lancaster, J. (1803) *Improvements in Education* London

Lawless, C.J. (1980) 'New chips but old problems' in Winterburn, R. and Evans, L. (eds) (1980) *Aspects of Educational Technology XIV* Kogan Page, London

Leedham, J.F. and Budgett, R. (eds) (1973) *Aspects of Educational Technology* Vol VII Pitman, London

Leith, G.O.M. (1968) *A Second Look at Programmed Learning* Occasional Paper No. 1, Council for Educational Technology, reprinted in Davies, I.K. and Hartley, J. (1972) (see above)

Lewin, K. (1958) 'Group decision and social change' in Maccoby, N. et al. (eds) *Readings in Social Psychology* Holt, Rinehart and Winston, New York

(7) Lewis, B.N. (1980) 'The professional standing of educational technology' in Howe, A. (ed) *International Yearbook of Educational and Instructional Technology 1980/81* Kogan Page, London

Lewis, B.N. and Woolfenden, P.J. (1969) *Algorithms and Logical Trees: A Self-Instructional Course* Algorithms Press, Cambridge

Lopez, F.M. (1966) *Evaluating Executive Decision Making* American Management Association, New York

Macdonald, B. and Ruddock, J. (1971) 'Curriculum research and development projects: barriers to success' in *British Journal of Educational Psychology* 41, Part 2, June 1971, reprinted in Hoyle, E. and Bell, R (1972) (see above)

Macdonald, F.J. (1971) 'A model of the decision-making process' in Glock, M.D. (1971) (see above)

Macdonald-Ross, M. (1972) 'Behavioral objectives and the structure of knowledge' in Austwick, K. and Harris, N.D.C. (1972) (see above)

(2) Macdonald-Ross, M. (1973) 'Behavioural objectives – a critical review' in *Instructional Science* 2, pp 1–52

Macdonald-Ross, M. (1976) 'Janus the consultant' in *British Journal of Educational Technology* 7, No. 1, pp 65–75

Mackenzie, N., Eraut, M. and Jones, H.C. *Teaching and Learning* UNESCO, Paris

Mackenzie, R. (1970) *State School* Penguin, London

Mager, R.F. (1961) 'On the sequencing of instructional content' in *Psychological Reports* 9, 1961, pp 405–413. Reprinted in Davies, I.K. and Hartley, J. (1972) (see above)

Mager, R.F. (1962) *Preparing Instructional Objectives* Fearon, Palo Alto, California

Mager, R.F. (1968) *Developing Attitude Toward Learning* Fearon, Palo Alto, California

Mager, R.F. and Beach, K.M. (1967) *Developing Vocational Instruction* Fearon, Palo Alto, California

Mager, R.F. and Clark, C. (1963) 'Explorations in student-controlled instruction', in *Psychological Reports* 13, 1963, pp 71–76

Maguire, J.S. (1971) 'Systematic concept teaching to pre-readers' in Packham, D. et al. (1971) (see below)

Mann, A.P. and Brunstrom, C.K. (1969) *Aspects of Educational Technology* Vol III Pitman, London

Mansell, J. (1981) 'Profiling must be a better way' in *Education* 29 May 1981

Marsh, P.E. (1964) 'Wellsprings of strategy: considerations affecting innovations by the PSSC' in Miles, M.B. (1964) (see below)

Marton, F. (1981) 'Phenomenography – describing conceptions of the world around us' in *Instructional Science* 10, pp 177–200

Maslow, A.H. (1954) *Motivation and Personality* Harper & Row, New York

McAleese, R. (ed) (1978) *Perspectives on Academic Gaming and Simulation 3* Kogan Page, London

McIntyre, D. (1970) 'Assessment and teaching' in Rubinstein D. and Stoneman, C. (1972) (see below)

McIntyre, D.I. (1980) 'Systematic observation of classroom activities' in *Educational Analysis* 2, No. 2, pp 3–30

McMurrin, S. (1970) 'Technology in education and education in a technological society' in Tickton, S.G. (1970) (see below)

Mechner, F. (1967) 'Behavioral analysis and instructional sequencing' in Lange, P. (ed) (1967) *Programmed Instruction* (The 66th Yearbook of the National Society for the Study of Education), University of Chicago Press

Megarry, J. (1978) *Perspectives on Academic Gaming and Simulation 1 and 2* Kogan Page, London

Megarry, J. (1979) 'Developments in simulation and gaming' in Howe, A. and Romiszowski, A.J. (eds) *International Yearbook of Educational and Instructional Technology 1978/79* Kogan Page, London

Mehrens, W.A. and Lehmann, I.J. (1978) *Measurement and Evaluation in Education and Psychology*, 2nd edition Holt, Rinehart and Winston, New York

Melnick, A. and Merritt, J. (1972) *Reading: Today and Tomorrow* University of London Press, London

Metfessel, N.S., Michael, W. B. and Kirsner, D.A. (1969) 'Instrumentation of Bloom's and Krathwohl's taxonomies for the writing of educational objectives' in *Psychology in the Schools* 6, No. 3, July 1969, pp 227–231, and reprinted in Stones, E. (1972) (see below)

Midwinter, E. (1972) *Priority Education: An Account of the Liverpool Project*, Penguin London

(7) Miles, M.B. (ed) (1964) *Innovation in Education* Teachers' College Press, Columbia University, New York

Miller, G. (ed) (1962) *Teaching and Learning in Medical School* Harvard University Press, Cambridge, Massachusetts

Miller, G.A. (1972) *Psychology: The Science of Mental Life* Penguin, London (first published 1962)

Miller, R. (1972) *Evaluating Faculty Performance* Jossey-Bass, San Francisco

Mitchell, P.D. (1981) Private communication with the author

Morgan, R.N. (1978) 'Educational technology: adolescence to adulthood' in *Educational Communication and Technology* 26, No. 2

Morrison, A. and McIntyre, D. (1969) *Teachers and Teaching* Penguin, London

Mort, P.R. (1964) Chapter 13 in Miles, M.B. (1964) (see above)

Morton, J., Bingham, E. and Cowan, J. (1974) 'A free-format course based on pre-recorded learning material' in Baggaley, J. et al. (eds) (1974) *Aspects of Educational Technology VIII* Pitman, London

Mosher, R.L. and Sprinthall, N.A. (1970) 'Psychological education: a means to promote personal development during adolescence' reprinted in Purpel, D.E. and Belanger, M. (1972) (see below)

MSC (1981) *An 'Open Tech' Programme: A Consultative Document* Manpower Services Commission, London

Munn, J. (1977) (Chairman of sub-committee of Scottish Education Department consultative committee on the curriculum) *The Structure of the Curriculum in the Third and Fourth Year of the Scottish Secondary School* HMSO, Edinburgh

Musgrove, F (1971) 'Curriculum objectives' in Hooper, R.S. (1971) (see above)

NAEA (1968) *The Essentials of a Quality School Art Program* National Art Education Association, Washington, DC

Nagarra, B. (1981) 'Libertarian or liberal' in *Libertarian Education* 30, pp 3–7

(4) Nash, R. (ed) (1976) *Teacher Expectations and Pupil Learning* Routledge & Kegan Paul, London

Natheson, M.B. and Henderson, E.S. (1980) *Using Student Feedback to Improve Learning Materials*, Croom Helm, London

Nehari, M. and Bender, I. (1978) 'Meaningfulness of a learning experience: a measure for educational outcomes in higher education' in *Higher Education* 7, p 1–11

Neil, M. (1970) 'A systems approach to course planning at the Open University' in Romiszowski, A.J. *The Systems Approach to Education and Training* Kogan Page, London

Nisbet, J.D. (1972) 'The Science 5/13 Project' pp 264–267, in Entwhistle, N.J. and Nisbet, J.D. (1972) (see above)

Noble, P. (1980) *Resource-based Learning in Post-compulsory Education* Kogan Page, London

(4) Northedge, A (1976) 'Examining our implicit analogies for learning processes' pp 67–78 in Rowntree (1976) (see below)

Oettinger, A.G. (1969) *Run, Computer, Run* Harvard University Press, Cambridge, Massachusetts

Open University (1972) Arts Faculty Correspondence texts (various authors) from Courses A100, A201, A203, A301, A302, A303, etc., Open University Press, Bletchley

(2) Ormell, C.P. (1974) 'Objections to Bloom's taxonomy' in *Journal of Curriculum Studies* 6, pp 3–18

O'Shea, T. and Self, J. (1982) *Learning and Teaching with Computers* Harvester Press, Brighton

Packard, V. (1957) *The Hidden Persuaders* Penguin, London

Packham, D., Cleary, A. and Mayes, T. (1971) *Aspects of Educational Technology* 5, Pitman, London

Page, E.B. (1958) 'Teacher comments and student performance' in *Journal of Educational Psychology* 49, 1958, pp 173–181, and reprinted in Glock, M.D. (1971) (see above)

Parkhurst, H. (1922) *Education on the Dalton Plan* Bell, London

Parlett, M. (1977) 'The department as a learning milieu' in *Studies in Higher Education* 2, No. 2, pp 173–181, and pp 6–22 in Hamilton et al. (1977) (see above)

Parlett, M. and Hamilton, D. (1972) *Evaluation as Illumination: A New Approach to the Study of Innovatory Programs* Occasional Paper No. 9, Centre for Research in the Educational Sciences, University of Edinburgh, Reprinted in Hamilton D. et al. (1977) (see above)

Pask, G. and Scott, B.C.E. (1972) 'Learning strategies and individual competence' in *International Journal of Man-Machine Studies* 4, p 217

Pateman, T. (ed) (1972) *Counter Course: A Handbook of Course Criticism* Penguin, London

Perry, W.G. (1959) 'Student use and misuse of reading skills' in *Harvard Educational Review* 29, No. 3 pp 193–200

Peters, R.S. (1969) 'Session Two Introduction' in *Conference on Objectives in Higher Education* University of London Institute of Education, London

(1) Pfeiffer, J. (1968) *New Look at Education: Systems Analysis in our Schools and Colleges* Odyssey Press, New York

Phenix, P.H. (1964) *Realms of Meaning* McGraw-Hill, New York

Pirsig, R.M. (1975) *Zen and the Art of Motor-cycle Maintenance* Bantam, New York

Plowden Report (1967) *Children and their Primary Schools* HMSO, London

(3) Plowman, P.D. (1971) *Behavioral Objectives* Science Research Associates, Chicago

Popham, W.J. (ed) (1971) *Criterion-Referenced Measurement* Educational Technology Publications, Englewood Cliffs, New Jersey

(*) Popham, W.J. and Baker, E.L. (1970) *Systematic Instruction* Prentice-Hall, Englewood Cliffs, New Jersey

Popper, K.R. (1972) *Objective Knowledge*, Oxford University Press, Oxford

Postlethwait, S.N., Novak, J. and Murray, H. (1971) *An Audio-tutorial Approach to Learning* Burgess, Minneapolis

Postman, N. (1970) 'Curriculum change and technology' in Tickton, S.G. (1970) (see below)

Postman, N. and Weingartner, C. (1971) *Teaching as a Subversive Activity* Penguin, London (first published 1969)

Powell, J.P. (1981) 'Helping and hindering learning' in *Higher Education* 10, pp 103–117

Preece, P.F.W. (1976) 'Associative structure of science concepts' in *British Journal of Educational Psychology* 46, pp 174–183

Pressey, S.L. (1964) 'Auto-instruction: perspectives, problems, potentials' in Hilgard, E.R. (ed) (1964) *Theories of Learning and Instruction* (63rd Yearbook of the National Society for the Study of Education), University of Chicago Press

(2) Pring, R. (1971) 'Bloom's taxonomy: a philosophical critique' in *Cambridge Journal of Education* 2, pp 83–91

Pronay, N. (1979) 'Towards independence in learning history: the potential of video-cassette technology for curricular innovation' in *Studies in Higher Education* 4, No. 1

Ramsden, P. (1979) 'Student learning and perceptions of the academic environment' pp 411–27 in HE (1979) (see above)

Reid, D.J. and Booth, P. (1969) 'The work of the Nuffield Individual Learning Project in Elementary Biology' in Mann, A.P. and Brunstrom, C.K. (1969) (see above)

Reif, F. (1978) 'Towards an applied science of education' in *Instructional Science* 7, pp 1–14

Reif, F., Larkin, J.H. and Brackett, G.C. (1976) 'Teaching general learning and problem-solving skills' in *American Journal of Physics* 44, pp 212–217

Reigeluth, C.M. et al. (1980) 'The elaboration theory of instruction: a model for sequencing and synthesizing instruction' in *Instructional Science* 9, pp 195–219

(*) Reimer, E. (1971) *School is Dead: An Essay on Alternatives in Education* Penguin, London

Richmond, K. (1969) 'A systems approach to educational reform: the Swedish example' Chapter 5 in *The Education Industry* Methuen, London

Roach, K. and Hammond, R. (1976) 'Zoology by self-instruction' in *Studies in Higher Education* 1, No. 2, pp 176–196

Roebuck, M. (1971) 'Floundering among measurements in educational technology' in Packham, D. et al. (1971) (see above)

Rogers, C. (1961) *On Becoming a Person* Houghton Mifflin, New York

(4) Rogers, C. (1969) *Freedom to Learn* Merrill, Columbus, Ohio

Rosenthal, R. and Jacobson, L. (1968) *Pygmalion in the Classroom* Holt, Rinehart and Winston, New York

Rosenzweig, M.R., Bennett, E.L. and Diamond, M.C. (1972) 'Brain changes in response to experience' in *Scientific American* 226, No. 2, February 1972, pp 22–29

Rothkopf, E.Z. (1968) 'Two scientific approaches to the management of instruction' in Gagné, R.M. and Gephart, W.R. (eds) (1968) *Learning Research and School and Subjects* Peacock, Itasca, Illinois

Rowntree, D. (1968) 'Tutorial programming: an integrated approach to frame writing' in Dunn, W.R. and Holroyd, C. (1969) (see above)

Rowntree, D. (1970) *Learn How to Study* Macdonald, London

Rowntree, D. (1971) 'Course production' from 'Symposium on Open University' in Packham, D. et al. (1971) (see above)

Rowntree, D. (1973) 'Which objectives are most worthwhile?' in Leedham, J.F. and Budgett, R. (1973) (see above)

Rowntree, D. (1975) 'Two styles of communication and their implications for learning' in Baggaley, J. et al. (1975) (see above)

Rowntree, D. (ed) (1976) Special Open University issue of *Programmed Learning and Educational Technology* 13, No. 4, October 1976

(4)   Rowntree, D. (1977) *Assessing Students: How Shall We Know Them?* Harper & Row, London

(*)   Rowntree, D. (1981) *Developing Courses for Students* McGraw-Hill, London

(*)   Rowntree, D. and Connors, B. (eds) (1979) *How to Develop Self-instructional Teaching* Open University, Milton Keynes

Rubinstein, D. and Stoneman, C. (eds) (1972) *Education for Democracy* 2nd ed, Penguin, London

(7)   Ruddock, J. (1980) 'Insights into the processes of dissemination' in *British Educational Research Journal* 6, No. 2, pp 139–146

Rushby, N.J. (1979) *An Introduction to Educational Computing*, Croom Helm, London

Saettler, P. (1978) 'The roots of educational technology' in *Programmed Learning and Educational Technology* 15, No. 1 February 1978

(5)   Salomon, G. (1978) 'On the future of media research' in *Educational Communication and Technology* 26, No. 1

(2)   Sanders, N.M. (1966) *Classroom Questions: What Kinds?* Harper & Row, New York

(3)   Satterly, D. (1981) *Assessment in Schools* Blackwell, Oxford

Schwab, J.J. (1969) *College Curriculum and Student Protest* University of Chicago Press, Chicago

(6)   Scriven, M. (1967) 'The methodology of evaluation' in Tyler, R.W. et al. (1967) (see below)

Shavelson, R.J. (1974) 'Methods for examining representations of a subject-matter structure in a student's memory' in *Journal of Research in Science Teaching* 11, No. 3, pp 231–249

Shipman, M.D. (1972a) *The Limitations of Social Research* Longman, London

Shipman, M.D. (1972b) 'Measuring success', pp 58–68 in Hoyle, E and Bell, R. (1972) (see above)

(4)   Shulman, L.S. and Keislar, E.R. (1966) *Learning by Discovery: A Critical Appraisal* Rand McNally, Chicago

Silberman, C.E. (1970) *Crisis in the Classroom* Random House, New York

Skinner, B.F. (1968) *The Technology of Teaching* Appleton-Century-Crofts, New York

Smith, M. (1977) *The Underground and Education* Methuen, London

Snyder, B.R. (1971) *The Hidden Curriculum* Knopf, New York

Stake, R.E. (1967) 'Introduction' in Tyler, R.W. et al. (1967) (see below)

Stenhouse, L. (1971) 'Some limitations of the use of objectives in curriculum research and planning' in *Paedagogica Europaea* 6 1970–71, pp 73–83

Stenhouse, L. (1975) *An Introduction to Curriculum Development and Research* Heinemann, London

Stephens, J.M. (1967) *The Process of Schooling* Holt, Rinehart and Winston, New York

Stern, G.G. (1970) *People in Context* Wiley, New York

(2,3) Stones, E. (1972) *Educational Objectives and the Teaching of Educational Psychology* Methuen, London

(4)   Stones, E. (1979) *Psychopedagogy: Psychological Theory and the Practice of Teaching* Methuen, London

Stratton, R.G. (1976) 'Ethical issues in evaluating educational programmes' Paper presented to Annual Conference of the Australian Association for Research in Education, Brisbane, November 1976

Tallmadge, G.K. and Shearer, J.W. (1969) 'Relationships among learning styles, instructional methods, and the nature of learning experiences' in *Journal of Educational Psychology* 60, No. 3, pp 222–230

Tansey, P.J. and Unwin, D. (1969) *Simulation and Gaming in Education* Methuen, London

Taylor, F.E. (1969) *Bluff Your Way in Teaching* Wolfe, London

Taylor, H. (1960) *Art and Intellect* Doulbleday, New York

Taylor, J.L. and Walford, R. (1973) *Simulation in the Classroom* Penguin, London

Taylor, L.C. (1971) *Resources for Learning* Penguin, London

Taylor, P.H. (1970) *How Teachers Plan Their Courses* National Foundation for Educational Research, London

TES (1976) Report of Prime Minister's speech at Ruskin College, Oxford, in *Times Educational Supplement* 22 October 1976

Thelen, H.A. (1969) 'Tutoring by students' in *School Review* 77, No. 3, September 1966

Thelen, H.A. (1972) *Education and the Human Quest* University of Chicago Press (first published 1960)

Thiagarajan, S. (1976) 'Learner verification and revision: what, who, when and how?' in *Audiovisual Instruction*, January 1976, pp 18–19

(*) Tickton, S.G. (ed) (1970) *To Improve Learning* (two vols) Bowker, New York

Tough, J. (1976) *Listening to Children Talking* Ward Lock, London

(*) Travers, R.M.W. (ed) (1973) *Second Handbook of Research on Teaching* Rand McNally, Chicago

Tribe, M. (1973) 'Designing an introductory programmed course in biology for undergraduates' in Austwick, K. and Harris, N.D.C. (1973) (see above)

Tyler, F. (1964) 'Issues related to readiness' in Hilgard, E.R. (ed) *Theories of Learning and Instruction*, the 63rd Yearbook of the National Society for the Study of Education, University of Chicago Press, Chicago

Tyler, R.W. (1934) *Constructing Achievement Tests* Ohio State University Press

Tyler, R.W. (1964) 'Some persistent problems in the defining of objectives', reprinted in Kapfer, M.B. (1971) and in Stones, E. (1972) (see above)

(*) Tyler, R.W. (1971) *Basic Principles of Curriculum and Instruction* (first published 1949) University of Chicago Press, London

(6) Tyler, R.W., Gagné, R. and Scriven, M. (1967) *Perspectives of Curriculum Evaluation* Rand McNally, Chicago

Tyler, R.W. and Wolf, R.M. (eds) (1974) *Critical Issues in Testing* McCutchan, Berkeley, California

Unwin, D. and Leedham, J. (1967) *Aspects of Educational Technology* Vol I Methuen, London

(*) Unwin, D. and McAleese, R. (1978) *Encyclopaedia of Educational Media, Communication and Technology* Macmillan, London

VanderMeer, A.W. (1965) 'Educational philosophies and communication' in Wiman, R.V. and Meierhenry, W. (eds) *Educational Media: Theory in Practice* Merrill, Columbus, Ohio

(4)   Verduin, J.R. (1967) *Conceptual Models in Teacher Education: An Approach to Teaching and Learning* American Association of Colleges for Teacher Education, Washington, D.C.

Walford, R. (1969) *Games in Geography* Longman, London

Warr, P., Bird, M. and Rackham, N. (1970) *Evaluation of Management Training* Gower Press, London

Warren Piper, D.J. (1969) 'An approach to designing courses based on the recognition of objectives' in *Conference on Objectives in Higher Education* University of London Institute of Education

Wastnedge, R. (1972) 'Whatever happened to Nuffield Junior Science?' in Hoyle, E. and Bell, R. (1972) (see above)

Watson, G. and Glaser, E.M. (1965) 'What have we learned about planning for change?' in *Management Review* November 1965

(3)   Webb, E.J., Campbell, D.T., Schwartz, R.D. and Sechrest, L. (1969) *Unobtrusive Measures: Non-reactive Research in the Social Sciences* Rand McNally, Chicago

(1)   Weston, P.B. (1980) *Negotiating the Curriculum: a Study in Secondary Schooling* NFER Publishing, Slough

Wheeler, K. (1971) 'Geography' in Whitfield, R. (1971) (see below)

Whitaker, F.G.P. (1965) *T-Group Training* Blackwell, Oxford

(3)   White, R.T. and Mayer, R.E. (1980) 'Understanding intellectual skills' in *Instructional Science* 9, pp 101–127

Whitfield, R. (ed) (1971) *Disciplines of the Curriculum* McGraw-Hill, Maidenhead

Wilhelms, F.T. (1967) 'Evaluation as feedback' reprinted in Hooper, R.S. (1971) (see above)

Wilson, J. (1971) *Moral Thinking*, Heinemann, London

Wilson, J. (1974) *Thinking With Concepts* Cambridge University Press, Cambridge (first published 1963)

(5)   Wiman, R.V. and Meierhenry, W.C. (1969) *Educational Media: Theory into Practice* Merrill, Columbus, Ohio

Wiseman, S. (1964) *Education and Environment* Manchester University Press

(3)   Young, M.F.D. (ed) (1971) *Knowledge and Control* Collier-Macmillan, London

Zimmer, R. (1981) Private communication with the author

Journals and Periodicals

The following is a *shortlist* of journals and periodicals that can be expected to contain articles of particular interest to some educational technologists in every issue. Those likely to have articles of interest to *all* educational technologists are asterisked (*). Many other educational journals will occasionally carry relevant articles. Unless otherwise stated, the publications are British.

     Alberta Journal of Educational Research (Canada)
     American Educational Research Journal (USA)
     Assessment in Higher Education
     Australian Journal of Higher Education (Australia)
     British Journal of Educational Studies
     British Journal of Educational Psychology
(*) *British Journal of Educational Technology*
     British Journal of In-service Education
     Cambridge Journal of Education
     Curriculum Inquiry (Canada)
     Distance Education (Australia)
     Educational Broadcasting International
     Educational Media International
     Educational Research
(*) *Educational Technology* (USA)
(*) *Educational Technology Research* (Japan) (published in English)
     Hard Cheese
     Improving College and University Teaching
(*) *Instructional Science*
     International Journal of Instructional Media (USA)
     Journal of Curriculum Studies
     Journal of Educational Technology Systems (USA)
     Journal of Educational Television and Other Media
     Journal of Experimental Education (USA)
     Journal of Further and Higher Education
     Journal of Personalized Education (USA)
     Libertarian Education
     McGill Journal of Education (Canada)
(*) *Programmed Learning and Educational Technology*
     Radical Education
     Simulation and Games (USA)
     Simulation/Games for Learning
     Studies in Higher Education
     Teaching at a Distance
     Times Educational Supplement
     Times Higher Education Supplement

Other Publications

Teachers and others interested in educational technology are advised to look out also for two less frequent publications:

     Aspects of Educational Technology and
     International Yearbook of Educational and Training Technology

which are both published (the first annually, and the second every other year) by Kogan Page of London. In addition, they may wish to be on the mailing lists of the Council for Educational Technology (London) and of the Scottish Council for Educational Technology (Glasgow).

INDEX